THE PR

MISTRESS

THE PRINCE'S MISTRESS

Perdita

A LIFE OF MARY ROBINSON

HESTER DAVENPORT

SUTTON PUBLISHING

This book was first published in 2004 by
Sutton Publishing Limited · Phoenix Mill
Thrupp · Stroud · Gloucestershire · GL5 2BU

This revised paperback edition first published in 2006

British Library Cataloguing in Publication Data
A catalogue record for this book is available from the British Library.

ISBN 0 7509 3228 7

Typeset in 10/12pt Goudy.
Typesetting and origination by
Sutton Publishing Limited.
Printed and bound in Great Britain by
J.H. Haynes & Co. Ltd, Sparkford.

Contents

List of Illustrations

Picture Credits

Mrs Robinson by Thomas Gainsborough, and Mrs *Robinson* by George Romney reproduced by kind permission of the Trustees of the Wallace Collection; *George, Prince of Wales*, by Jeremiah Meyer, and *Mrs R— sitting for her picture* by Thomas Rowlandson, The Royal Collection © 2006, Her Majesty Queen Elizabeth II; Front of Drury Lane Theatre and *The Dramatic Enchantress* and *The Doating Lover* © The British Library; Traditional costume of Perdita in the eighteenth century, from Thomas Jeffrys' *Collection of the Dresses of Different Nations* (1757) (© The British Library); *David Garrick* by courtesy of the National Portrait Gallery, London; *Richard Brinsley Sheridan* © Novosti/Bridgeman Art Library; Mrs Robinson as Amanda, Scene from *The School for Scandal, Vauxhall Gardens, Florizel and Perdita, Perdito and Perdita, The Thunderer, Perdita on her Last Legs* and Frontispiece to *Poems* by Mrs Robinson, © The British Museum; Playbill © V&A Picture Library; Masquerade at the Pantheon © Guildhall Library, Corporation of London; *Lieutenant Banastre Tarleton* by Sir Joshua Reynolds © National Gallery Picture Library; Dr Awsiter's Baths © from the Collection of the Royal Pavilion Libraries and Museums; Mary Robinson's Grave © Olivia Davenport.

Traditional costume of Perdita

Preface and Acknowledgements

In the churchyard of Old Windsor, not far from where I live, lie the remains of the beautiful Mary Robinson, actress, royal mistress, poet, novelist, and feminist. The grave is shaded by trees on the north side of the church and the stone is green from damp; the area has a melancholy feel. Hers is not the only tomb on the shady side, but nevertheless seems cut off from the crowded gathering in the sunshine, as if shunned by the morally righteous in death as in life. An old photo shows that wrought-iron railings once protected the grave, but they disappeared in the Second World War. Shortly afterwards the inscription changed too; it originally read 'Mrs. Mary Robinson, Author of Poems and other Literary Works, died the 26th December, 1800, at Englefield Cottage, in Surrey, aged 43 years', but in 1952 a great-great niece had it re-inscribed:

MARY ROBINSON
BORN 27TH NOVR 1758
DIED 26TH DECR 1800
'PERDITA'
(BORN DARBY)

She imposed the nickname by which Mary is certainly best known, but which would not have been her choice for her monument. Rather than recalling the notoriety of her early years she wished to be remembered as a poet and yearned for the laurels of authorship, once writing to a friend that she did not care what ill fortune she might suffer, if only 'Fate would grant that o'er my tomb/*One little Laurel* wreath might bloom'. So, on a golden evening in July 2004, a gathering of friends and villagers assembled in the churchyard to grant her wish, as part of the launch of the hardback version of this book. With due ceremony a laurel wreath was placed on her grave, the church bells rang a joyful peal, and flower petals were strewn over the tomb to create a colourful, scented carpet. Next week the billboard for the local paper read 'OLD WINDSOR'S FOND FAREWELL TO ACTRESS PERDITA'. After two hundred years!

Although the name Perdita translates as 'the lost girl', Mrs Robinson was never totally forgotten, only pushed into the footnotes of history just as her grave was tucked into an obscure corner of the churchyard. Her writings were largely ignored, but the story of the pretty actress who briefly shone as a royal mistress remained. Prudish Victorians thought her history best ignored too: one mid-century moralist commented that 'No woman could look upon *her* grave without a blush or a tear'. Nevertheless her tale got told, though early accounts tended to the semi-fictional and sentimental as Stanley V. Makower's *Perdita: A Romance in Biography* (1908), or Marguerite Steen's *The Lost One* (1937). Steen is surprisingly obtuse about her, dismissing Mary as a woman with neither 'brains' nor 'strength of character', and she is so patronising about her poetry that it is surprising she wrote about her at all. Philip Lindsay in both *The Loves of Florizel* (1951) and *A Piece for Candlelight* (1952) presents her as a saucy little madam. A new era of serious biographical study was opened in 1957 by the publication of Robert D. Bass's *The Green Dragoon: The Lives of Banastre Tarleton and Mary Robinson*, though in this Mary takes second billing to the man who was her lover for fifteen years, a British hero, Yankee villain, of the American War of Independence. Bass struggles to understand Mary and is naïve in taking her on her own terms, but his book is an invaluable source on Tarleton and includes a great deal of material about Mary, printing many poems, letters and newspaper references in full. There have been scholarly short biographical studies more recently; Judith Pascoe's biographical section in her introduction to *Mary Robinson: Selected Poems* (2000) is a succinct, lively, and scrupulously researched account. M.J. Levy wrote an informative chapter in his *The Mistresses of King George IV* (1996); he had previously edited Mary Robinson's *Memoirs* (1994), though he seems not to have consulted the manuscript which shows interesting variations from the version published by her daughter in 1801. This is kept in a private collection in a stately home not open to the public, and it was one of the privileges of my research to be able to examine it. Up to the middle of 2005 there had not been a serious, full-scale biography: then, suddenly, there were three. My book was followed three months later by one by Paula Byrne and three months after that came Sarah Gristwood's; both take *Perdita* as their primary titles.

This clutch of biographies, however unwelcome to the individual author, shows the current interest in the lives of feisty eighteenth-century women, among whom Mary Robinson claims attention. Her lovers or admirers included some of the foremost men of the late eighteenth century – George Prince of Wales, Richard Brinsley Sheridan, Charles James Fox, William Godwin and Samuel Taylor Coleridge. David Garrick tutored her in acting, and Sir Joshua Reynolds, Thomas Gainsborough and George Romney all painted her portrait. Likewise, during recent years, academics have been rediscovering women writers of the period, many of them well-known in their own day but whose reputations became submerged in the dominance of male romantic writers of the late eighteenth and early nineteenth centuries. Pascoe's anthology of Robinson's poems in 2000, the bicentenary of her death, is an indication of the attention now given to Mary Robinson the writer, the role she forged for herself after a devastating illness left her a helpless cripple. Many recent books and academic articles have considered her as Romantic poet, novelist, feminist and autobiographer; in the year 2000 an academic conference was wholly devoted to her.

I have not, however, written a literary biography. For most readers it would be pointless to do so since her works are hard to come by outside specialist libraries. I have not therefore entered into detailed literary analysis of the texts, but have tried to give some idea of the nature of Mrs Robinson's writings, suggest how they were received at the time, and use them to help understand and illustrate the life of a woman whose chameleon career encompassed many different roles. Her fame as a writer mattered to her; at the end of her life she wished for literary recognition as she had once wanted theatrical applause. For that reason she fought against the stigma of immorality with which she had been marked since her brief affair with the Prince of Wales. But, as Judith Pascoe in her introduction to the *Selected Poems* writes: 'It is probably impossible to overplay the role of Robinson's affair with the Prince of Wales in her later literary and social reception' (p.38). However, even though she allowed Coleridge and others to think her a penitent Magdalen, I do not believe that, secretly, she was ever ashamed that once upon a time she had been wooed and won by a handsome Prince.

It has been fascinating to follow her life as it was presented in the newspapers of the day and these have been an important source of information. There are obvious comparisons to be made with today's media treatment of celebrities (not to mention attention-seeking behaviour by such celebrities, royal scandals, the sale of royal love letters, and so on). But these I have left to the reader. When journalists and pamphleteers wanted an image for Mary Robinson at the height of her fame they looked to the heavens, comparing her to a comet, meteor, star or sun; I have tried to convey something of the brilliancy that so dazzled her contemporaries.

With quotations I have followed modern practice in printing them as they were originally, though it was tempting to remove some of the capital letters from the poetry. Mary was addicted to them as a device for emphasis – they are there on her gravestone – but they can make her poems read with the insistency of an old-fashioned telegram. Nor have I tried to represent prices in current terms. The £20,000 promissory note which she received from the Prince should probably be thought of as the equivalent of £2,000,000, but simply to multiply all prices by 100 not only ignores inflation over the period of her lifetime, but also the difference in values of goods between then and now. The top price for a ticket to Drury Lane then, for example, was five shillings [25p]: this would become £25, cheap in comparison to today's prices, but not startlingly so. Apply the same rule to the cost of a copy of Mary's 1791 volume of poems and the guinea price converts into £105! (A guinea was a pound and a shilling [1*s* = 5p]; there were 20 shillings in every pound, and twelve old pence in every shilling. A half-crown was two shillings and sixpence [2*s* 6*d*], 12½p today.)

Many people have been of great assistance to me in preparing this biography. I owe a large debt to Dr Judith Pascoe of Iowa University, a most generous scholar, who helped enormously by sending across the Atlantic her copies of some of Mary's and her daughter's novels, and other writings unobtainable outside specialist libraries; she has answered queries and been consistently encouraging. I have also benefited greatly from her own exemplary and stimulating writing.

To many other friends I am likewise indebted. Dr Lorna J. Clark most kindly posted material which was hard to obtain here from Canada. I am very grateful to Catherine Dolman for her detailed commentary on the dresses worn by Mary in her portraits, and for answering other queries. Professor Katharine Worth has kindly checked the sections on the theatre. I am particularly grateful to Dr Lynn Mucklow for her careful analysis of Mary's medical problems in so far as they are known, and for the expert suggestions of Dr Kerry Thomas and Kathleen Whelan.

Janet Martin was most helpful in undertaking preliminary research in Liverpool library into Tarleton family history. Geraldine Lillicrap kindly likewise looked for material in Bath library. I am very grateful to Dr Brigitte Mitchell who brought back historical material from Aachen and translated it for me. Lucy Norman checked some information in Brighton, and kept my computer healthy.

To Janet Kennish's meticulous recording of her research I am indebted for the discovery of Thomas Robinson's death. Graham Dennis of Blacklock Books in Englefield Green obtained books and gave valuable advice in trying to establish the whereabouts of Englefield Cottage. I should like to thank John Handcock for answering legal questions and for trying to find some record of Thomas Robinson at the Law Society. For the paperback edition corrections kindly supplied by Professor Jonathan Bate and David Gilson have been incorporated.

I am most grateful to Jean Higgins for hospitality and company on an expedition to Talgarth, and to Edwina Higgins for information. I am likewise appreciative of the encouragement and many helpful suggestions made by Alison Haymonds. Ellen Dollery, Margaret Gilson, Jeanette Obstoj, Jasmine Tarry and Professor W.M.S. Russell all lent books or provided other valuable help. Margaret Gilson also made the laurel wreath. My daughter Olivia kindly allowed me to use her drawing of Mary's grave.

I should like to express my very great gratitude to owners of private collections of material, including the manuscript of her memoirs, for allowing me access and giving me permission to quote from their holdings. Her Majesty The Queen has given gracious permission to quote from papers in the Royal Archives. Broadview Press, Peterborough, ON, Canada, has very kindly given permission to quote from *Mary Robinson: Selected Poems*, edited by Judith Pascoe, 2000; *A Letter to the Women of England* and *The Natural Daughter*, edited by Sharon M. Setzer, 2003; *Walsingham*, edited by Julie A. Shaffer, 2003. Peter Owen Publishers has generously allowed quotation from *Perdita: The Memoirs of Mary Robinson* (1758–1800), edited by M.J. Levy, 1994. The following institutions have also given permission to quote from their archive holdings: The Abinger Collection at the Bodleian Library; The Carl H. Pforzheimer Collection of Shelley and His Circle, The New York Public Library Astor, Lenox and Tilden Foundations; The Huntington Library, California; Hertfordshire County Council; Westminster City Archives.

I am also grateful for the help in various ways of Miss Pamela Clark, Registrar of the Royal Archives, Christopher Lloyd, Surveyor of The Queen's Pictures, Dr Bruce Barker-Benfield at the Bodleian Library, Stephen Wagner and Laura O'Keefe of the New York Public Library, Alison Williams of Bristol Record Office, Ruth Hobbins and staff at Liverpool Library, Ali Burdon at the City of Westminster Archives, Rosemary Fisher of Worcestershire Library and History Centre, Frances Younson at Gwent Record Office, Angela Bolger of Taplow Court, Buckinghamshire, and Graham Snell of Brooks's Club.

My biggest debt, however, has been to my husband Tony, patient reader and most valued commentator during the writing. To him, and to all friends who have helped and encouraged me, I dedicate the book.

1

Bristol Belle

She possessed surprising beauty, such as I have rarely seen equalled in any woman, and might well rescue her and my native city, Bristol, from the imputation of producing females deficient in that endowment.
(Nicholas Wraxall, *Historical and Posthumous Memoirs*)

According to her own note, it was on Sunday 14 January 1798 that Mrs Mary Robinson began to write her memoirs. A striking-looking woman in her early forties, tall and elegant, she was living with her daughter Maria at 1 Clifford Street in London's fashionable West End. The furnishings of the room where she sat would have matched the elegance of her appearance. But she was not to be envied, for she was pitiably crippled. Even with crutches she could scarcely move around, and she was dependent on servants to carry her up and down stairs, or to her coach for an outing. Frequent bouts of illness incapacitated her further; only ten days later a newspaper, the *Oracle*, reported that she was in bed 'with a nervous fever, which threatens the most serious consequences'.[1] There are few women whose health is the subject of press bulletins, but Mrs Robinson was a celebrity, in the news for her fifth and most ambitious novel, *Walsingham*, which the *Morning Post* described as 'one of the most entertaining [novels] ever published . . . full of interest, full of anecdote of fashionable life', its satire rendering 'a service to society'.[2] The paper printed extracts, and on 3 January a 'tribute of praise' to her verse (which was also appearing regularly in the *Post*) by one 'FRANCINI', a pseudonym of the young Samuel Taylor Coleridge. Mrs Robinson sent him a set of the four-volume *Walsingham* by way of thanks.[3]

But she was only too aware that the *Morning Post*, the newspaper most loudly trumpeting her literary fame, had nearly two decades earlier been equally loud in vilifying her. In 1780 she had left her husband and her profession as an actress for an affair with the seventeen-year old George, Prince of Wales. Predictably it had not lasted, but the scandal while it did, Mary's flamboyant behaviour and the liaisons she subsequently engaged in, had not only fuelled the gossip columns but had left a residual stain, however hard she sought to remove it through her poetry, and as a novelist peddling conventional morality and satirising the fashionable follies in which she herself had once indulged (though she had never been guilty of gambling, principal target of attack in *Walsingham*). She thought herself misunderstood, and planned her memoirs to be a 'vindication' of her life.[4]

The impulse for this self-justification may have stemmed from talking with William Godwin, whose *Memoirs of Mary Wollstonecraft* were published shortly after she began her own. Mary knew Godwin and had known his wife, who had died the previous autumn after giving birth to the future Mary Shelley. She too had had a notorious reputation, as a supporter of the French Revolution and as the author of the feminist *A Vindication of the Rights of Woman* (1792). Godwin thought that an honest presentation of his wife's life story could not fail to rouse public sympathy; instead, his revelation that she had had an illegitimate child by an American businessman, Gilbert Imlay, that she had twice thereafter attempted suicide, and that she was pregnant before her marriage to Godwin, proved a disaster. Even former supporters were horrified, and the hostile press Godwin received may have given Mary pause. Too much honesty might be counter-productive. Nevertheless, she declared in the *Memoirs* that 'These pages are the pages of truth, unadorned by romance'.[5]

Precept and practice are two different things however. Most autobiographers require some rose-tinting to the mirrors in which they observe themselves; memory is fickle, and 'truth' compromised when untruths have been claimed for years. The laudanum which she took to dull the pain of her illness must also have blunted her sense of reality. *Memoirs of the Late Mrs Robinson*, posthumously published, has to be approached with caution, though it is the primary source of most of the information about her early life. She once addressed a poem to a friend 'who desired to have my portrait', offering a verbal one instead. In it she recognised her faults and virtues – quick-tempered, ambitious, particular in friendship and unforgiving if betrayed, readily sympathetic, sometimes obstinate but never self-interested, a lover of

Genius. All of this is true, but it is to a biographer's raised eyebrows that she also declares:

E'en from the early days of youth,
I've blessed the sacred voice of TRUTH;
  And Candour is my pride:
I always SPEAK what I BELIEVE;
I know not if I CAN deceive;
  Because I NEVER TRIED.[6]

She had probably convinced herself of the truth of what she wrote: tales repeated often enough become established fact. And, of course, truth is to be found in the *Memoirs*; 'unadorned' however, her memories are not, in either content or style.

Bristol, where Mary's story begins, was second only to London as a trading port, and likewise river-based; its ships fanned out to Ireland, France, Spain, Africa, America, the Baltic and the Caribbean, and it was better placed than London for the cross-Atlantic trade. It served as a distribution point for West Country raw materials and was itself heavily industrialised with glass manufactories and sugar refineries. Horace Walpole, who disliked its mercantilism, described the city as 'the dirtiest great shop I ever saw, with so foul a river, that had I seen the least appearance of cleanliness, I should have concluded they washed their linen in it'.[7] But Bristol had another identity, being also an ancient city; the towers of religious foundations matched the belching chimneys of its manufactories and the forests of masts in its river basins. Even Walpole admitted that the cathedral was 'neat . . . and has pretty tombs', and with prosperity the town was pushing out beyond the city walls and creating elegant squares and streets of houses. A further aspect of Bristol life and money-making was found a mile downstream where the Hotwells attracted invalids to drink the mineral waters, and fashionable society to attend its summer season. However, Bristol's wealth had its sinister side; until 1747 when it was overtaken by Liverpool, it was the foremost port engaging in the slave trade. But Mary's merchant father, Nicholas Darby, was unconnected with that trade of human degradation, making his endeavours in the chilly waters of the North Atlantic with its abundance of fish, furs and seal oils.

Mary says that her father's family was originally Irish, with the name of MacDermott, altered to Darby for the sake of an estate. But Nicholas appears to have been born around 1720 in what is now Canada, then part of America.[8] He engaged as a ship's captain in the Newfoundland fishing trade, at some time coming to Bristol where he established himself, the town serving as a winter base. There was great rivalry with the French over the fishing gounds and, during what became known as the Seven Years War, Darby represented the Society of Merchant Venturers of Bristol (set up in 1552 and still in existence) in informing the British Board of Trade of French activities in the region. He made useful contacts with influential men, such as the elder Pitt, the Earl of Bristol, Sir Hugh Palliser (who was appointed Governor of Newfoundland), and the Lord Chancellor, Robert Henley Earl of Northington, who became Mary's godfather. Nicholas was a fearless, single-minded man from whom Mary inherited her ambitious streak: her liaison with the Prince might be called her own bold merchant venture.

Mary describes her mother, Hester Vanacott, as the 'mildest, the most unoffending of existing mortals'; she took her vivacious manners from her and, the other side of the coin, the melancholy which she stresses in the opening pages of the *Memoirs*. Hester came from Bridgwater in Somerset, though it was in the tiny village of Donyatt near Ilminster in the same county that, on 14 July 1749, 'Hatty Venecot' married 'Mr Nicol's Derby of Bristol'. In writing about her ancestry on her mother's side Mary emphasises the female line, proud that 'My mother was the grand-child of Catherine Seys, one of the daughters and co-heiresses of Richard Seys, Esq., of Boverton Castle in Glamorganshire' (to the west of Cardiff, now demolished). She also makes much of a very slight connection through the marriage of Catherine's sister with a nephew of the philosopher John Locke.[9] This Catherine Seys, whose daughter (Mary's grandmother) was called Elizabeth, must have married a man with the surname of Petit since on 30 July 1723 Elizabeth Petit married James Vinicot (spellings of surnames show much variation at this period) in St Mary's Church Bridgwater; on 22 May in the year following Hester was baptised. A son, James, was born the following year. Mary was fond of her grandmother but says nothing about her grandfather or great-grandfather, probably because their births and occupations were nothing to boast of: Petits and Vinicots seem to have been small-town tradesmen in Bridgwater.[10] She lets it be known, however, that the godmother of her grandmother Elizabeth was Lady Tynt of Haswell (south of Bridgwater), and that she spent her days in good works with her godmother, visiting the sick and indigent.

Nicholas and Hester went to live in Bristol, where John, their first-born, was baptised on 9 June 1752; a daughter Elizabeth was baptised 12 January 1755, but at only eighteen months she died of smallpox. She was buried on 29 October 1756, only three weeks after a Mary Darby had been interred, perhaps likewise a smallpox victim and possibly Nicholas's mother; that would explain why the next daughter to be born was called Mary.[11] After her would come two more brothers, William, baptised on 13 October 1760, and George, for whom no baptismal record was found.[12] Except for William's, all these births and deaths were recorded at the cathedral church of St Augustine the Less, and the family in fact lived in Minster House, hard against its walls; it was thought to have been the Prior's lodging of the Augustinian Abbey, whose church became Bristol cathedral after the dissolution of the monasteries. This building straddled past and present in combining new construction with the old, and though Mary writes of it 'sinking to decay' in 1798, a painting of 1821 shows a cheerful little house with small front garden giving onto the Green, with a blend of Georgian sash and Gothic dormer windows. Minster House was demolished in 1868 when the cathedral was given a nave, which it had previously lacked.[13]

Mary herself would still recognise the chancel and transepts of the cathedral, its monuments and flagstone memorials, its cloister and ancient chapter-house, and it is these surroundings which she invokes when describing the night of her own birth:

> In this awe-inspiring habitation . . . during a tempestuous night, on the twenty-seventh of November 1758, I first opened my eyes to this world of duplicity and sorrow. I have often heard my mother say that a more stormy hour she never remembered. The wind whistled round the dark pinnacles of the minster tower, and the rain beat in torrents against the casements of her chamber. Through life the tempest has

> followed my footsteps; and I have in vain looked for a short interval of repose from the perseverance of sorrow.[14]

That ominous storm is all too convenient to her theme. As many have observed, this is the language of a Gothic novel, and much in the mode of *Walsingham* whose eponymous hero-narrator declares: 'I was born to sorrow; I was nursed with tears'.[15]

Mary's date of birth seems innocent enough, but in this 'world of duplicity' it proves not so. In 2002 Alix Nathan published her discovery that Mary Darby was not born in 1758.[16] She quotes a baptismal register of St Augustine's which for 19 July 1758 reads 'Polle Daught. of Nicholas and Hester Darby', with the added note: 'Born nov.27.th 1756' (Polly is a diminutive of Mary). It thus appears that Mary took two years from her life, the assumption being that she wanted to suggest that at the time of her marriage she was only fourteen, scarcely out of the nursery and a passive participant in a ceremony into which she had been thrust by her mother. The problem with this, however, is that in the *Memoirs* she indicates that her age at marriage was *fifteen* (in 1773), while on her tombstone it is given as forty-three years, both of which imply a date of birth in 1757. It is then startling to discover that the date 1758, quoted above and for 200 years the accepted year of birth, does not appear at all in the original manuscript of the *Memoirs*. Mary herself actually wrote that 'during a tempestuous night on the twenty-seventh of november [*sic*], I first opened my eyes to this world of duplicity and sorrow', giving no year at all.[17] She is therefore not guilty of claiming that she was born in 1758, a date which must have been wrongly calculated by her daughter and added before publication.

Was Mary nevertheless lying in taking one rather than two years off her age by implying, if not stating, that she was born in 1757? The situation is further complicated because it turns out that what Nathan saw was a *copy* of the baptismal register, not the original which records the baptism on 19 July 1758 without any note of birth-date.[18] There are a number of cases where the actual date of birth was considerably earlier than baptism (perhaps because fathers were away at sea); in these cases it is recorded in a line underneath, and the copyist follows that practice, except in Mary's case where, because it was not in the original register, he squeezed it in as an afterthought at the end of the line. All that can confidently be stated therefore is that Mary Robinson was *not* born in 1758.

One has the choice consequently of believing her, or the copyist. The fact that no actual date was given in the original register might be taken as an argument that she was still a babe in arms at baptism. But since the copyist knew the exact day and month of Mary's birth it would be logical to assume that he knew the year too; moreover, he had no reason to lie, while Mary did have reason to want to be thought younger than she was. The fact that she does not put 1757 as the year of her birth when it would have been logical to do so, has been taken in this biography as a strong indication that she shied away from telling an absolute lie, and that 1756 is accurate. But it is open to those wishing to exonerate Mary from deception to choose the later date.

This confused situation illustrates the difficulty in considering Mary's childhood, since evidence apart from her own is sparse. She portrays herself, for example, as being different in both appearance and nature from her brothers. The boys were 'fair and lusty, with auburn hair, light blue eyes, and countenances peculiarly animated and lovely'; she however was 'swarthy', with large eyes and 'features peculiarly marked with the most pensive and melancholy cast'.[19] Maybe, but she grew up with blue eyes and auburn hair like her brothers, and donated them to most of her heroines. (A further red herring is that she claims a 'striking likeness' to the family of her god-father, Lord Northington, as if hinting that he was her natural father; this must be counted part of a tendency to fantasise – in *The False Friend* (1799), written in the same year as the *Memoirs*, the heroine's guardian does indeed prove to be her father.) Mary also conveys a marked difference of temperaments, her brothers outgoing and active while she was sensitive and inward-looking. When they played on the Green, she sought out the cathedral gloom, where she crouched under the eagle lectern and thrilled to the deep tones of the organ and the chanting choristers; after she had learned to read, her 'great delight' was of memorising the inscriptions on Walpole's pretty tombs.

The mixture of modern commercialism and ancient spirituality, present both in the nature of the home and in the city at large, must have helped to shape the woman she became, but since she had been labelled a commercial adventuress she wanted in her memoirs to distance herself from the trading elements of her background. Claiming the studious cloister as her natural environment, she cast herself in the same childhood mould as her fellow-Bristolian, the poet Thomas Chatterton, born in 1752. He took the pillared aisles of St Mary Redcliffe as his boyhood playground, and later claimed to have found the poetic works of a medieval monk, 'Thomas Rowley', among its ancient lumber. These poems are remarkable creations, even if forgeries, and Chatterton's apparent suicide in his London lodgings at the age of eighteen made him for Mary the model of neglected genius starving in an attic.[20] She too was a Chatterton before she was a Nicholas Darby.

Nicholas was an indulgent father, however, and ambitious for his daughter. He engaged various tutors, including a distinguished organist, Edmund Broderip, who taught her to play and sing on an expensive Kirkwood harpsichord. Though she is vague about dates, she was also educated at a boarding-school, a popular alternative to a live-in governess or privately hired tutors.[21] Such schools provided women teachers with an opportunity for independent income, but were hit-and-miss affairs for the pupils; had Mary been unlucky she might have found herself at such a one as the Bristol school where

> YOUNG LADIES are genteelly boarded, and carefully taught to read their MOTHER-TONGUE with PROPRIETY and CORRECTNESS, and are also instructed in all kinds of NEEDLE-WORK, and every other branch of polite and useful Education; of which the forming their tender Minds in Sobriety and Virtue will be most strictly attended to.[22]

This was the kind of school where, as she wrote in *Walsingham*, a girl 'read authors, whose works she did not comprehend; prattled a foreign jargon, without knowing the meaning of the words she uttered [and] finished needle-work which in half a century would only adorn the lumber-room of her grand-daughter'.[23]

Mary was fortunate, however. A highly-regarded 'School for Young Ladies' was then found at 6 Trinity Street, near the cathedral, which enabled her to sleep at home. It was run by the More sisters, Mary, Elizabeth and Sarah, who were later joined by Martha and Hannah. It had opened in 1758, advertising its curriculum as 'French, Reading, Writing, Arithmetic, and Needlework', that essential 'polite' accomplishment at least relegated to the bottom of the list.[24] Hannah, the youngest and cleverest of the sisters, was to write plays, novels, works about female education, and as she grew older a stream of religious tracts; she became the friend of Dr Johnson, David Garrick and Horace Walpole, for whom she 'redeem[ed] the credit of Bristol'.[25] The irreproachable sisters were reputed to be less than pleased when in later life Mrs Robinson revealed that she had been their pupil, but Hester Thrale Piozzi was much amused to discover that 'Hannah More *la Devote* was the Person who Educated fair *Perdita la Pecheresse*'; she asked Miss More if it was true and she 'owned it as a fact'.[26] Maria may have known of their embarrassment, for another discovery in the manuscript of the *Memoirs* is that several lines about the More sisters have been scribbled over and not included in the published version. Much can still be read however, and it is in no way offensive, merely noting that the five sisters each managed a 'separate department with zeal, good sense and ability' and that Hannah More the 'accomplished authoress of Percy [her drama] divided her hours, between the arduous tasks of "teaching the young ideas how to shoot" and [exemplify ?] by works of taste and fancy'.[27]

At the time, bright little Mary must have been a star pupil. She loved to perform, reciting poems such as Pope's 'Elegy on the Death of an Unfortunate Lady', which she claims to have known by heart before she was seven. It would have been a huge excitement when the Misses More, who were theatre enthusiasts, took the whole school to a performance of *King Lear* at Bristol's newly opened Theatre Royal, with the actor-manager William Powell in the lead. It may seem a strange choice for young girls, but it cannot have been too disturbing as the eighteenth-century version of the play had a happy ending, with Cordelia saved from the hangman's noose and Lear surviving too. Mary remembered the performance with sufficient clarity later to be critical of Powell's wife for playing Cordelia with insufficient '*éclat*'.[28] Powell's daughters were at the school, and, among other players' children, Priscilla Hopkins, daughter of the Drury Lane prompter, with whom Mary would later share the stage.

All seemed well at home. Nicholas Darby's trading concerns had flourished and Mary was treated to fine clothes from London, and a bed furnished with 'the richest crimson damask'.[29] They had moved into a larger house in the area known as St Augustine's Back; entertainment was lavish, and the household provided with 'the luxuries of plate, silk furniture, foreign wines, etc.', which created the pseudo-aristocratic life-style to which the merchant class aspired. But Darby was restless and ambitious (because he was American, thought his daughter), and in 1765 he embarked on a 'wild and romantic' scheme to set up fisheries for whale, cod, salmon and seal along the south coast of Labrador, a project made possible when the land was ceded to Britain in the Treaty of Paris of 1763. For his plans he obtained backers, including the Governor, Sir Hugh Palliser, but it would mean overwintering. Darby proposed leaving his three younger children in England (the eldest son John had been established in a trading business in Leghorn), but to take his wife with him. Hester, however, would neither consent to be parted from her children, nor to undertake the hazardous voyage. Nothing would deter her husband, and investing £8,000 in the venture he set sail with 170 men and, unknown to the family, a mistress willing to brave the venture. From this time Mary dated the 'sorrows' of her family.

However, for the time being the carefree life continued for Mary, and 'To sing, to play a lesson on the harpsichord, to recite an elegy, and to make doggrel [*sic*] verses, made the extent of my occupations'.[30] Letters from Labrador were reassuring as Darby established headquarters at Cape Charles. But then they grew infrequent, and Hester suffered a terrible blow when six-year-old William died from measles.[31] Next year there was worse news: the Labrador scheme had failed when a marauding band of Inuit 'most barbarously and treacherously . . . killed three of [Darby's] men and drove the rest to the Mountains burnt and destroy'd his Boats Stages and Dwellings and wasted his Salt'. These words come from a petition to the King for compensation for his losses, amounting to £4,677 3*s* 6*d*.[32] His ambitions ruined, Darby ordered his wife to sell the family home and all its contents. The subsequent auction took place over five successive days, from 7 to 11 March 1768; among the 'elegant' household goods offered were 'two fine Pieces of India painted Silk, two beautiful Italian Marble Slabs in curious carved Mahogany Frames [and] a very curious Italian Marble Chimney Piece finely executed'.[33] There was also 'a very fine-toned' Kirkman harpsichord.

A letter from her husband summoned Mrs Darby to meet him in London, bringing Mary and George with her. It proved a painful reunion, as Nicholas announced that he intended to live with his mistress, though willing to pay for his wife's 'board' and the continuing education of his son and daughter. At the age of eleven, Mary found that her secure world was destroyed for ever; for the rest of her life she would be subject to constant changes of address and financial insecurity.

However apprehensive she felt about the outcome, it must have been exciting for Mary to go to the capital, the largest city in Europe. Standing on the south bank of the Avon she would have been able to see most of Bristol, population 50,000, spread over the hill opposite, and have a sense of it as a self-contained community; but London was vast and impersonal, its population over half a million and stretching some 5 miles from Hyde Park in the fashionable west to the wharfs, yards and foetid streets of Limehouse in the east. Growth was unrestricted, and it was spreading inexorably through the fields and market gardens with which it was fringed. It was a dirty, polluted city, dark with soot in winter, hazed by dust in summer, foul with the stench of street refuse. Noisy too; in a poem of the last year of her life, Mary would evoke its early morning sounds and activities:

> Who has not wak'd to list the busy sounds
> Of summer's morning, in the sultry smoke
> Of noisy London? On the pavement hot
> The sooty chimney-boy, with dingy face
> And tatter'd covering, shrilly bawls his trade,
> Rousing the sleepy housemaid. At the door
> The milk-pail rattles, and the tinkling bell
> Proclaims the dustman's office; while the street
> Is lost in clouds impervious. Now begins
> The din of hackney-coaches, waggons, carts;
> While tinmen's shops, and noisy trunk-makers,
> Knife-grinders, coopers, squeaking cork-cutters,
> Fruit-barrows, and the hunger-giving cries
> Of vegetable venders, fill the air . . .[34]

Mary had been used to spending the summers in Clifton, famed for its pure air. Clean air was harder to find in London, but she and

George were placed in a school in Chelsea, detached from the city and considered a healthy place for educational establishments.

Of Meribah Lorrington, her new teacher, Mary wrote in her *Memoirs* that 'All that I ever learned I acquired from this extraordinary woman'.[35] This must be counted exaggeration, but Mary may have been thinking that it was from her that she had her introduction to classical learning, normally denied to girls, which had recently helped her to create a viable sense of Walsingham's educational background.[36] If Mrs Lorrington was an extraordinary woman, so was her father, an Anabaptist who frightened the children with his strange Persian robe and fierce look, but who had been a teacher himself and had given his daughter a 'masculine', classical education, which she passed on to her pupils. Mary became her favourite because of her capacity for study, and her enthusiasm for writing verses, tales of pastoral love and death in landscapes of crystal fountains and flow'ry meads (later published in her first volume of poems). But Mrs Lorrington had a weakness: addiction to drink, the consequence, she said, of widowhood. That and her father's odd behaviour led to the school's closure. Mary was sent to another, across the river in Battersea, but her father's failure to keep up with remittances (he was again pursuing his American dream) worried her mother, and she took her daughter away.

Mrs Darby then had the bright idea of starting her own school, and found suitable accommodation in Chelsea. Mother-and-daughter combinations were quite common, and as well as engaging assistants Hester asked Mary to undertake the English teaching, read the lessons at prayers, and superintend the children's dressing. Mary may have found some aspects of the new life tiresome: in her novel *The Natural Daughter*, the patience of the heroine Martha Morley is tested when teaching 'by the stupidity of some; the infantine impertinence of others; the budding pride of the high-born [and] the pert vulgarity of the low'.[37] According to Mary the school acquired ten to twelve pupils, but it did not survive Nicholas Darby's return from another failed commercial venture; he had lost money again after being out-manoeuvred by local rivals, and in his embittered state felt the school an insult to his capacity as husband and father, and ordered its closure. Hester obediently took lodgings in Marylebone, and assistant-teacher Mary became a pupil again, at a nearby establishment called Oxford House.

Before the school closed, however, Mary had witnessed a sad sight. One evening, sitting at the window, she heard 'a deep sigh or rather a groan of anguish'. Realising that there was a woman in distress Mary went to help:

> She, bursting into tears, asked whether I did not know her. Her dress was torn and filthy; – she was almost naked; – and an old bonnet, which nearly hid her face, so completely disfigured her features that I had not the smallest idea of the person who was then almost sinking before me. I gave her a small sum of money, and inquired the cause of her apparent agony: she took my hand and pressed it to her lips.– 'Sweet girl,' said she, 'you are still the angel I ever knew you!'[38]

It was Meribah Lorrington. Mrs Darby was not at home, but with the help of the French assistant Mary cleaned her up and gave her clothing. Mrs Lorrington refused to say where she was living, and years later Mary heard that she had died in the Chelsea workhouse. This Hogarthian history of descent from intellectual superiority and independent means to physical degradation provided Mrs Lorrington's pupil with a different sort of lesson.

Mary's sympathies could always be engaged; what she lacked was strong guidance in the ways of the world as her developing beauty became a magnet to men. She says that, being tall, she looked older than her years, and tells of a naval captain, a friend of her father's, who drank tea with her and her mother one Sunday evening and was so taken with her that he afterwards made a proposal of marriage. Hetty asked how old he thought her daughter was; to his answer 'about sixteen', she replied with a smile 'not quite thirteen'.[39] Nicholas too was aware of his daughter's attractions. He took Mary to call on the son of his old friend Lord Northington, who had died in January 1772; Robert Henley, the second Earl, became an astute politician, but like his friend Charles James Fox had the reputation of a rake. Mary says she received from him the 'most marked attention and politeness', but Darby no doubt noticed appraising glances. When he disappeared from England again, he left with a chilling threat to his wife: 'Take care that no dishonour falls upon my daughter. If she is not safe at my return I will annihilate you.'[40] We know nothing of what happened to Nicholas in the years that followed. Could he have found himself in jail in the far north for trading irregularities, on some charge of a rival? Or did he get caught up in the American War of Independence, perhaps on the Yankee side? Bristol merchants generally supported the Americans, for the sake of maintaining trade. All that Mary says of her father thereafter is that he was 'out of the country' when she was on the stage; there must be a reason for her silence.

Mrs Darby's difficulties of chaperonage were no doubt compounded by her daughter's inheritance of Nicholas's strong personality. Mary loved her mother, but she would not have been meek and biddable; she liked attention and was beginning to feel her power to command masculine attention. It must have been with considerable agitation that after her husband's departure Hetty heard a proposal that her daughter should make a career in the theatre. She had caught the eye of Oxford House's dancing master, John Hussey; he was also ballet master at Covent Garden Theatre, and it was his suggestion that, with 'her extraordinary genius' for performance, she should make trial of the stage. The girl was wildly excited, contemplating 'a thousand triumphs'; Mrs Darby was only partly reassured by those who could cite actresses who had preserved 'an unspotted fame' in a profession constantly the subject of scandal.[41] One can readily imagine the cajolings, pleadings, tears, perhaps tantrums, with which the teenage girl sought to overcome her mother's reluctance. Hetty eventually agreed to an audition before Thomas Hull, a Covent Garden stalwart of reassuring stolidity, though she may have winced at Mary's pieces – speeches of Jane Shore from Nicholas Rowe's play of that name, and the story of a repentant whore. Mary's choice shows both her ambition and her confidence, for Jane Shore was one of the great roles for tragic actresses; she records that the actor 'seemed delighted' with her attempt. However it was not to Covent Garden Theatre that she went but, after an introduction by a mutual friend, to the Theatre Royal Drury Lane, and its great actor-manager David Garrick. (The 1737 Licensing Act permitted only two theatres in London for the main season, a measure brought in by Robert Walpole when drama was being used to attack his government.)

Garrick had recently moved into a grand house, part of Adelphi Terrace designed by Robert Adam, and it was in this impressive building, with painted ceilings and views over the river, that Mary auditioned again. Garrick had always encouraged new talent and in this same year of 1772 he put forward three aspirants. Success was not guaranteed however, and of one young woman given trial the prompter noted that 'she is a piece of still life, sings out of tune and will never make an actress'.[42] Mary would have to pass such hard-headed professional scrutiny if she were to make the stage her career.

Garrick himself had made a triumphant entry into the London theatrical scene in 1741, when his sensational performance of Richard III popularised a new 'natural' style of acting to replace the static, declamatory one of the previous generation. More importantly however for Mrs Darby's peace of mind, he had as manager of Drury Lane (from 1747) purged the theatre of much of its disreputable image. He had written unexceptionable plays himself, and bowdlerised some of the grosser Restoration comedies; while he had not managed to rid the theatre of prostitutes touting for custom, he had stopped arrogant young bloods from seating themselves on the stage itself, or pursuing actresses back-stage; he had increased his company's professionalism by insisting on rehearsals and encouraging ensemble acting. Through the example of his own scandal-free life after marriage, he had helped to give his profession respectability. His energetic little figure dominated the theatrical world; in entrusting her daughter to him, Mrs Darby must have hoped she had found a safe pair of hands (they were certainly more to be trusted than those of George Colman at Covent Garden).

Richard Brinsley Sheridan, Mary's future manager, would have advised otherwise however, though at this time he was unknown. He had his first success in 1775 with *The Rivals* and also became known for his marriage to the beautiful singer Elizabeth Linley. Elizabeth had a seventeen-year-old sister Mary, and both theatre managers tried to obtain her father's consent to her joining their companies; in 1775 Garrick thought he had been successful. But Sheridan was bitterly opposed, and he wrote a long, though unfinished letter to his father-in-law warning him against a stage career in language which would have unnerved Hester Darby. Not only does Sheridan (unfairly) declare Garrick 'one of the most artful and selfish Men that ever imposed on Merit or Honesty', but what he had to say about the 'Indecency of the Profession' shows how morally dubious the stage could still appear, even allowing for exaggeration to further his own ends. To safeguard this other Mary he wrote:

> What is the *modesty* of any Woman whose trade it is eternally to represent all the different modifications of Love before a mix'd Assembly of Rakes, Whores, Lords and Blackguards in Succession! – to play the Coquet, the Wanton, to retail loose innuendos in Comedy, or glow with warm Descriptions in tragedy; and in both to be haul'd about, squeez'd and kiss'd by beastly pimping Actors! – what is to be the Fate of a Girl of seventeen in such a situation?[43]

Yet Mary Robinson was younger than Mary Linley when Garrick offered to engage her, and apparently made her something of a pet:

> Garrick was delighted with everything I did. He would sometimes request me to sing the favourite ballads of the day; but the circumstance which most pleased him, was my tone of voice, which he frequently told me closely resembled that of his favourite [Susannah] Cibber.[44]

He wanted to appear with her himself for her first performance, and decided that she should play Cordelia to his Lear.

Garrick's Lear was passionate and kingly, terrifying in the curse and storm scenes, moving to tears in his reconciliation with Cordelia. In the following year, 1773, Fanny Burney could not decide whether it was with '*pain or pleasure*' that she had witnessed his 'exquisitely great' performance.[45] But she regretted that she saw the play in its altered form, Shakespeare's language interwoven with the inferior verse of Nahum Tate. He had re-written the play in 1681 to conform with neo-classical ideas of the unities, removing the Fool because comedy and tragedy should not mix, and giving Cordelia a larger role. In Tate's version she does not marry the King of France and disappear from the action for a long time, but has a romance with Edgar and is given a companion, Arante, with whom she appears in the storm scene, declaring

> Blow winds, and lightnings fall,
> Bold in my virgin innocence I'll fly
> My royal father to relieve or die. [III, ii, 66–8]

Cordelia and Edgar, who had quarrelled, have a long scene of reconciliation which culminates in Cordelia's calling 'Come to my arms, thou dearest, best of men' and embracing whatever 'beastly pimping' actor – in Sheridan's terms – was playing the part. At the end of the play Cordelia and Edgar prepare to rule, while Lear plans a comfortable retirement with Gloucester. In fact the version which Fanny saw and Mary rehearsed had been 'improved' by Garrick, who restored much of the original poetry. Nevertheless he did not restore the Fool, and the happy ending was set in moral stone, for the eighteenth-century audience required virtue to triumph over vice, and Garrick's *King Lear* was to hold the stage until 1838.

Unfortunately Mary says next to nothing about the preparations for her role, noting only that Garrick was 'most sanguine in his expectations of my success, and every rehearsal seemed to strengthen his flattering opinion'.[46] Nevertheless, it was not all honeyed sweetness; Garrick's was the most powerful personality Mary had yet met, but to add to his 'fascinating' smile she found that he 'had at times a restless peevishness of tone which oppressively affected his hearers'. Overworked and losing his health, Garrick was becoming something of a tetchy Lear himself. Maybe he was also losing his judgement. Given that Cordelia in this version is a more substantial role than the one we are familiar with, was it a wise introductory choice for a girl who only reached her sixteenth birthday in November? Or was the childless actor indulging himself with the company and admiration of a very pretty girl, aware that her mother's opposition (and Nicholas Darby's potential return) made a début uncertain? It does not sound as if these 'rehearsals' were on stage with other players.

Nevertheless Garrick encouraged Mary to frequent the theatre as much as possible, and probably provided tickets to his box. The stage-struck girl was only too willing, soon drawing attention to herself. In eighteenth-century theatres the audience was almost as much illuminated as the performers, and the framed boxes became miniature theatres themselves for the display of fashion and beauty. Mrs Darby's anxieties multiplied as admirers, young and old, made their way to their seats. One handsome officer, denied admission by her mother's frown, managed to slip the girl a passionate love-letter; he also subsequently ingratiated himself so well with Hester that she thought to save her daughter from the theatre by marrying her to him. It then transpired that the accomplished captain was already married. Neither mother nor daughter learned as much as they might have done from this lesson.

In the event, Mary did not make her mark on theatrical history by appearing with Garrick as his last Cordelia. Instead, answering a different cue, 'Satan appeared to her in the form of an Attorney's clerk, all glittering with spangles, and bedaubed with lace'.[47] This fine fellow's name was Thomas Robinson.

2

The Disastrous Marriage

O . . . *that that Woman had but been married to a noble Being, what a noble Being she herself would have been.*
(Samuel Taylor Coleridge to Thomas Poole, 1 February 1801)

Mary Darby and Thomas Robinson began their acquaintance in exchanges of glances across the street; the Darbys were then living in Southampton Buildings off Chancery Lane. He was a clerk in legal offices, lodging with one of the partners, John Vernon, and had been ill; gazing out of the window he was caught by a pretty face and answering looks opposite. The cross-street pantomime ended when Hester found out and firmly closed the window shutters. The young man was not so easily deterred however; some time later Mrs Darby was persuaded by a solicitor friend, a Mr Wayman, to join a pleasure party to Greenwich and to allow her daughter to accompany her. Mary was delighted and prepared her costume with care, remembering, with a precision to which readers of her *Memoirs* become accustomed, that she wore 'a nightgown of pale blue lustring, with a chip-hat [straw], trimmed with ribbands of the same colour'.[1] (A night or bedgown was an informal dress, not for sleeping in, and lustring a light crisp silk.) To her 'consternation', and her mother's indignation, who should be waiting to hand her from the coach but the young neighbour. Mr Wayman had to work hard during the evening to reconcile Mrs Darby to the acquaintance, persuading her of the many good qualities and bright prospects of his young friend, heir to a 'rich old uncle' in South Wales.

It is a pity that he did not write this testimonial down, for Thomas Robinson's character and reputation need help. He never told his own story and appears only in his wife's *Memoirs* where the failure of the marriage is blamed on him, and in a few scurrilous, anonymous accounts in which he is presented as her pimp. No letters of his have been preserved, nor anything to qualify her portrait of a weak, lazy profligate. Robinson is elusive in other ways too; he does not appear in legal records because he never completed his articles; he was contemporary with Sheridan at Harrow, but the school kept no records of pupils then. Sheridan was born in 1751, which may be the year of Robinson's birth, but the exact date remains unknown, as does the identity of his mother. Yet of his father there are plentiful records, for he was in fact none other than the rich old uncle in South Wales.

Thomas Harris, born in 1705 in Talgarth (in Brecknockshire), was the second of three brothers, all of whom distinguished themselves. Joseph Harris, the eldest, became Assay-master at the Mint, while Howell Harris, the youngest, was one of the founding fathers of Welsh Methodism, a charismatic figure who preached hell-fire through England and Wales. Thomas was the brother who made money, starting life as a humble tailor in London but amassing a fortune, much of it from lucrative army contracts. A characteristic tale of eccentricity describes how one morning he came across three drunkards amusing themselves by breaking windows; he joined in and broke one himself, saying that the owner of the house kept a good cellar and inviting his companions to share a bottle with him. When they discovered that he had broken his own window they were so impressed that thereafter they set themselves to put business his way.[2] Harris spent forty years in London, never marrying, but forming a relationship with a woman who bore him three children – William, Thomas and Elizabeth Robinson. Since Harris did not give them his own name, Robinson was presumably the mother's surname, and perhaps she too was an Elizabeth. The only other clue to her identity comes in an account written in 1781 to discredit Mary, by John King, a money-lender and former friend; he is not to be trusted but he correctly identifies Thomas's father as a tailor, describing his mother as a 'Jolly Laundress'.[3]

Naturally, young Mr Robinson did not tell Mrs Darby any of this, but from a bad beginning he swiftly rose in her esteem, visiting the family in their new lodgings in York Buildings, Villiers Street, and establishing seriousness of purpose by presenting her with books such as James Hervey's *Meditations among the Tombs*. Hester became convinced that she had found a suitable son-in-law, and pressed Mary to accept him in marriage. His suit was strengthened when first

George and then Mary contracted smallpox, the terrifying disease which had killed Hester's first daughter. This time the strain of the illness was only mild, but it was at risk to his own health that Thomas continued his visits. This disinterested conduct helped him plead his cause with Mary, who says she was induced to allow banns to be published while still lying on her sickbed. (Hester should have been suspicious when Thomas asked that the wedding be kept secret from his uncle until he had come of age and completed his training.) Though Mary claims to have begged for a postponement of the marriage after the banns were read, which took place on 28 March, 4 and 11 April 1773 at St Martin-in-the-Fields, the wedding following on the very next day, 12 April. The signature 'Thos Robinson' on the register is the only physical relic there is of him; it is joined by the neat signature of Mary Darby, and Hetty Darby's as witness.

Even as she knelt at the altar, Mary says her thoughts strayed 'to that scene where I had hoped to support myself with éclat and reputation'.[4] Garrick was sent a letter informing him of her 'advantageous marriage', which he took in good part, offering congratulations when he later met her in the street. In her *Memoirs* she makes much of her youth and inexperience as justification for consenting to the marriage: she was young, but was no child bride. Though she says that 'only three months before I became a wife, I had dressed a doll', she had also at much the same time delivered a mature performance of speeches from *Jane Shore*. Moreover, a girl of strong personality could have exerted her will forcibly if totally opposed to the match; like Lydia Bennett in *Pride and Prejudice* Mary probably thought that it would be 'very great fun' to have a handsome husband and the status of a married woman. She would have enjoyed the dressing up too; she wore a demure Quaker outfit for the ceremony, changing for the wedding breakfast (at the home of 'a female friend') to a white muslin dress, 'a chip hat adorned with white ribbons, a white sarsnet [fine silk tissue] scarf-cloak, and slippers of satin embroidered with silver'.[5]

In the strange period which followed, Mary, her mother and George went to live in a grand house near Lincoln's Inn Fields, while Thomas went back to his old lodgings. Too late Mrs Darby's suspicions were aroused, and she learned some unpleasant facts: the truth of his relationship with his 'uncle', that he was already of age but without the enhanced income he had claimed would follow, and that the period of his clerkship was not near expiry. Hester insisted on the marriage being acknowledged to his relations, particularly, Mary says, because she was now pregnant. This was not true however, as Maria Elizabeth was not born for another year. Though apprehensive about making the confession, Robinson yielded and with Hester they set out for Bristol where Mary was to wait until he summoned her into Wales. Both women were glad to see old friends and familiar places again and Mary gratified an urge to sit once more under the brass eagle lectern in the cathedral.

A letter eventually reported Mr Harris's grudging willingness to see a moneyless girl whom he thought too young for marriage (he was told she was seventeen, thus establishing a precedent for telling untruths about her age); Thomas also asked Mary to write to money-lender John King to borrow what she would need for the journey. Mary describes King as a man 'whom I had seen in his company' but denies that she knew anything about her husband's financial transactions.[6] She might not have made this reference at all, but for awareness that there were those who might recall the *Letters from Perdita to a Certain Israelite*, published anonymously in 1781 at the height of the scandal with the Prince of Wales. The book was a malicious attempt to blacken Mary's name by printing letters dated between 21 September and 23 November 1773, which purport to reveal an illicit relationship between her and a Jew, since identified as John King.[7] What King appears to have done was to intersperse genuine letters with forged ones, adding his own fabricated answers. Sheep and goats among the correspondence are easily distinguished: five of the seven letters to 'our very worthy friend' engage in friendly but unexceptional exchange, as in the one in which she asks for the loan for her journey:

> Since I wrote my last letter, I received one from my dear Mr. R— wherein he desired me to inform you, that if you please to answer my drafts, he shall not want till he returns to *London*; the Money I can assure you is for me, and I really shall find it extremely welcome as soon as you can conveniently send it.[8]

The term of endearment attached to her husband conveys a fondness for him found nowhere else. Yet in another letter King claimed she had written she inconsistently wrote, 'How can I love that stupid Thing R—!'[9] The Israelite's answers are constructed to fit with the real ones while lingering lasciviously on the delights of her body which he supposedly enjoyed. King must have lusted after Mary, but these letters acquit her of any impropriety with him. Nevertheless they show that she was neither so innocent of involvement in her husband's borrowing, nor of knowing the man from whom he obtained it, reminding him in one letter that they are to make a party to Drury Lane Theatre on their return.

Robinson came to fetch his wife, and they crossed the Severn to Chepstow. The route then took them through the rugged landscape of the Black Mountains to the rich pastures of the Wye Valley, before climbing through the parkland of Thomas Harris's Tregunter estate. From the terrace in front of the grand house he was building there was a spectacular view of a mountain, Mynydd Troed, which Mary calls the 'Sugar-loaf' because of its shape.[10] Much of the land between house and mountain belonged to her husband's 'uncle', as Thomas persisted in calling him. Mr Harris greeted his son's bride cordially enough, but the cold reception she received from her sister-in-law Elizabeth, and Mary Edwards, the house-keeper, Mary would never forget or forgive. If Thomas had been singing the praises of his wife's beauty and social graces it had soured their hearts against her, and Mary's carefully prepared outfit of 'dark claret-coloured riding-habit, with a white beaver hat and feathers' impressed neither of them.[11] Miss Betsy and Mrs Molly, as Mary dubbed them, made it clear that a poor lawyer's wife had no business with fashion, or artistic fancies such as playing their ancient spinet, no doubt to them exhibitionism. Mary took her revenge in the *Memoirs*, mocking her sister-in-law's snub nose, red face, squat figure and antiquated clothes. How offensive the pair really were, and how justified the unkind portrait, cannot be known. Mr Harris, however, took a fancy to his pretty daughter-in-law, declaring that he 'should have liked me for his wife, had I not married Tom'.[12] She describes the 'Squire' riding his small Welsh pony around his estate, in his costume of 'brown fustian coat, a scarlet waistcoat edged with narrow gold, a pair of woollen spatter-dashes [gaiters], and a gold-laced hat', chivvying the rustics for their swearing while embroidering his own language colourfully. Mary felt that she was in a beautiful landscape, peopled by barbarians.

To her surprise, when they set off to return to Bristol, Mr Harris came too. He was introduced to her mother, made the rounds of Bristol society, and occupied himself in purchasing furnishings for Tregunter, for which he sought Mary's advice: 'Choose them as you like them, Mrs Robinson, for they are all for you and Tom when I am no more.' The pair would have done well to remember, however, that the will was not yet written.

Back in London Thomas rented a new property, 13 Hatton Garden, and furnished it 'with peculiar elegance'. He also acquired that essential for the man-about-town, a two-seater phaeton with horses to match. Servants were hired, friends entertained, tickets for entertainments bought, new clothes purchased. Any pretence that Robinson was preparing to be a lawyer disappeared as the couple launched themselves into fashionable London life, borrowing money no doubt on the expectation of the handsome property soon to be his. Mary dissociates herself from his financial dealings, saying that he became irritated if she questioned him about them, and insisting that she was still but a 'child', of an age 'when girls are generally at school, or indeed scarcely emancipated from the nursery', and therefore not to be held accountable.[13] This next year was one for which she particularly sought to justify herself, by chronicling her husband's descent into debt and infidelity while she preserved an inviolable chastity in the face of attacks on her honour by his libertine friends. Nevertheless she was as hedonistic as he, admitting that 'Dress, parties, adulation, occupied all my hours'.[14]

The 'adulation' resulted from her appearances at the long-established pleasure gardens and the recently opened Pantheon in Oxford Street, a venue for concerts and masquerades. There were over sixty pleasure gardens in and around London for evening entertainment, of which Vauxhall Gardens was the most popular, and Ranelagh the most exclusive (and therefore to some a little dull). Riff-raff were deterred by the half-crown entrance fee at Ranelagh compared with Vauxhall's shilling, though entrance money at Ranelagh included the refreshments, which always consisted of tea, coffee, and bread and butter. At both Gardens there were formally laid-out gravel walks and flower-beds; Ranelagh, situated where the Chelsea Flower Show is now held, had a canal and Chinese temple, but could not compete outside with Vauxhall's tree-lined and ornamented avenues hung with 10,000 oil lamps. At Ranelagh the glory was indoors in the Rotunda, a dome 150 feet across. In Smollett's *Humphrey Clinker* there is a description by Lydia Melford, whose enthusiasm might be Mary's:

> Ranelagh looks like the enchanted palace of a genius, adorned with the most exquisite performances of painting, carving and gilding, enlightened with a thousand golden lamps, that emulate the noonday sun; crowded with the great, the rich, the gay, the happy, and the fair; glittering with cloth of gold and silver, lace, embroidery and precious stones.[15]

When her chance came to join the gilded throng Mary prepared herself with a view to being noticed by contrast, choosing a light brown 'singularly plain' gown, with no ornament, and leaving her auburn hair undisguised by fashionable white powder. All eyes were consequently upon her (she says).

In both Gardens the crowds were entertained by popular singers, at Vauxhall serenading the company from a balcony above the walks, while at Ranelagh the company listened to the singing while promenading around and around the rotunda in twos, threes and fours, 'like so many blind asses in an olive-mill', according to Lydia Melford's more cynical uncle.[16] The same 'eternal circle' was found at the Pantheon. Modelled by James Wyatt on the Pantheon at Rome, it too had a dome, with a coffered ceiling, ornate plaster-work and classical statuary in niches, and was illuminated with coloured lamps placed on the cornices. Dress for the Pantheon was formal court attire, with hooped petticoats and high feather headdresses; Mary wore pale pink satin with sable trimmings, costly wear. On her first, undated, visit Mary was observing the fashionable assembly, when she was herself observed by two men, one of whom asked 'Who is she?' A third man joining them said 'I think I know her': it was Lord Northington.[17] He came to speak to her; she introduced her husband to the Earl, and he presented his companions, Lord Lyttelton and his cousin Captain Ayscough. Next day the men paid a formal visit to the Robinsons and from then on Lord Lyttelton was constantly with them at social occasions; he made a friend of Thomas, probably (certainly in Mary's view) with the aim of seducing his wife.

Thomas, the 'wicked Lord Lyttelton', born in 1744, was the son of George, the 'good Lord', who had been Chancellor of the Exchequer and also a literary man; he was a friend of Pope and author of much now-forgotten poetry, which Mary admired. She recalled that at seven she could render a musical setting of his poem 'The Heavy Hours' so pathetically that it always reduced her mother to tears. His son wrote verse too, and much was expected of him in youth, but he turned to dissipation and was alienated from his father. He was an able politician and, his biographer says, no worse a rake than most young men then; nevertheless he had made himself notorious in 1773 for having abandoned his wife of less than a year and run off to Paris with a barmaid. He returned following the death of his father in August, but his reputation was such that for a woman to be constantly in his company was to invite only one conclusion. Rather than set tongues wagging Mary would have been well advised to stay at home, especially if she found him, as she claims, 'uniformly my aversion' and 'the most hateful of existing beings'.[18]

John King also writes of Mary's relationship with Lord Lyttelton in the *Letters from Perdita*, reporting the first meeting much as she does, except that he says it took place at a masquerade where she appeared as an orange girl (hinting at Nell Gwynn). Subsequently their intimacy progressed

> till at length his Familiarity with her became the topic of the whole Town. They were continually together at every Place of Amusement; and the Husband trudged after them, as stupid and tranquil as any Brute of the cornuted Creation.
>
> They were frequently in a Carriage, with the Blinds up, and Mr. R— a Mile or Two behind on horseback; so far was he from taking Umbrage at this Intimacy, that he continually boasted among his Acquaintance . . . [of] his Wife's Ascendancy over every fashionable Gallant.[19]

True or false? The source is untrustworthy, though a foolish husband might have made such boasts, and King's tale appears to have backing in the *Town and Country Magazine*. Each month this magazine presented an irregular union in its popular *tête-à-tête* series, disguising the names, illustrating the article with a pair of portrait miniatures, and recounting the circumstances of the liaison. In October 1773 'Mrs R—' and 'The Libertine Macaroni' [a foppishly dressed man] were featured. Lord Lyttelton is identified as the Macaroni through his recognisable history and the listing of his former amours, 'but presently we find him captivated by a female of a superior species, who bears the name of R—n', to whom it is said that he had laid long, but ultimately successful siege.[20] It would be an extraordinary coincidence for there to be another Mrs R—n to link with Lord Lyttelton, but apart from the total dissimilarity of the woman's past history from Mary's there are other difficulties in accepting the story. The false history could be discounted: in *tête-à-têtes* what was not known was made up, as in two quite different and both inaccurate accounts featuring Elizabeth Armistead, the courtesan who was to follow Mary in the Prince's affections.[21] The real problem is that Lord Lyttelton was out of the country until August and then appears to have stayed at the estate he had inherited in Worcestershire until late October, when the article appeared.[22] So there does not seem to have been an opportunity for a relationship to develop.

The curious case of Mrs R—n and The Libertine Macaroni is seemingly prescient rather than retrospective, for there was some sort of relationship even if not the sexual gropings in a closed carriage of King's tittle-tattle. Mary's expressed repugnance for Lord Lyttelton, his manners 'overbearingly insolent . . . language licentious . . . person slovenly', is so exaggerated as to suggest actual attraction. She would have been drawn to him because of his father, his rank and his wit, and is unlikely to have found totally disagreeable one who was 'the life and delight of every circle he joined'.[23] A man who sets out to seduce a woman does not do so by behaving obnoxiously; in any case the worst she can find to demonstrate uncouth behaviour is his declaration that 'no woman under thirty years of age was worth possessing' (altered to the tamer 'admiring' in the published *Memoirs*).[24] He hoped he had not made 'the *pretty child*' angry by saying so. There may well have been times when Lyttelton found Mary irritating and wanted to provoke her back. But he wooed her in terms of her interests, giving her a copy of the poems of Anna-Laetitia Aikin (later Mrs Barbauld), which she read 'with rapture', and teasingly calling her 'the poetess Corry' with reference to Cordelia, the part she might have played. That there was anything illicit between them she vehemently denies, with repeated versions of 'GOD can bear witness to the purity of my soul'.[25] But she was young, heedless and indiscreet; she played with fire and was scorched by rumour.

While she claims to have loathed Lord Lyttelton, Mary admits that George Robert Fitzgerald, the volatile Irish duellist nicknamed Fighting Fitzgerald, possessed manners she defined as 'beautifully interesting'. She recounts various incidents of his pursuit of her, one when she became separated from her husband during an evening at Vauxhall Gardens. Claiming that he had seen Robinson outside, Fitzgerald accompanied her there and attempted to abduct her in his waiting coach; she broke away and discovered Thomas in the nick of time. This narrative reads so much like fiction (as in Richardson's *Sir Charles Grandison* or Burney's *Evelina*), as to be scarcely believable, yet the incident follows immediately after the declaration that 'these are the pages of truth', and such events did sometimes occur. (The 'late unfortunate Fitzgerald', as she calls him, came to a sorry end, executed in 1786 for murdering a magistrate; wanting a quick death by breaking his neck he leapt off the scaffold – but the rope snapped and he had to do it again.)

It was Lord Lyttelton who for his own purposes told Mary of her husband's adultery, naming the woman as Harriet Wilmot, and giving Mary her Soho address. In another scene where the remembered dialogue, though not necessarily its import, is unconvincingly melodramatic, Lyttelton urged her to 'Leave him! Command my powers to serve you'.[26] Instead, the betrayed wife rushed speechless from the room and set out for Soho. Could she really, a quarter of a century afterwards, remember so precisely that her rival wore 'a dress of printed Irish muslin, with a black gauze cloak and a chip hat, trimmed with lilac ribbons', not to mention her own costume of 'a morning *dishabille* of India muslin: with a bonnet of straw: and a white lawn cloak bordered with lace'?[27] A stagey scene followed, with a penitent Miss Wilmot, who noted Mary's pregnancy, swearing that she would never see Mr Robinson again. Next day Thomas admitted the offence, throwing the blame on Lord Lyttelton. That was not the limit of his infidelity, however. Mary learnt from her brother George, who went riding on his pony with Thomas, that he visited a lady in Marylebone; there the boy saw his sister's watch hanging by her chimney. Assuming the story is true, Robinson must have taken the watch as a love-offering because he was now deeply in debt. They had moved out of their expensive home in Hatton Garden to a house 'lent by a friend' in Finchley, and had been deserted by most of their (unpaid) servants. Matters grew so desperate that, fearing arrest by his creditors, Thomas decided to escape to Tregunter, even though Mary's time was near.

If her first visit to her father-in-law had been disagreeable, the second was humiliating. Thomas Harris, who had made his money through hard work, was angry with his wastrel son, unprepared to help him, and ready to blame his high-spending daughter-in-law for her share in his ruin. Mary records indignantly that at a dinner party, when one of the company congratulated him on having finished his house in time for it to become a nursery, Mr Harris answered, 'No, no, they came here because *prison doors* were open to receive them'.[28] She fails to see the hurt and bitterness of a proud old man. Harris refused to allow the baby to be born in his house (the pair may have hoped a grandchild would mollify him and loosen the purse-strings). He packed Mary off to Trevecca House, where a Methodist seminary (still existing) had been set up by the Countess of Huntingdon and Howell Harris at the foot of the mountain; workshops, including a flannel manufactory, were also attached. It was there, on 18 October 1774, that Mary's beloved daughter, Maria Elizabeth Robinson, was born.

One wonders whether Maria knew much of the circumstances of her birth before encountering her mother's manuscript; it would have made painful reading if not. But there was a kind nurse present, Mrs Jones, and it was at her urging that two days after the baby's birth Mary wrapped her in a piece of their own Welsh cloth and carried her to the workers in the manufactory. They greeted 'the little *heiress* to Tregunter' with unsophisticated joy. When she was a week old, Maria was christened at the church on the hillside above Talgarth; Mary does not mention this, so we do not know which, if any, of Mr Harris's household stood godparents. There is a plaque in memory of Thomas Harris in the church, which records that 'in him the Poor always found a most bountiful Benefactor, his Heart and Mansion being ever open to the feelings of Humanity, by releiving [*sic*] the Distresses of the Indigent'. The unyielding old man did not count his son among the indigent, and when he first came to see the baby the conversation reputedly ran:

'Well!' said Mr Harris, 'and what do you mean to do with your child?'
I made no answer.
'I will tell you,' added he; 'Tie it to your back and work for it.'
I shivered with horror.
'Prison doors are open,' continued Mr. Harris. 'Tom will die in a gaol; and what is to become of you?'
I remained silent.[29]

It seemed that this prophecy might come true sooner rather than later when shortly afterwards Robinson heard that creditors had discovered his whereabouts. The couple retreated to Monmouth, where Mary's grandmother lived; she at least was delighted to welcome her great-granddaughter. They spent about a month at Monmouth, during which time Mary suffered anguish when the baby was found in convulsions, brought on, her mother believed, when she overheated herself at a ball and her milk was affected. But with the help of a visiting clergyman who dosed her with a spoonful of aniseed spirit and spermaceti oil, Maria recovered. A month later Robinson was arrested for debt; the couple had to return to London in the company of the sheriff, where Robinson was able, temporarily, to sort out his affairs, and Mary was reunited with her mother. Despite their increasingly precarious financial position they also resumed their pleasure-going, Mary continuing to coquette with both Fitzgerald and Lyttelton.

But while still tripping the light fantastic, in quieter moments her more pensive self was dedicated to poetry and, already ambitious for literary fame, she decided to print the collection of her poems to which she had been adding since her schooldays. The volume which was eventually published contains thirty poems; she herself later recognised that they are 'trifles, mere trifles', and hoped that no copy remained apart from her mother's: it may be the one held by the British Library, as its back page contains 'Erata' [*sic*], initialled M.R. The collection is characterised by earnestness, with several elegies, and poems of exemplary sentiment including both a Hymn and an Ode 'to Virtue' ('Hail daughter of th'etherial Sky,/Hail everlasting purity').[30] If Lord Lyttelton saw the verses on the death of his father it would have added confirmation to his view that women could not write poetry: he once declared that he was 'not very partial to literary ladies', finding them 'generally, of an impertinent, encroaching disposition'.[31] Could he have had Mary in mind? One of her poems, 'Letter to a Friend on leaving Town', takes up a familiar theme, the worth of rural retreat compared with the frivolities of town life:

> Gladly I leave the town, and all its care,
> For sweet retirement, and fresh wholesome air,
> Leave op'ra, park, the masquerade, and play,
> In solitary groves to pass the day.[32]

But it was to a very different place of retreat that Mary Robinson was about to go.

Inevitably there came a time when Robinson could juggle with money-lenders no longer; he was arrested for debt and on 3 May 1775 committed to the Fleet prison.[33] It was Mary's opinion that had Mr Harris helped at this stage, his son would subsequently 'have pursued a discreet and regular line of conduct', though nothing about Thomas Robinson suggests that redemption on this occasion would have led to a life of strict sobriety, within the limits of his purse.[34] He was in receipt of a small allowance from his father, probably amounting to the £100 annuity which was all that was willed to him by his father, when Harris eventually died in 1782.[35] It is extraordinary that even on his death-bed, 'being far advanced in years and sick and weak in Body but of sound Mind Memory and understanding (praised be God)', Thomas Harris was still unprepared to acknowledge his illegitimate children, terming them 'friends'. Thus 'my friend Elizabeth Robinson' received an annuity of £20, plus a lump sum of £200 and accommodation in Tregunter mansion for life; 'my friend William Robinson', a lieutenant in the marines in the East India Service and based at Bombay, received £500. 'My Servant Maid Mary Edwards', Mary's 'Mrs Molly', was left an annuity of £60 and the sum of £500 (perhaps she had been something more than a servant). The bulk of the estate went to his niece, the daughter of Joseph Harris, and her husband; money was also left to provide ten poor men of Talgarth with new suits every St Thomas's Day. The 'little heiress of Tregunter' inherited nothing. It would have been without compassion that in 1775 the old man heard of the imprisonment of his son.

When Thomas Robinson entered the Fleet it was to become a

member of a strange society, and not one immediately suggesting incarceration for, as a foreign visitor noted, 'neither bolts, nor irons, nor gaoler are to be perceived; nothing . . . to denote a prison'.[36] Moreover the debtor, provided he paid four guineas for his 'habeas' (writ of Habeas Corpus), could choose his own gaol; Robinson opted for the Fleet rather than the King's Bench prison favoured by the upper classes. The Fleet, an ancient prison, got its name from the river which ran beside it, its stinking waters fouled by blood and waste from Smithfield Market, fortunately largely covered over. A striking feature of these gaols was that though presided over by a warden (who made his income from the prisoners' fees, and some greasing of his palm), they were self-governing, classless republics, ruled over by a committee and an elected president who made 'laws' and handed out punishments if necessary. But however democratically run, they were still prisons, and the newly arrived debtor had his likeness taken so that the 'jigger', or door-keeper, knew him and could prevent escape. He also had to hand over a 'garnish', either his overcoat or money in lieu.

The long four-storey building was forbidding, even if not of the squalor of a criminal gaol like Newgate. Passages and stairways were dark and encrusted with dirt, and in the penultimate scene of *The Rake's Progress* Hogarth pictures Tom Rakewell, the spendthrift heir who has squandered all his money, slumped in despair in a wretched bare brick room in the Fleet. Tom Robinson was more fortunate; he had means enough to secure 'good' accommodation for himself, his wife and his child. There was no obligation for Mary to be incarcerated with her husband; she could have lived with her mother. But she determined not just to stay in the Fleet, but to impose upon herself the same custodial conditions and never leave it till he did. It was a brave decision for an eighteen-year-old: she must have cared about Thomas more than she would admit when writing her memoirs later.

As it happens, the prison reformer John Howard visited the Fleet both in 1774, and on 6 April 1776, when the Robinsons were inmates; we therefore know that on that day Thomas was one of 243 prisoners (thirty of them 'Commoners' with no money or rights and obliged to beg at a grille for subsistence); their wives and children numbered 475.[37] Howard details the accommodation, so that when Mary says they obtained an 'apartment' on a favoured upper floor, we know that it was a room measuring 14 feet by 9½ feet, provided with a window and fireplace but otherwise unfurnished, and costing one shilling and threepence a week in rent. Days and nights were spent in this confined space, which Mary did her best to keep clean and orderly. On a lower floor was a chapel, a coffee room with newspapers and a tap room; at night the corridors echoed with drunken rowdiness.

Though she had her baby to look after and amuse, the days must have seemed very dreary. Their room overlooked the racquet court, where men could play at various sports, as Thomas did. For Mary it was the only place of exercise, and it was here that one evening Maria spoke her first words, pointing to the moon when clouds suddenly obscured its brightness and saying 'All gone', a poignant phrase in the circumstances, which she had picked up from a nursery maid who would hide things from her with these words. Mary gave herself some sense of purpose by publishing her little volume of *Poems*. Though she says that publication took place before her husband's imprisonment it cannot have done, because the title page is illustrated with a charming engraving – belying her current circumstances – of cherubs and wreaths of roses, by Angelo Albanesi, an Italian artist whom the Robinsons met as a fellow inmate. Moreover, one of the poems, 'The Linnet's Petition', must have been written in the Fleet. It is the plaintive song of a bird begging to be released from its cage:

> Ah! pity my unhappy fate,
> And set a captive free,
> So you may never feel the loss,
> Of peace, or liberty . . .[38]

A compassionate girl catches 'the flutt'ring thing' and gives it freedom. But for Mary there was no kind hand to open the prison door; few former friends even made enquiries, and she was bitter that her women friends appeared to have abandoned her.

She gave expression to her feelings in a long poem called, simply, *Captivity*, which evokes the 'black Despair' of the prisoner. When it was published in 1777 it too had a striking, if not literal, engraving by Albanesi which images Mary's state: in the darkness of a dungeon a bare-breasted woman is chained hand and foot to a pillar, gazing steadfastly at a brightly burning lamp which stands on it. Mary was offered an escape route in letters from the libertine lords; had she been the profligate woman of her later reputation she would have taken it. That was the urging of Albanesi's wife Angelina, a woman of easy virtue herself, who in contrast to Mary lived outside the prison and visited her husband sumptuously dressed. She 'laughed at my folly in wasting my youth', pictured the splendid life she might be enjoying and told her that the Earl of Pembroke, having heard of her circumstances and her person, was ready to offer his 'services'. She also discovered that Albanesi himself was helping her husband to the services of prostitutes, a personal humiliation.

Though she was given guarded encouragement in a review which said that she '*sometimes* expresses herself decently enough', her poems sold poorly.[39] Then someone suggested that she might seek the patronage of the Duchess of Devonshire, who was known to have literary interests, so she boldly parcelled up a copy and gave it to her brother George to deliver at Devonshire House in Piccadilly. It must have been quite an undertaking for him to go to the imposing mansion, mount the steps, enter the great hall and seek an audience with the most celebrated figure of London society, but he managed it. He also so engaged the Duchess's sympathy for his sister that she sent an invitation to Mrs Robinson to visit her next day. Mary could not deny herself this opportunity, and, dressing herself with an eye to her situation in a 'plain brown satin gown', for a brief while exchanged the 'dark galleries' of prison for the splendour of the Duchess's elegant apartments.[40] This, she says, was exactly nine months and three weeks after she had entered the Fleet.

Georgiana, Duchess of Devonshire, though from a different social sphere, was of a compassionate disposition. She was just seven months younger than Mary and had not been married long either, but since her wedding to the Duke she had become society's darling and the leader of the 'ton', the fashionable set.[41] Her appearances were avidly reported in the daily newspapers, especially the extravagant fashions she created, like the single ostrich feather which reared up above her head before curling gracefully down (Queen Charlotte banned the wearing of these feathers at court). But though Georgiana was far above her in station, there were reasons unknown to Mary why she would be sympathetic. She too was not very happy and led a frantic social life in consequence; she had suffered miscarriages and was aware that for her husband her only value was in providing an heir. One of the activities to which she had turned, gambling, had left her with massive debts by the spring of 1776, and she knew what it was to have creditors pressing for payment. She responded to Mary's sad situation by inviting her to come frequently and to bring her daughter with her, and though it never became an intimate friendship, Mary was to maintain good relations with the Duchess for the rest of her life. She showed *Captivity* to the Duchess and it was dedicated with permission to her, with a prefatory address:

> Madam,
> YOUR Grace's Partiality to these imperfect Lines has emboldened me to use your kind Permission, of dedicating them to you, the friendly Patroness of the Unhappy. To paint those Virtues, which dignify your Grace's exalted Situation, would appear in me an idle Presumption; but I cannot publish these Verses, and not take the occasion of repeating my Thanks to you, for the unmerited Favors your Grace has bestowed upon,
> Madam,
> Your Grace's
> Most obliged,
> And most devoted Servant,
> MARIA ROBINSON

It was during Mary's visits to the Duchess that Thomas betrayed her, with Albanesi's connivance. In her *Memoirs*, Mary reminded him of her own contrasting loyalty:

> Mr Robinson knows what I endured . . . He knows that neither poverty nor obscurity, neither the tauntings of the world nor his neglect, could tempt me even to the smallest error: he knows that I bore my afflicting humiliations with a cheerful, uncomplaining spirit; that I toiled honourably for his comfort; and that my attentions were exclusively dedicated to him and to my infant.[42]

She was proud to have shown such unwavering devotion.

Finally a time came when 'by setting aside some debts, and by giving fresh bonds and fresh securities for others', Thomas obtained his liberty.[43] On 3 August 1776, fifteen months after the prison doors had closed behind him, he was released, his wife and child with him.[44] Maria, who had been a babe in arms when they first entered the Fleet, left it as a walking, talking child. Her mother was at a landmark age too as she neared her twentieth birthday, and she likewise had learned at least one lesson in discovering the importance of self-reliance. She had been given plenty of evidence that men are ever deceivers, but their company and admiration was something she would continue to enjoy. On stage four years later she would declare (in Elizabeth Craven's *The Miniature Picture*) that 'all women are born coquets, and nothing but a great passion for one object, can cure that natural propensity we all have to coquetry'. In Thomas Robinson she had not found that object.

3

Garrick's Girl

Mrs Robinson looked Ophelia most beautifully, and for so young a theatrical adventurer, play'd it very pleasingly.

(*Morning Chronicle*, 1 October 1777)

Released from prison he might be, but Thomas Robinson still had no means with which to support his family, and Mary became pregnant again; appeals for funds to his father went unanswered. The couple took modest lodgings above a confectioner's shop in Old Bond Street but nevertheless plunged back into the social whirl, where they quickly re-encountered old acquaintances. In Vauxhall Gardens Mary met Lord Lyttelton, 'who insolently remarked "that notwithstanding all that had passed I was handsomer than ever"'.[1] She gave him a withering look. Another encounter was more productive. Walking in St James's Park the Robinsons met William Brereton, a young actor from Drury Lane Theatre whom Mary had known before. They invited him to dine, and during the evening Brereton suggested that Mrs Robinson should try her luck on the stage again.

During the dreary year just past Mary must often have wondered what her life might have become if she had made a marriage with the theatre rather than a man without means or morals. Now the idea was proposed again, holding out an opportunity not only to indulge that side of her nature which loved to perform, but also to earn an independent income. The combination of 'fame and independence' (in that order) are what she cites in her novel *The Natural Daughter* as the reasons why the heroine, Martha Morley, chooses to become an actress.[2] Even before a settlement was made the couple moved to 'a very neat and comfortable suite of apartments in Newman-street' on the northern edge of town, where one morning Brereton arrived unexpectedly with the new manager of Drury Lane, the 24-year-old Richard Brinsley Sheridan; he would have known Robinson from school-days. The meeting went well, Sheridan no doubt shrewdly noting Mary's good looks and, even in the early stages of pregnancy, fine figure. Wearing his manager's hat he was unassailed by those doubts about engaging a young woman that had concerned him when it had been his wife's sister under discussion, and he invited Mary and Thomas to a meeting in Drury Lane Green Room. There they also found her former mentor, David Garrick.

In her *Memoirs* Mary mistakenly says that Garrick had retired some seasons earlier; in fact the highly charged days of his farewell performances had taken place in June while she was still in the Fleet. Garrick had sold his half-share in Drury Lane to Sheridan (his antagonism forgotten) and his father-in-law, the musician Thomas Linley; there were two other shareholders, but for practical purposes Sheridan was the day-to-day manager. The theatre had changed too. Before retiring Garrick had commissioned the Adam brothers to renew Wren's old building; they had replaced bulky pillars with slender columns inlaid with plate glass, raised the height of the ceiling to improve acoustics, and redecorated the whole auditorium, ornamenting the edges of the boxes and galleries with elegant festoons of flowers and medallions.[3] On the theatre's reopening the previous September the audience had burst into spontaneous applause.

Trial was made of Mary in the role of Juliet, with Brereton reading Romeo, and Shakespeare's play was chosen for her début. She wrote to the Duchess of Devonshire seeking her approval, and received an encouraging letter. Articles of agreement were then drawn up setting out terms and obligations on both sides. A paylist exists for 16 December 1776 which records her being paid £20, a sum representing payment for the season thus far at a weekly rate of £2, even though she had only performed twice by that date.[4] This was appropriate pay for a novice; the highest-paid actress was the tragedienne Mary Ann Yates, who earned £26 a week, while Frances Abington, the second-highest paid, received £12. Young Mrs Robinson thus became a member of the extended Drury Lane family, which that season consisted of fifty actors, thirty-seven actresses, nineteen dancers, six singers and several orchestra members, in addition to the army of scene-changers, painters, carpenters, charwomen, dressers, door-keepers, and so on, down to Mrs Beckham the candle woman, who earned 12 shillings a month.[5]

Seemingly bearing no grudge for efforts thrown away four years earlier, David Garrick was happy to coach Mary again. He took her through her part, himself performing Romeo even to the point of exhaustion. Garrick was famed for his 'naturalness' on stage, for seeming to be at one with his character at all times, anticipating in every bodily movement and facial expression the feelings to be expressed. He had made a habit of studying gesture and behaviour, but knew that acting was more than mimicry. He may have said to Mary, as to others, and in words which would have appealed to her poetic sensibility:

> Listen to what I say, but do not copy me; this is the situation you have to paint. As you enter into it, your soul will provide you with all the right nuances for the feelings you wish to express.[6]

It is a pity that Mary did not write more about what she learnt from Garrick, and how she learnt it, but in *The Natural Daughter* the terms in which she describes Martha Morley's acting must represent what Mary absorbed from Garrick as the aim, and suggest how she viewed her own stage performances:

> She was the pupil of Nature; her feelings were spontaneous, her ideas expanded, and her judgement correct . . . She was lively and unaffected: her smiles were exhilarating; her sighs were pathetic; her voice was either delicately animating or persuasively soothing: she neither giggled convulsively nor wept methodically: she was the thing she seemed, while even the perfection of her art was Nature.[7]

The fictional Martha's acting is intuitively brilliant, but for Mary there was much of a practical nature to learn. She must pitch her voice to be audible in a large auditorium (judging from reviews this was her principal weakness at first); she must learn how to move on a raked stage, avoiding tripping on the raised grooves in which the scenery 'flats' ran; she must absorb the conventions of ensemble acting, be ready to curtsey to the audience at any applause (mid-speech if necessary), and master the curious art of the exit, which required a graceful springing step 'with a glance at the pit'.[8]

The season's programme was not published in advance. Next night's performance was announced from the stage at the end of every evening's entertainment; bills, printed and distributed on the day, named the plays and the casts scheduled to appear. The night's programme was also announced on the front pages of the daily papers, so on the morning of 10 December 1776 play-goers could read that that evening they would have a choice of *Caractacus* by William Mason at Covent Garden, a work 'Written on the model of the ancient Greek Tragedy', or *Romeo and Juliet* at Drury Lane with 'a YOUNG LADY (Being her first appearance upon any Stage)' as Juliet. It is uncertain who played Romeo; the play-bills named William Brereton, but the newspapers announced it would be William Smith, at forty-six rather old for Romeo, though age and even advanced pregnancy were not barriers then. In terms of revenue Drury Lane came out the better, with box-office receipts of £170 8*s*, compared to Covent Garden's £131 18*s* 6*d* (a full house at Drury Lane, which accommodated 1,800, would have realised more than £250).

Shakespeare's play was not all that the audience went to see; every night the five-act 'mainpiece' would be succeeded by a two-act 'afterpiece' – a farce, musical or pantomime. On Mary's début night it was *Selima and Azor*, an extravaganza with special scenic effects, and music by Sheridan's brother-in-law, another Thomas Linley. Even before the mainpiece a black-clad player normally came forward with a Prologue, a lively piece of rhyming verse fitted to the occasion; an Epilogue rounded the evening off. In addition a band would accompany both a Dancing and a Singing, which were interpolated between acts (notoriously a 'Hornpipe in Wooden Shoes' in the middle of *Hamlet*), though in *Romeo and Juliet* the Dancing was a Masquerade suitably fitted to the end of Act I, and the Singing accompanied Juliet's funeral procession. Garrick had written the words for this dirge, and that was not all. He had composed a scene which he thought improved on Shakespeare, where Juliet wakes *before* Romeo feels the full effect of the poison. In this version, therefore, Romeo carries Juliet from the vault where she has lain in a drug-induced trance to a front-stage awakening:

Juliet I know that voice. Its magic sweetness wakes
My tranced soul. I now remember well

	Each circumstance. O! my lord, my Romeo! Had'st thou not come, sure I had slept forever; But there's a sovereign charm in thy embraces That can revive the dead. O honest friar! Dost thou avoid me Romeo? Let me touch Thy hand, and taste the cordial of thy lips. You fright me – speak! O let me hear some voice Besides my own in this drear vault of death Or I shall faint. Support me!
Romeo	O! I cannot! I have no strength, but want thy feeble aid, Cruel poison!
Juliet	Poison! What means my lord, thy trembling voice? Pale lips! And swimming eyes! Death's in thy face!
Romeo	It is indeed. I struggle with him now . . .[9]

After Romeo's protracted death Juliet kills herself as Shakespeare intended, with her cry 'O happy dagger!'

In performance this death-scene took place on a green carpet (put down by the scene-changers in full view of the audience) since the stage was dirty, costumes precious, and women about to die traditionally wore white. Mary recalled that

> my monumental suit, for the last scene, was white satin and completely plain; excepting that I wore a veil of the most transparent gauze, which fell quite to my feet from the back of my head, and a string of beads round my waist, to which was suspended a cross suitably fashioned.[10]

An indulgent manager may have allowed her new costumes, but this privilege was usually reserved for the top performers such as Mrs Abington, who had a purchasing allowance, and was so much the fashion-leader that milliners and mantua-makers came to the theatre purely to observe them. Lesser-ranked performers chose from the wardrobe stock whatever took their fancy (and whatever fitted them). Wherever it came from, for the earlier part of the play Mary wore a dress of 'a pale pink satin, trimmed with crape, richly spangled with silver', while her head was 'ornamented with white feathers'. This costume sounds startling enough without knowing that it would have been held out by an enormous hoop in a showy version of contemporary dress: there was little attempt at historical accuracy.

Mary was very nervous as she made her first entry on the stage. Audiences were kind to new performers, but conditions were intimidating since there could never be any dimming of the chandelier-hung auditorium, so she could plainly see the faces gazing assessingly at her. Moreover it was a noisy, restless audience. At the beginning of the play late-comers were still coming in, banging doors and chattering: no eighteenth-century audience expected to sit still and silent. Making her entry 'with trembling limbs and fearful apprehension', Mary clung to the Nurse's arm, and, after she had dared to take a look, never forgot her first impression of the 'gradual ascent of heads' in the pit, all eyes fixed on her (the pit was where critics and theatre enthusiasts were to be found, paying four shillings for the privilege of sitting on backless benches upholstered in green baize). Among them she made out 'the keen, the penetrating eye' of David Garrick. To her amazement, 'thundering applause' greeted her first appearance, and though she confessed that she deserved none since nothing that she subsequently said could have been heard, after the first scene she drew courage and finally acquitted herself so well that her performance concluded to 'peals of clamorous approbation'.

Or so she says. William Hopkins, the prompter (a position more akin today to stage manager), wrote more soberly in his notes: 'Juliet by Mrs Robinson – a genteel Figure – a very tolerable first Appearance, and may do in time'.[11] The critics echoed his view, noting that Mrs Robinson had an attractive appearance and promised well. The *Morning Post* of 11 December commented:

> A Lady, whose name is *Robinson*, made her first appearance last night at this theatre, in the character of *Juliet*; – her person is genteel, her voice harmonious and admitting of various modulations; – and her features, when properly animated, are striking and expressive.

But the critic warned of work to be done:

> At present she discovers a theatrical genius in the rough; which, however, in elocution as well as action, seems to require a considerable polishing, before it can be brought to perfection.

Two days later, when she had performed again with greater confidence, the same critic wrote that she possessed 'a considerable share of untutored genius, and may, under proper instructions become an acquisition to the stage'. The word 'genius' was one to relish, but Garrick may have started at the suggestion that she had not yet received tuition.

Altogether Mary played Juliet four times before the end of December. These, plus single occasions in two other years, were her only performances of the role. The ever-changing repertory (49 mainpieces that season) did not allow for many repeat performances: actors had to be quick studies and develop a large repertory of parts to play at a day or two's notice. But had she been a phenomenal success she would have been asked to play Juliet more often. Despite her claim in the *Memoirs* that it was one of her most popular roles, Juliet and Mrs Robinson was not a combination that made theatrical history.

In January 1777 Mary did not appear at all, but in late February (when six months pregnant) Sheridan cast her in contrasting plays, one a declamatory tragedy, the other a comedy of modern life; in both she played the part of a wronged wife. Statira in *Alexander the Great* is enraged by the great conqueror's unfaithfulness with his former wife Roxana; Amanda in Sheridan's *A Trip to Scarborough* realises that her husband is in pursuit of her best friend Berinthia. For *A Trip to Scarborough* there were new dresses, and, in the first portrait ever published of her, Mary can be seen as 'Amanda'. This Amanda, however, is a character from *Love's Last Shift* by Colley Cibber, a role she never played. It accompanies the text of the play in the series *Bell's British Theatre*, in which every play is illustrated by a costumed performer, but since a portrait of Mary Ann Yates as Berinthia had already illustrated *A Trip to Scarborough*, the publishers chose Mrs Robinson for a different Amanda. She wears a huge bell of a dress which is strikingly ornamented with loops of diamond-patterned braid, tassels and ribboned bows, with her hair in the fashionable 'high' head-style, adorned with ribbons and sprouting a crop of feathers.

Exotic eastern dramas were costumed differently. Mary recalled that for *Alexander the Great* her attire was 'white and blue, made after the Persian *costume*, and though it was then singular on the stage, I wore neither a hoop nor powder; my feet were bound by sandals richly ornamented; and the whole dress was picturesque and characteristic'.[12] Clad thus, she had to burst into the first scene, exclaiming in furious despair:

> Give me a knife, a draught of poison, flames!
> Swell heart, break, break, thou stubborn thing!

There could have been no drooping or murmuring on this occasion. The play ends with Roxana stabbing Statira to death (another call for the green carpet), and Mary claims that her performance received an 'éclat which flattered my vanity'. But truth to tell, this production was put on for one night only, and no doubt at the insistence of another shareholder in the company, Willoughby Lacy, who had a high opinion of his own talents and who played Alexander. Neither of the two principal tragediennes, Mrs Yates and Miss Younge, was called on, so Mary got her chance.

Alexander the Great was a bowdlerised version of Nathaniel Lee's *The Rival Queens* (1677); Sheridan's *A Trip to Scarborough*, however, was counted a new play and intended for a run. Though it was announced as a rewriting of Sir John Vanbrugh's comedy *The Relapse; or, Virtue in Danger* (1696), the change of title seems to have confused the audience into expecting greater novelty. Moreover, purged of its spice, the play became duller (one of the funniest moments of the original occurs when Berinthia is carried off by Amanda's husband crying pianissimo 'Help! Help! I'm ravished, ruined, undone!'; in Sheridan's tamer version Amanda arrives in time to prevent the seduction). One critic welcomed the attempt to keep Vanbrugh in the repertory by removing the play's 'heap of indecency', but found the result 'languid and dragging'.[13] He was not the only objector, and during the performance the audience grew restive. Hissing began and came to a pitch in a scene between Amanda and Berinthia. Audiences had been known to riot when offended, ripping up the benches and tearing down the chandeliers, throwing whatever came to hand at the actors and even mounting the stage in physical attack.

All too aware of what might follow, Mrs Yates hurried off stage, leaving a terrified Mary to face 'the critic tempest' alone:

> I stood for some moments as though I had been petrified: Mr Sheridan, from the side wing, desired me not to quit the boards: the late Duke of Cumberland, from the stage-box, bade me take courage – 'It is not you, but the play, they hiss,' said his Royal Highness. I curtsied; and that curtsy seemed to electrify the whole house; for a thundering peal of encouraging applause followed, – the comedy was suffered to go on, and is to this hour a stock play at Drury-lane theatre.[14]

Alone, she saved the play. Reviews next day suggest, however, that it was the performance as well as the play which had displeased. The *Morning Post* commented on the actors generally seeming unfamiliar with their parts; the *Morning Chronicle* was more specific and, while criticising others, suggested that Mrs Robinson brought her trouble on herself:

> Indeed, it is but justice to say, that the audience were put out of temper by the want of importance in Mrs Robinson, who though her beautiful face and form suited well for the poet's description of Amanda, spoke so low during the beginning of the play, that the company in the front boxes could hardly hear a syllable she uttered.

But the *Gazetteer*'s critic supported her, feeling that her acting 'had certainly a just claim to the encouragement of the audience', and that 'success cannot fail to attend her theatrical abilities'.[15]

Despite its initial problems, *A Trip to Scarborough* was repeated several times in March and early April, but Mary was now heavily pregnant and her final performance for the season took place on 10 April. This was her benefit night. All players looked forward to their benefits, when they received the takings of the evening and could sell tickets themselves for whatever they could get (normal prices ranged from five shillings for a box seat to one shilling for the top gallery).[16] The other advantage was that players could choose the whole evening's programme, selecting a part they were anxious to play. On this occasion Mary made the sensible choice of Fanny in

Garrick and Colman's comedy *The Clandestine Marriage*. Fanny, who has married secretly, is pregnant; she has to fend off unwanted admirers, and inform and reconcile her crotchety father to the match. The afterpiece was Garrick's *A Christmas Tale*, which sounds an odd choice for April, but it was a tale of magic and an audience draw because of the special scenic effects by Drury Lane's remarkable scene-designer, Philippe de Loutherbourg. He thrillingly fulfilled such stage directions as 'The rocks split and discover the castle of *Nigromant* [the wicked magician] and the fiery lake', and not long afterwards, 'The flames and the ruins of the castle vanish away and discover a fine moonlight scene'. The box-office took £189 10*s*; usually the player paid a theatre charge of £105, but since none is listed it may all have gone to Mary, plus whatever ticket money she took herself – if as she says her benefit was 'flatteringly attended', the boxes filled 'with persons of the very highest rank and fashion', she must have done very well.

After this performance Mary retired from the stage to await her confinement, which unfortunately meant that she missed the theatrical event of the decade – the opening night on 8 May 1777 of Sheridan's *The School for Scandal*. Sheridan wrote the play with particular players in mind, and had intended the part of Maria for Mary, but she knew that she would be too 'unshaped' by then. Instead the role went to Priscilla Hopkins (Mary's former companion at school), but the dramatist had no great opinion of her talents, which he later said was the reason why he had not written a love scene between Maria and Charles Surface.[17] The first performance was a triumph; someone passing the theatre heard such a mighty roar coming from the building that he assumed it was about to collapse, and ran away – but it was the spontaneous acclamation which greeted that moment when the screen falls in Joseph Surface's library, revealing Lady Teazle (Mrs Abington) to her husband Sir Peter (Thomas King, noted for his performances of crusty old gentlemen). The success of *The School for Scandal* was exceptional, and it was repeated eighteen times before the season ended on 7 June. Mary thus lost the chance to be associated with the play, and her pregnancy explains to all actresses since why the part of Maria offers them less than they might have expected.

The first night took place shortly before Mary's second child, Sophia, was born. The Robinsons had moved to the Covent Garden area to be near the theatre, and Sophia was christened on 24 May at St Paul's Covent Garden (the 'actors' church').[18] But unlike Maria Elizabeth this baby did not thrive, and the tiny body was taken back for burial less than a fortnight later, on 10 June. Mary says that the child died in convulsions in her arms, and that as she watched over her in 'agonising anxiety' Sheridan called. He had a baby son himself, and was readily sympathetic:

> I had not power to speak. All he uttered was, 'Beautiful little creature!' at the same time looking on my infant, and sighing with a degree of sympathetic sorrow which penetrated my soul. Had I ever heard *such a sigh* from a husband's bosom?[19]

Mary may do her husband less than justice in implying that he was unmoved by the fate of their child, but he had resumed his womanising and was said by Mary to be keeping two women, one a dancer, the other a prostitute.

The reader feels great sympathy for Mary as a mother in the loss of her child, but the scene of Sophia's death, with Sheridan visiting in her husband's absence, provokes the question: what exactly was the relationship between actress and manager? Sheridan was promoting her career, encouraging her to try both comedy and tragedy (which she saw as her natural bent), but in the *Memoirs* she is cagey about him, conscious of contemporary gossip. She does not deny that 'the happiest moments I then knew were passed in the society of this distinguished being' and that he paid her 'flattering and zealous attentions' which contrasted with Thomas's neglect. In a contorted passage in which Sheridan is not even named she attempts to define her feelings, confusingly using the word *soul* to convey both what they were and what they were not:

> I was complimented on all sides [after her début]; but the praise of one object, whom most I wished to please, was flattering even to the extent of human vanity . . . I heard one of the most fascinating men and the most distinguished geniuses of the age honour me with partial approbation: a new sensation seemed to awake in my bosom: I felt that emulation which the soul delights to encourage, where the attainment of fame will be pleasing to an esteemed object. I had till that period known no impulse beyond that of

> friendship; I had been an example of conjugal fidelity; but I had never known the perils to which the feeling heart is subjected in an union of regard wholly uninfluenced by the affections of the soul.[20]

By choosing words like 'bosom', 'feeling heart', and 'affections', she comes close to admitting falling in love but swerves aside to define the relationship solely as 'an union of regard'.

This passage is as Mary wrote it, but when she reaches the year 1779, sixteen lines about Sheridan have been scored over and do not appear in the published *Memoirs* of 1801. They follow a paragraph beginning 'Mr Sheridan was still my most esteemed of friends', continuing on the subject of his warnings against the 'temptations' of extravagance and flattery.[21] The last sentence is 'There was a something beautifully sympathetic in every word he uttered: his admonitions seemed as if dictated by a prescient power, which told him, that I was *destined to be deceived*'. However, this paragraph originally concluded with two sentences which are mostly readable:

> I believe that, through life, no one has ever more tenderly or more sincerely esteemed me than he did at that period. Indeed I have never at any period since had reason to suppose, that I did not possess his most friendly [one word].

The next paragraph begins with 'The powerful interest which Mr Sheridan . . .', but the two following lines are heavily obliterated. They must suggest a dangerously growing attachment, for what can next be read is:

> I reflected that he was married to a very charming woman, that I was also united to an husband, though to a neglectful one . . .

At the end it is possible to make out: 'every hour effected a [one word] from his own domestic attractions; and I resolved on alienating my heart from [two or three words] fascinations'. The printed version then reverts to the manuscript as Mary notes that the resolution was not easy to achieve because her situation made it 'difficult to avoid the society of Mr Sheridan', but the full context is lost in publication.

The passage erased by Mary's daughter (it must be assumed) is not an admission of infidelity, but it does admit temptation – and who could blame her for finding the charming, vivacious Sheridan attractive? That there was gossip at the time is shown by correspondence in the *Morning Post* in that summer of 1779. A letter signed 'Squib' alleged that three actresses – Miss [Margaret] Cuyler at the Haymarket, Mrs [Jane] Lessingham at Covent Garden and Mrs Robinson at Drury Lane – had all been unnaturally '*pushed forward*' by their respective managers, implying that it was for sexual favours. Mary wrote at once in self-exoneration:

> Mrs Robinson presents compliments to *Squib*, and desires that the next time he desires to exercise his *wit*, it may not be at her *expense*. Conscious of the rectitude of her conduct, both in public and private, Mrs Robinson does not feel herself the least hurt, at the ill-natured sarcasms of an anonymous detractor.[22]

Perhaps her openness and willingness to answer the accusation carries conviction. Sheridan acquired a reputation as a womaniser, though Linda Kelly, a recent biographer, says that at this period he was 'in theory' faithful to Elizabeth. She makes no mention of Mrs Robinson, suggesting that if his eye was straying at all it was towards the beautiful Frances Crewe, to whom he dedicated *The School for Scandal*.[23] However, if a chance was offered with another beautiful woman in need of consolation, Sheridan was probably not the man to resist it. They may have been lovers, if only briefly.

After the loss of Sophia, Mary withdrew to the spa-towns of Bath and her native Bristol to recuperate, but she was back in London for the re-opening of the play-house, her salary increased to £2 10*s* a week.[24] Her initial role was that of Ophelia to the Hamlet of John Henderson, making his Drury Lane début; he became a much-admired principal (and a close friend of Mary's) until his early death in 1785. On this occasion, however, he struggled with the unfamiliar Garrick version of the last act. This reduces the body count considerably: Hamlet never gets to England, so Rosencrantz and Guildenstern survive; Ophelia goes mad but there is no grave-yard scene; nor is there any duel or poisoned pearl. Instead, Hamlet stabs Claudius and then runs upon Laertes's drawn sword before uniting the hands of

Laertes and Horatio. The reception of Henderson's performance was coloured by critics' dislike of Garrick's alterations; Mary, however, received approving notices, though one critic thought that she ruined Ophelia's 'beautiful woodlark notes' by singing out of tune.[25] She and Henderson played together again in *Richard III*, with Mary cast as Lady Anne. Once more her playing won approval; the critic of the *Morning Chronicle* said it afforded 'hopes that a person and face so agreeable and engaging may be well-employed in the service of the tragic muse'.[26]

In this season and the next Mary expanded her repertoire, Sheridan casting her in a variety of roles in plays new and established, comic, tragic, and romantic. In the season 1777–78 she took on nine new parts, the one in which she appeared most frequently (sixteen times) being The Lady in the afterpiece, *Comus*. This was an adaptation by George Colman of Milton's masque of sexual temptation, in which the virtuous Lady, armed with her chastity, resists the blandishments of Bacchus' son Comus; Mary's role with its triumphant virtue was to acquire ironic overtones in time. In the following season, which again opened with *Hamlet*, she added a further eleven roles, and appeared in breeches for the first time in Benjamin Hoadly's comedy *The Suspicious Husband*, as Jacintha who adopts a boy's disguise in order to elope. An actress had to have confidence to appear in breeches, knowing that all the men would be concentrating their gaze on her lower half; Mary showed her complete self-possession afterwards when she attended a masqued ball striding 'like an Adonis' in Jacintha's scarlet costume.[27]

The part which she performed most often of any during her theatrical career (in the 1778–79 season) was in Sheridan's popular new afterpiece *The Camp*, where she played the small role of Lady Plume thirty-one times, and also later appeared as Lady Sash. *The Camp* is a slight piece, but it appealed to patriotic fervour when, following the American Declaration of Independence, France recognised the new state and a French invasion of the south coast was feared. The play was a spectacular de Loutherbourg recreation on stage of the military camp at Coxheath; Lady Plume and Lady Sash are fashionable ladies come to inspect it (Lady Plume a glance at the Duchess of Devonshire, who had spent some weeks 'camped' with the Duke, playing at soldiers).[28] The plot uses the comic situation that an artist, visiting the camp from Drury Lane to take a view of it for just such a scenic display, is overheard muttering 'O.P.' (Opposite Prompt) and 'P.S.' (Prompter's Side) and is arrested as a Jacobite spy (Old Pretender and Pretender's Son), and threatened with hanging. There is also a girl called Nancy looking for her sweetheart while disguised as a soldier; Mary was to play this breeches part in the next season.

In *The Camp* Sheridan gave the public what they liked best – new comedy and expensive scenic effects; unfortunately for him as manager, would-be dramatists were more anxious to write blank-verse tragedies. But he could not refuse to stage Robert Jephson's *The Law of Lombardy* as his previous dramas had done quite well; it was first performed on 8 February 1779, and for eight nights subsequently. Mary played Alinda, handmaid to Princess Sophia of Lombardy (Miss Younge), who through her love for the villainous Bireno (Henderson) betrays her mistress; he then orders Alinda's murder to ensure her silence. But the biter is bit and the dying Alinda reveals the truth. Critics were unimpressed and the play was never revived; scorn was poured on such muddles with scenery as resulted in a tree appearing in the middle of a prison cell. The actors fared better, though one critic said with double-edge that 'Mrs Robinson made a considerable impression on all who heard her'.[29]

When the two main play-houses closed for the summer season it was customary for players to accept engagements either at a provincial theatre or at the Haymarket, the theatre licensed for the summer months. Sheridan, with her career in mind, had urged Mary to take up an offer in 1778 from the Haymarket manager, George Colman. Mary agreed, provided she could approve in advance the parts she was to play. The first was Nancy Lovel in Colman's own comedy *The Suicide*. But she discovered that the part had been billed to another actress, Elizabeth Farren. Miss Farren, then only sixteen, was to take over from Mrs Abington as principal comedy actress in the 1780s and '90s, but at this time she was at the outset of her London career. Mary, insulted, demanded that the part be returned to her before she would play anything else. Colman refused, and equally refused to release Mary from her engagement, so she spent the summer smouldering, performing in nothing, though nevertheless in receipt of her weekly salary of £3.[30] She might not have out-performed Miss Farren, but would have pleased the oglers more, as Nancy Lovel was a breeches part, and in that department, according to Charles James Fox, the willowy Elizabeth Farren was deficient:

> D— n it, she has no prominence either before or behind – all is a straight line from head to foot; and as for her legs, they are shaped like a sugarloaf.

His objections, however, did not deter Fox from bedding her for a time.[31]

Mary never appeared anywhere other than Drury Lane, which, if she had been wanting to develop her career, was a mistake. Yet for her benefit earlier that year she had shown that she was not without ambition, playing Lady Macbeth to William Smith's Macbeth. This was a substitute production, as she had originally planned to play Cordelia with John Henderson as King Lear, no doubt hoping that Garrick would come to see her. But three days beforehand she was obliged to place a notice in the press: 'Mrs Robinson presents her most respectful compliments to her Friends and the Public in general, and is extremely sorry she is under the disagreeable necessity of changing her Play on account of Mr. Henderson's indisposition'.[32] The sudden switch of play illustrates how swiftly the repertoire could be changed, but three days' rehearsal for Lady Macbeth hardly seems adequate. Critics, however, chose to review only her afterpiece, a musical farce called *The Lucky Escape* which she had written herself, taking the music from established songs. Unfortunately it did not fare well with them, the *Post* likening the play to 'a kind of flies . . . called *Ephemeris*, which do not live but for a day', its plot 'the history of a vapour'.[33]

The prompt copy of *The Lucky Escape* survives in the Huntington Library in California, so the butterfly nature of its plot can still be judged. Sir Toby Stedfast is father to Maria, who is in love with Edwin, but their happiness is threatened by Venture, 'a Sharper', who is after Maria's £10,000. He has her father's consent to marriage, but her spirited friend Letitia steals a suit of Venture's clothes for Edwin; thus disguised, Sir Toby accepts him as his future son-in-law, and when the real Venture appears threatens him with the stocks. All ends happily. It is an insubstantial piece, though the critics might have been kinder towards a first attempt by a very young woman.[34]

The following year Mary did play Cordelia for her benefit, but by then she could no longer look for Garrick's 'keen eye' in the audience. He had died on 20 January 1779; when the news came the evening's performance was cancelled, and Drury Lane Theatre darkened its doors in respect. The great actor was laid to rest near the monument to Shakespeare in Westminster Abbey, with Sheridan as principal mourner. Later a *Monody* to Garrick's memory by Sheridan was spoken on stage by Mrs Yates, hair dishevelled and dressed in a flowing robe of purple. Mary too commemorated the actor in verse; in her *Elegy to the Memory of David Garrick* she tried to capture evanescent dramatic genius by suggesting that its most fleeting manifestations were for the spectator what made it most enduring:

> Who can forget thy penetrating eye,
> The sweet bewitching smile, th'empassioned look?
> The clear deep whisper, the persuasive sigh,
> The feeling tear that Nature's language spoke?[35]

Garrick's art, she suggests, was an empathic one, a complete assimilation of his character's identity. For the theatre his death marked the end of an era.

Mary's star was rising however, both theatrically and socially, and with it the difficulties of preserving an 'unsullied reputation'. In this her task was made difficult even by her address. When she advertised her benefit that year, on 14 April 1779, she placed a notice in the *Public Advertiser* announcing that tickets for it were to be had 'of Mrs Robinson, Great Piazza, the corner of *Russel Street*, *Covent Garden*'. Most players lived in this area, since they needed to be in reach of the 'call-man' who summoned them to morning rehearsals; non-attendance was fined. But Covent Garden was considered a disreputable place. Created in 1631 by Inigo Jones (a stretch of the original arcading can be found in the south-west corner), it was designed to provide elegant housing for aristocrats, but after fruit and vegetable stalls were introduced it deteriorated socially; taverns, brothels and gambling houses established themselves around its edges and by the beginning of the eighteenth century it was a notorious hell-raising area. Its reputation had become less vicious, but it was not a salubrious place to live.

Some of the players had risen from the Garden itself. Thomas King's parents had run three shacks as coffee-houses, as seen in Hogarth's *Dawn*, in which an angular spinster makes her way to St Paul's Church past the coffee-house, eyeing through her fan sticks the young rakes still fondling their wenches. Fanny Abington first came to notice as 'Nosegay Fan', singing ditties and selling bunches of flowers in the market by day and, it was said, herself in the taverns at night. The theatre was still associated with loose morals, and all actresses were regarded by men as fair game. Hester Darby could never reconcile herself to her daughter's profession, and when Mary's merchant brother John came to watch her he left precipitately the instant she appeared. Perhaps he had overheard salacious comments from the men around him. The play-house audience produced an endless stream of predatory males who assumed that the stony defences of any theatrical Venus would eventually crumble before their drip of monetary temptation. Moreover, as Mary's professional reputation increased so did her value in the flesh market; the bids became greater and the bidders of loftier pretensions. The Duke of Rutland offered her £600 a year to become his mistress; other sugar-coated propositions came from a '*royal* Duke [no doubt King George III's disreputable brother the Duke of Cumberland], *lofty* Marquis, and a City Merchant of considerable fortune'.[36]

Mary did not help to keep the pursuing pack at bay by adopting an extravagant life-style. This was one of the things which Sheridan had warned her against, but she was beginning to enjoy the heady pleasures of display, and no wise finger-wagging would deter her. At the same time Thomas was eating up both their incomes gambling and keeping his mistresses; consequently he decided once more to attempt reconciliation with his father.[37] So in the summer Mary went to Tregunter again. There she found herself received more warmly than before, and gratifyingly consulted on fashion by her sister-in-law, the supposed immorality of her profession tolerated because of the money it made. But the old man remained obdurate, with the result that on their return journey Thomas was re-arrested for debt, and Mary's virtue put on trial again; George Brereton, a racing acquaintance to whom Robinson owed money, offered to release him if she would yield to him. She tells the tale at some length, with righteous indignation and much 'remembered' dialogue.[38] Yet despite this further evidence of men's duplicity, she claims that still she 'knew as little of the world's deceptions as though [she] had been educated in the deserts of Siberia'.

Mary's life now centred around her social activities, with pleasure parties and her own morning 'levées'.[39] One of those coming regularly to her house in the autumn of 1779 was the twenty-year-old baronet and man of the turf, Sir John Lade, the nephew of the brewer Henry Thrale and his wife Hester, who had inherited great wealth. On the young man's coming of age in the following summer, the Thrales' friend Dr Johnson wrote *A Short Song of Congratulation*, foreseeing his ruin, but Sir John was losing money at Mary's card tables a year earlier, some of it filling Thomas Robinson's pockets. He was to become a crony of the Prince of Wales, one of those condemned as a disreputable hanger-on, yet he is one man whom Mary never accuses of making improper advances to her.[40] Cynics might argue that this was because his proposals were acceptable, and newspaper gossip did link the two of them, one reporting a 'kind of bo-peep play' between them in the theatre.[41] On the other hand, in a magazine more interested in reporting than refuting scandal it was said that Sir John had offered her an 'establishment' which she had 'smilingly' refused.[42]

If Mary had been as concerned to protect her reputation in 1779 as she was to defend it at the end of her life, she would have behaved with more discretion. Instead she encouraged social callers such as Sir John, and with her 'circle of friends increas[ing] almost hourly' found her time so occupied that she was scarcely able to find 'a quiet hour for study'. While she was never accused of not knowing her parts, it seems that Mrs Robinson was becoming less interested in her dramatic roles than in establishing herself as a social celebrity and, whether on- or off-stage, attention-seeking was becoming a dangerous addiction.

4

Enter the Prince

He will either be the most polished gentleman or the most accomplished blackguard in Europe, possibly an admixture of both.
(Richard Hurd, Bishop of Coventry and Lichfield, Preceptor of George, Prince of Wales)

Had the gods been in portentous mood on 12 August 1762 at the birth of George Frederick Augustus, eldest son of King George III and Queen Charlotte, and from his first cry Duke of Cornwall, Lord of the Isles, Great Steward of Scotland, etc., they might have produced a summer storm with echoes of a Bacchanalian rout. But unlike the night when Mary was born, no omens were discerned. The birth was untroubled, and the good news carried, rather incompetently, to the 25-year-old King, who expressed himself delighted to be father of a girl, only discovering the mistake when he reached the Queen's bedside.[1] Five days later the baby boy was pronounced Prince of Wales.

The nation rejoiced, with bells rung and prayers said. Thereafter royal births were to become almost annual events and the palace population grew rapidly. Frederick, created no less than the Bishop of Osnaburg at seven months (much later Duke of York), was born in 1763, William, later Duke of Clarence and eventually William IV, in 1765, and so on, until the royal brood reached fifteen, though two boys died young. The King wanted fresh air for his children, away from the pernicious influences of the capital, so the family was housed in the royal residence known as the White House, on the banks of the Thames at Kew.[2] But as children multiplied this building became too small, so when their formal education began Prince George and Prince Frederick were placed with their tutors in the nearby Dutch House (Kew Palace today). Here they were cloistered from the outside world, and though they played among themselves, none of the children had friends of their own age; occasional pleasure outings were always in the company of adults.

The two princes followed a strictly time-tabled day which lasted from seven in the morning till three in the afternoon, under clergymen-tutors more animated by zeal than imagination. The curriculum, however, was impressive (and more wide-ranging than any school's), covering the classics, religion, mathematics, history, government, law, literature, philosophy and the modern languages of French, German and Italian. There were practical lessons too; the Prince and his brother were taught the processes by which the nation was sustained, sowing the grain, harvesting the crop, and baking their own loaves. Specialists taught them the more refined arts of drawing and music (the Prince developed a fine singing voice and could play the cello), and they learnt to ride, to fence and to box. But it was reported that unlike his brothers, George lacked physical daring; he refused ever to skate again after he had tumbled on the ice a few times. Such reports displeased the King, who was also disturbed by stories of untruthfulness and laziness. The tutors were licensed to punish any misdemeanours with severe beatings.

Above all, the royal parents were anxious to instil moral virtue, an aim which seems to have taken priority over affection. The Queen was especially fond of her eldest son, but it hardly shows in a letter sent to him on his eighth birthday in which she urged him to

> Abhor all vice, in private as well as in publick, and look upon yourself as obliged to set good examples. Disdain all flatery [*sic*]; it will corrupt your manners and render you contemptible before the world. Do justice unto everybody and avoid partiality. The first will acquire to you happiness in this world as well as hereafter: the latter will make you unhappy, because it leaves after it an unhappy conscience – a situation which seems to me the most wretched in life, as it deprives us of the greatest enjoyment of life, that is, peace of mind.[3]

There is much more along these lines, concluding with a recommendation that the boy show 'the highest love, affection and duty toward the King'. Unfortunately this was something which became increasingly difficult the older he grew. He was later to say that the King had 'hated' him from the age of seven, and he was well aware that while Frederick, his father's favourite, could do no wrong, he could do no right. Yet Mrs Papendiek, daughter of the Queen's hairdresser, thought that at the age of sixteen the boy had 'an elegant person, engaging and distinguished manners, added to an affectionate disposition and the cheerfulness of youth', with a 'sweetness and intelligence quite irresistible'.[4]

George, Prince of Wales possessed faults of vanity, self-absorption and sensuality that no upbringing could have eradicated, but a less rigid, kindlier environment might have mitigated the worst of his failings. When he reached physical maturity and 'entered the vestibule of the Temple of Venus', as an early biographer Robert Huish puts it, rumours of liaisons were soon circulating.[5] In her memoirs Mrs Papendiek put some of the blame for the Prince's escapades on attendants who should have known better; these, she says, 'introduced improper company when their Majesties supposed them to be at rest, and after the divines had closed their day with prayer'.[6] But on another level the Prince's view of women was highly romantic and idealistic. He was looking for a woman to worship, and this led him between April and December 1779 to address no fewer than seventy-five love letters to his sisters' sub-governess, Mary Hamilton.

Miss Hamilton was a descendant of the 3rd Duke of Hamilton, twenty-three years old and very pretty; Sir Joshua Reynolds once said that whenever he read of a beautiful woman in a novel, it was Miss Hamilton who came into his mind.[7] Modest and conscientious in her duties, she had struck up a friendship with the likeable young Prince. She listened sympathetically when he told her confidentially that he was in love, but she must have been dumbfounded when he revealed to her in a letter that the object of his adoration was 'y^{r} dear, dear, dear Self'.[8] For a day or two she made no reply, probably hoping it would all go away, but her silence only encouraged him further. Trying to sound maturely reflective, he assured her that 'After the impetuous ardor of youth, and the violent impulse of passion is passed, then it is that one wishes to find in a companion for life, such sentiments and such feelings as you possess'.[9] This time she hastened to reply and disabuse him of any thought that she could offer more than 'pure, sacred and totally disinterested' friendship. But other women were to discover that one discouraging letter would not extinguish the Prince's passion once aroused. Despite agreeing to call her 'friend and sister', letters poured from his pen and remained very much those of a would-be lover.

He planned an exchange of love's symbols, instructing her to present him with a lock of her hair in a setting engraved on the back with her birth date, and on the front his own sentiments 'Toujours aimée'. In turn she was to receive a bracelet with his hair, bearing the legend 'Gravé à jamais dans mon coeur'.[10] The Prince was in love with being in love, and little concerned with the difficult situation in which he was placing Miss Hamilton. He was to be her 'Palemon', her knight, while on a less elevated level he wanted her to advise him in all things, stick pins in pieces of fabric to choose for his waistcoats and tell him what she disliked about his conduct so that he might amend it (she said that she disapproved of his swearing). In mid-September the Prince presented his 'dearest, dearest, dearest, Sister, Friend' (and future biographers) with a verbal self-portrait which, while self-conscious and immature, is also engagingly honest. He describes himself as 'upon ye whole well made, tho' rather too great a penchant to grow fat'; feature by feature his face meets with his approval except for his 'uggly [*sic*] ears'. Then comes the tricky business of moral assessment. After his noble aspects – open and generous sentiment, good heart, strict notion of honour – he deals with his 'vices' in one long breathless sentence which, while quickly relabelled as weaknesses, shows some self-knowledge:

> Now for his vices, or rather let us call them weaknesses – too subject to give loose or vent to his passions of every kind, too subject to be in a passion, but he never bears malice or rancour in his heart, as for swearing he has very near cured himself of that vile custom, he is rather too fond of Wine & Women, to both which young men are apt to deliver themselves too much, but w[h] he endeavours to check to ye utmost of his power, but upon ye whole his Character is open free & generous, susceptible of good impressions, ready to follow good advice, especially when he receives it from so affectionate & friendly a Sister as you are.[11]

Though Mary Hamilton exclaimed, 'My God, what will become of you if you suffer yourself to be led away with such impetuosity', she could not stem the epistolary tide. In November the Prince's preoccupation was a suit for the New Year's celebrations, and he sent her a sample of the material to be made up 'with a white Ermine lining with a White

Sattin Waistcoat embroidered with Cheneal' (the Prince's spelling was a weak point). He wanted to know whether the coat should be plain or with a 'light Cheneal embroidery' to match.

Then, suddenly, everything changed. On 5 December Miss Hamilton received a letter which horrified her: the seventeen-year-old Prince confessed that he had fallen in love with an actress, a Mrs Robinson. He concluded 'Adieu, Adieu, Adieu, *toujours chère*. Oh! Mrs Robinson'. Two days later another letter informed his 'sister' that he was 'in good health, tho' over head & ears in love, & so much so y[t] I do not know to what lengths it will carry me'.[12] By this date Mrs Robinson, who had just passed her twenty-third birthday, was wondering that herself.

The Drury Lane season of 1779–80 had opened on 18 September in a theatre so recently redecorated that the paint 'takes the company by the nose very uncivilly'.[13] The mainpiece launching the season was as the previous year *Hamlet*, with the *Morning Chronicle* finding Mary again a 'natural and affecting' Ophelia. The *Morning Post* also applauded her performance, though it was still unimpressed by singing which was 'rather too discordant even for madness itself'.[14] But there was a major difference between this year and the previous one: John Henderson and Elizabeth Younge had deserted Drury Lane for Covent Garden and better terms. William Smith took over the role of Hamlet, but the critics were won over neither by Smith nor the continuing use following his death of Garrick's version of the play, which was described as contrary to 'taste, reason and common sense'.[15] It was an inauspicious beginning to the season. Moreover, audiences followed the star players, and though there had been a profit of almost £4,000 the previous season, 1779–80 saw it cut to only just over £130, while Covent Garden made more than £6,000.[16]

Matters might have been worse had there not been a new afterpiece by Sheridan, *The Critic; or, a Tragedy Rehears'd*. This opened on 20 October, though its expensive scenic effects were another reason for reduced profits. Spain had just joined France in declaring war on the British, and the final scene of the play raised a cheer by staging the destruction of the Spanish Armada to the accompaniment of 'Rule Britannia' and other patriotic tunes. But *The Critic* is really a light-hearted satire on the theatre and press of the day; it is also Sheridan's revenge on the 'irascible tribe' of tragedy-writers, their persistence in proffering bad plays, and petulance when they were rejected.[17] Most of it consists of a disastrous rehearsal of a tragedy written by Mr. Puff, the critic; the play is dated and rarely performed today, but the absurdities of character and action can still reduce an audience to helpless laughter. One often-quoted moment is when the heroine Tilburina (daughter of the Governor of the fort) 'comes in stark mad in white satin' following the death of her lover Don Whiskerandos (son of the Spanish Admiral). 'Why in white satin?' Mr Puff is asked. 'O Lord, sir,' he replies, 'when a heroine goes mad she always goes into white satin' (closely followed by her confidant 'stark mad in white linen'). On the play's first night this would have been all the funnier for following *Hamlet*, with Ophelia in the traditional white for her mad scenes, though on this occasion she was not played by Mary.

But although she was not in *The Critic*, Mary's dramatic career flourished in this, her last season. It had been well managed, giving her the opportunity to extend her range and take on more parts each year, in this season performing eighteen roles, eight of them new to her. As well as Ophelia, which she played four times, she repeated the role of Lady Anne in *Richard III* (twice) and Juliet (once), and also played for the first time Viola in *Twelfth Night* (five times), Rosalind in *As You Like It* (three times) and Imogen in *Cymbeline* (once). These are all 'breeches' parts, and would have shown off her figure, but she must have been equal to their demands or she would not have been cast in them. However, the Shakespearean role which she played most frequently (fourteen times), and with which she became indissolubly linked, was that of Perdita in *The Winter's Tale*.

The version of *The Winter's Tale* was not the one we know today but Garrick's again, and strictly speaking should not have been advertised as *The Winter's Tale*, since he called it *Florizel and Perdita*. Shakespeare's play had been found unacceptable because it broke the so-called unities, being in two halves with a sixteen-year bridge of time between them, shifting the action from Sicily to Bohemia, and mixing the comic and tragic modes. Shakespeare's first three acts, set in the Sicilian court of King Leontes, are of wintry passions, with the King accusing his Queen, Hermione, of adultery with King Polixenes of Bohemia, and disavowing their baby daughter; the last two are a summer pastoral of love in the kingdom of Bohemia between a shepherd, Florizel (the disguised son of Polixenes), and a shepherdess who is truly the daughter of Leontes and Hermione. As a baby she had been adopted by shepherds who found her exposed on Bohemia's sea coast [*sic*], her name pinned to her wrappings: Perdita, Latin for 'the lost girl'. Recognition of her true identity leads ultimately to reconciliation and renewal. Garrick adapted the last two acts, prefacing them with one character telling another the past history (a dramatist's trick mocked in *The Critic*). All the action takes place in Bohemia, including the moving final scene when a statue of the supposedly dead Hermione comes to life; this curtailing of Hermione's story, the audience denied its emotional resonances, is the greatest weakness of *Florizel and Perdita.*

There is also the objection that Garrick's version sanitises the role of Perdita. Shakespeare's shepherdess, 'the queen of curds and cream', is sweet and good, but she is also a girl who knows her own mind and whose country upbringing has made her aware of the facts of life. Garrick's Perdita is a more saccharine miss. She has no spirited exchange with Polixenes about breeding, and her best-known speech wishing for the flowers of spring to give her guests ('O Proserpina/For the flowers now that, frighted, thou letst fall/ From Dis's waggon') is cut because it is a story of rape. But Garrick's Perdita retains her charm, and the part was in many ways perfect for Mary, with her fresh beauty and graceful bearing. She would also have conveyed the seriousness and melancholy which underlie the character, fearful that her happiness cannot last because of Florizel's parentage. The first performance took place on 20 November with William Brereton as Florizel, William Smith as Leontes, and Mrs Elizabeth Hartley, a Covent Garden actress, appearing as Hermione. The critics admired her 'transcendent grace and beauty' as she made the transition from statue to living being; subsequently Miss Farren played the part to objections that she was too young (indeed younger than her daughter). The play was newly costumed, but with money tight it was not spent lavishly. The critic of the *Gazetteer* grumbled:

> Florizel and Perdita have hitherto appeared in beautiful dresses, covered with flowers of both the same pattern, and she wore [*sic*] an ornamented sheep hook, instead of which Mrs Robinson appears in

> a common jacket, and wears the usual red ribbons of an ordinary milk maid, and in this dress she also appears with the King to view the supposed statue of Hermione, after she is acknowledged his daughter.[18]

Nevertheless the piece had been 'well cast and ably performed'. The *Morning Post*, ready to snipe at Mary, was not entirely complimentary, saying that her Perdita would have been 'very decent, except for that strange kind of *niddle to noddle* [head waggling] that she now throws into every character, comic as well as tragic'.[19]

A week after the opening performance of *The Winter's Tale* there occurred an event which must have shocked both the Robinsons: the sudden death in strange circumstances of Lord Lyttelton. According to the *Post*, he had had a dream three days previously in which a 'female spectre, in white raiment, presented herself, and charged him to depend on his dissolution within three days'.[20] He boldly challenged the apparition on the shortness of the warning, little time being left for 'reparation after so disorderly a life'. On Saturday 27 November, the third after the dream, he went to Epsom races in good spirits, joking with friends that 'he should jockey the ghost, if he escaped a few hours'. But while preparing for bed that night he was seized with convulsions and died. The story was made the more chilling in that a friend declared that the nobleman had appeared to him at daybreak saying 'My dear friend, it is all over, you see me for the last time'. Mary cannot have been unaffected by such a tale, although when the report appeared on 6 December she had other matters on her mind.

The Winter's Tale made a double bill with *The Critic* and it is likely that when the King commanded a royal performance on 3 December, it was for *The Critic*, the dramatic event of the year, that the royal party came, not to watch Mrs Robinson in *The Winter's Tale*. King George III was an enthusiast for the theatre and there were frequent command performances, the King's preference being for modern comedies. *The Clandestine Marriage* seems to have been his favourite, for he saw it more often than any other play, but he also saw *The Rivals* six times and *The School for Scandal* five.[21] The King and the Queen would happily have taken their seats in the festooned royal box, while their attendants, male and female, prepared to stand behind their Majesties for the whole performance. Accompanying their parents, but in their own box, were the Prince of Wales and Prince Frederick.

Mary was nervous about performing before royalty – she had done so before but in less conspicuous roles – but she was rallied in the Green Room by William Smith who exclaimed, 'By Jove, Mrs Robinson, you will make a conquest of the Prince; for to-night you look handsomer than ever.'[22] Smiling at the compliment and, as she put it with understatement, little foreseeing 'the vast variety of events that would arise from that night's exhibition', Mary moved to take up her position in the wings, where at once she came under the Prince's scrutiny. The royal boxes were not in the centre of the auditorium but, following the command of the poor-sighted George II, in the first tier immediately beside the stage, the King's on one side, the Prince's directly opposite. The royal family therefore not only watched the action side-on, but commanded direct views into the wings where performers and scene-shifters gathered. Mary, waiting for her entrance, was in full view of the Prince of Wales and could see that his gaze was fixed on her and that he frequently exchanged words with his equerries, while still regarding her with apparent admiration. That would have been distraction enough, but Mary had another. She had just been introduced to a young aristocrat, George Capel, Viscount Malden, who accompanied her to the wings and engaged her in conversation whenever she was off-stage.

In the circumstances Mrs Robinson's performance is likely to have been very self-conscious and niddle-noddling. She says she hurried through her first scene in embarrassment, and was aware throughout of the Prince's admiring glances and audibly flattering remarks. There were no curtain calls then, but at the end of the play the performers bowed or curtseyed and the royal family responded in kind. As the curtain fell, Mary's eyes met those of the Prince of Wales, whereupon

> with a look that I never shall forget, he gently inclined his head a second time; I felt the compliment, and blushed my gratitude.[23]

She endured some teasing in the Green Room afterwards for the Prince's marked attentions. They were not yet over. At the end of the evening, as the royal family crossed the stage where Mary was waiting (deliberately?) for the chair to take her home, the Prince made her a 'very marked and low bow'. Then she hurried home for a 'little supper party' she had arranged, where the whole conversation, she says, 'centred in encomiums on the person, graces and amiable manners, of the illustrious heir apparent', little seen in public before this date. The illustrious heir himself meanwhile, his heart beating with the promise of Mrs Robinson, returned with his parents to the Queen's House, which he was later to transform with much gilt and many mirrors into Buckingham Palace.

Mary's account of the evening raises questions: did the Prince suffer a *coup-de-foudre*, or did he come to the theatre primed to look out for Mrs Robinson? Had his Uncle Cumberland told him of the beautiful actress, as an actress more likely to be compliant than the frustrating Mary Hamilton? Was Lord Malden a plant, sent to hold her in conversation and ply her with favourable reports of his handsome friend? Did Mary herself set out to attract his attention? Mary's past history (and what was to come) suggests that long-distance coquetry was an art she had perfected, and she knew where the Prince would be sitting. A few days later Malden came to Mary's house in her husband's, perhaps organised, absence. He seemed embarrassed – he 'paused, hesitated, apologized' – for what, Mary knew not. Eventually he pulled a small letter from his pocket and handed it over. Addressed to 'PERDITA' it 'contained only a few words, but those expressive of more than common civility', and was signed 'FLORIZEL'. As Mary recorded it, the scene then continued:

> 'Well, my Lord, and what does this mean?' said I, half angry.
> 'Can you not guess the writer?' said Lord Malden.
> 'Perhaps yourself, my Lord,' cried I gravely.
> 'Upon my honour, no,' said the Viscount. 'I should not have dared so to address you on so short an acquaintance.'[24]

Eventually he confessed that the letter came from the Prince of Wales. Mary must have felt a momentary thrill, a sense of triumph, but what she records is her cautious response. Could she be sure that the letter, the 'partial but delicately respectful' letter, did indeed come from the Prince, or was she being tested by Lord Malden? She expressed her reservations (though she did not refuse further communications), with the result that on the following day Malden brought her a second letter in which the Prince begged her to come to the Oratorio, where he would 'by some signal convince me that he was the writer of the letters'. However, the Oratorio referred to in her account in the *Memoirs*, a command performance at Drury Lane of Purcell's setting of *Alexander's Feast* (a poem by Dryden), did not take place until 11 February in the following year. Mary must have telescoped two occasions; there was another command performance on 11 December at Covent Garden for Sheridan's *The Duenna*, a date that would fit. Mary was not on stage that night so could go with her husband, and take a box in view of the Prince's. As soon as he observed her, she says, he began making signs such as 'moving his hand on the edge of the box as if writing'. He called for a glass of water and saluted Mary with it, causing heads to turn.

Perhaps this latter gesture did belong to the February Oratorio, as it was there that public attention began to be drawn to the pair, though there was as yet no understanding that the charade which took place was more than a matter of Mrs Robinson making a fool of herself in a manner the *Morning Post* thought typical of her:

> A circumstance of rather an embarrassing nature happened at last night's Oratorio: – Mrs R—, deck'd out in all her paraphernalia, took care to post herself in one of the upper boxes, immediately opposite the Princes, and by those wanton airs, peculiar to herself, contrived at last so to *basilisk* a certain heir apparent, that his fixed attention on the amorous object above, became generally noticed, and soon after astonished their M—s, who, not being able to discover the cause, seemed at a loss to account for the extraordinary effect. No sooner however were they properly informed, but a messenger was instantly sent aloft, desiring the *dart-dealing* actress to withdraw, which she complied with, tho' not without expressing the utmost chagrin at her mortifying removal.
>
> Poor *Perdita*!
> 'Queen it not an inch further,
> But milk thy ewes and weep!'[25]

Mary's version in her *Memoirs* makes no reference to this humiliation, though she acknowledges the buzz of curiosity.

Oeillades apart, there had been no meeting. But Mary's very willingness to go to the Oratorio, and her behaviour there, shows that she had crossed a barrier and was moving towards acceptance of the Prince's proposals. The transformation of Mrs Robinson into 'The Perdita', her public persona, was under way. This Perdita was a being the reverse of Shakespeare's, not the pure modest girl of lost identity, but a morally lost woman who brazenly exploited her physical charms.

In the two-month interval before the Oratorio it can be assumed that there was a great deal of correspondence, letters arriving (via Lord Malden) almost daily. Mary seems to have consulted no one about her dangerously enticing situation, although the Prince had confessed his passion to Mary Hamilton and received her dismayed response. She had seen no romance, only depravity, and on 14 December made a dramatic plea:

> For the love of Heaven, Stop, O stop my friend! & do not thus headlong plunge yrself into vice. Y^{r} last Note made every nerve of me thrill with apprehension. I had determin'd to say nothing further upon ye subject fearing it w^{ld} be in vain & hoping y^{r} reason w^{d} be a sufficient guard, but you listen not to the voice of reason – & Alas! will not longer, I fear, to that of friendship.[26]

She had found out something of Mrs Robinson, and what she discovered appalled her. This was not just an actress, bad enough in itself, but one married and with a child (the 'Mrs' could have been an honorary title), and already suspected of irregular liaisons.[27]

Could she have brought herself to do so, Mary Hamilton would have done better to write directly to Mary herself (or even speak to her) and tell her of her own correspondence with its vows of eternal fidelity, but for her Mrs Robinson was no more than an intriguing wanton with whom communication would have been contamination. Knowing nothing therefore of the Prince's recent fervent pursuit of another woman, Mary says she found 'a beautiful ingenuousness in his language, a warm and enthusiastic adoration . . . which interested and charmed me'. Had she discovered that sentiments such as 'love you more than words or ideas can express', 'doat upon & adore beyond the idea of everything that is human', 'her whom alone I can love', were being recycled, she might have have been less impressed.[28] Even so she claims to have responded with extreme caution:

> [I] always offered his Royal Highness the best advice in my power; I disclaimed every sordid and interested thought; I recommended to him to be patient till he should become his own master; to wait till he knew more of my mind and manners before he engaged in a public attachment to me and, above all, to do nothing that might incur the displeasure of his Royal Highness's family.[29]

She must have remembered, may even have quoted, Perdita to Florizel:

> Oh, but dear sir,
> Your resolution cannot hold, when 'tis
> Oppos'd, as it must be, by th' power o' th' king.[30]

She would have recalled the warnings given to Ophelia by her father and brother concerning Prince Hamlet's protestations of love, 'springes to catch woodcocks'. But Mary should have needed no one to tell her, 'When the blood burns, how prodigal the soul/Lends the tongue vows'. She could never seriously have thought that a seventeen-year-old would remain faithful unto death to a woman with whom he had never spoken, and indeed she declares that she 'entreated him to recollect that he was young, and led on by the impetuosity of passion' (which must have sounded too much like Miss Hamilton for the Prince's taste), begging him to remember that should she leave her husband and profession for him, 'I should be thrown entirely on his mercy' (which was more promising). Why therefore, knowing the risks she ran, did she eventually yield?

In the first place because he was the Prince; it was one thing to brush aside the attempts at seduction of known libertines like Lord Lyttelton and George Fitzgerald, another to disdain an eager, fairy-tale Florizel. Such a flood of love-letters she had never received before, and her poetic self responded to their ardour. It was reported that he once 'pricked a vein in his arm that he might sign a letter with his own blood', and while the story is not authenticated, it is the kind of histrionic gesture that would appeal to him, and impress her with the belief that he was genuinely in love.[31] And so he was – for the moment. Knowledge of the Prince in later life makes Mary's behaviour appear astonishingly foolhardy, but the Prince's image was not only untarnished then, but bright with promise. Mary's rational self was wary, and for many weeks she refused any assignation: if she had truly been the scheming courtesan Miss Hamilton (and later historians) thought her, she would not have hesitated, but grabbed what she could for fear that the Prince *would* change his mind. But her vanity, always her Achilles heel, was flattered, and prudence was overmastered. Moreover, each letter exchanged with the Prince enmeshed her with him further. His later affairs, particularly that with Mrs Fitzherbert, show how relentlessly he pursued his quarry.[32] Once Mary had nibbled the bait by attending the theatre, once she had replied to a letter, she was hooked if not yet landed.

Nevertheless, still believing herself a free agent, she must have thought long and hard about her course of action. Against a liaison were the unsure long-term outcome, certainty of the monarch's disapproval, and the placing of herself in a category of women which until then she had just about managed to avoid. She must also have recognised the possibility of pregnancy (there was a shop near Covent Garden where 'cundums' made of sheep's gut or treated linen were sold in packets tied up by ribbons, but they were to protect not against pregnancy but venereal disease). Royal bastards were usually provided for – the descendants of Nell Gwyn, actress turned King's bedfellow, were still Dukes of St Albans – but pregnancy would be a very unwelcome complication. Moreover her stage career was flourishing; to hazard all that she had worked for during four years must at some moments have seemed madness. One thing she does not admit, though her future behaviour proves it, is that the 'fairy visions' which filled her mind included seeing herself as leader of the social world, leapfrogging over even her patroness, the Duchess of Devonshire, as fashion icon, wearing the finest silks and riding in splendid carriages.[33] At all stages of her life Mary Robinson desired to excel, to be foremost: the role of Prince's mistress was one she thought she could play to perfection.

Mary's decision-making gained an added complication when Lord Malden, the go-between, confessed that he too had fallen in love with her: Pandarus had turned Troilus. George Capel, Viscount Malden until 1799 when he became 5th Earl of Essex, was unrelated to

Elizabeth I's favourite, the family tracing their origins to Sir William Capel, Lord Mayor of London in 1503. He had been born in 1757, and educated at Corpus Christi College Cambridge, from which he graduated in 1777. Thereafter he set out on the traditional Grand Tour in France and Italy; there is no evidence that he profited greatly from it. In the previous year he had become Tory MP for Westminster, but was more man-about-town than politician, and until he inherited money from his grandmother in 1781, had little to spend on his pleasures. But in the spring of 1780 his attendance on Mrs Robinson at masquerades fuelled the gossip columns, and acted as a smoke-screen to the true state of affairs.

The King had forbidden his son from attending masquerades which he saw as a licence for vice, but their popularity had been long established, and when he came of age the Prince would make up for lost time. The essence of masquerade is disguise, the adoption of a different identity in costume matched by behaviour and speech; the excitement was the freedom to act a part behind the security of a mask. For moralists, masquerades permitted a dangerous blurring of identity and sexual restraint as normal conventions of social behaviour were set aside. Revellers would accost each other with 'Do you know me?', and act out their costumed roles (though many were unequal to the demands of improvisation). A Witch might cast a spell on a silent Milk Maid, a Harlequin tease a Shepherdess, a Nun reprove a gourmandising Friar. At a designated hour masks were removed for all to be revealed, when the old Witch might prove to be a young man, the Milk Maid too. Identity change was not compulsory however, and Mary, who spent much of her life dressing to play parts either in her professional or private life, preferred to be recognised. She might wear a domino (a hooded cloak, usually black and worn with a mask), but sometimes she did not hide her identity at all.

There were two principal London venues at this date for masquerades. One was at the King's Theatre, the opera house, where the stage was extended over the orchestra and decorated as a ballroom. The other was the Pantheon, which was transformed, as the German visitor Baron von Archenholtz wrote, into a 'temple of Comus'.[34] For the masked ball he attended, mirrors to the value of £36,000 had been hired to decorate the rooms and add to the sense of confusion. Tickets were twice the price of those for the King's Theatre; nevertheless 1,500 tickets at two guineas each were sold for the 'Grand and Only Masquerade' at the Pantheon that season, on 3 April 1780, three of them to Mr and Mrs Robinson and Lord Malden. With so many revellers expected, instructions were issued for a one-way coach system, horses' heads towards Hyde Park. Nevertheless, the streets around became wedged in with coaches, with the consequence that few of the company had reached the Pantheon when the doors opened at half-past ten and those that did had to wait till one o'clock in the morning for the supper rooms to be opened. This bad start left the reporter from the *Morning Post* disgruntled and disinclined to enter into the masquerade spirit. He found few costumes of note, only the usual collection of 'Nuns, Flower Girls, Milk Maids, Shepherds and Shepherdesses, Friars, Turks, and Persians innumerable; all very fine, and all tongue-tied'.

The journalist was on the lookout for those of rank or notoriety, and had no difficulty in recognising Mary with Malden and Robinson, but the tensions he observed in their behaviour he was less able to interpret, though tart about Mrs Robinson's exhibitionism and her husband's apparent willingness to be cuckolded:

> Mrs R—n, with a pink jacket and coat, with a loose gauze thrown over it, appeared melancholy from the provoking *inattention* of the company, and after a few parting parings [*sic*] round the room, retired with her *pliant* spouse on one side, the *Malden* hero on the other, who sympathetically *sulked* with his *acknowledged half*.[35]

How long the trio stayed discontentedly circling the room is not recorded, but it was well after dawn before the last of the revellers had drunkenly departed. The older Mrs Robinson pictures a comparable scene in *Walsingham*:

> Many a fair sylph . . . here made her *debut* in the mazes of deception, or the flowery paths of modern gallantry, till the festoons of coloured lamps glimmered their last rays, and the morning came, to discover the weary group half asleep, half dressed, half dirty, and more than half dissatisfied with their night's entertainment.[36]

The younger Mrs Robinson was probably only half-aware of any dissatisfaction.

Mary and her two companions would have gone to this masquerade straight from the theatre, as she had been on stage that evening. A fortnight later the trio attended a masked ridotto (a ridotto included more entertainment than a masquerade) at the King's Theatre, even though Mary would next day, for the first and only time, play Imogen in *Cymbeline*, and there would be a rehearsal in the morning. Maybe she had already decided to leave the stage and was indifferent to her career. Again on 1 May all three went to a ridotto at the Opera House, and here it was said that 'Mrs Robinson shone with unusual lustre, exhibiting a rich fruit of diamonds, beautifully contrasted with a *ruby* head'.[37] The unasked question was, who gave it her? The answer appeared to be Lord Malden.

The May issue of the *Town and Country Magazine* therefore featured the couple in their *tête-à-tête* series of irregular unions, as 'The Dramatic Enchantress' and 'The Doating Lover'. As with Lord Lyttelton before, a long history of sexual conquests is given for Lord Malden, but the Enchantress is described as 'not so easy a conquest as many imagined'. Information for *tête-à-têtes* was often gathered from servants (most evidence in divorce cases then came from servants who knew exactly what their masters or mistresses had been getting up to). In this case, since details of Mary's childhood and early history are inaccurate but her years on stage largely correct, the magazine's informant was very likely a servant, supplying anecdotes of events which she/he had witnessed. These support Mary's contention in her *Memoirs* that many would-be lovers tried to tempt her through female emissaries. One narrates how a 'lady abbess' (a brothel-keeper), pretending to apply for benefit tickets, placed in front of her a hundred-pound bank-note from a nobleman as payment in advance; another woman brought a baronet's promise of 'a new chariot' with her cypher:

> Even this bait did not take; Mrs R—n listened, shook her head, and retired. Mrs T—d rung the bell, and when the servant entered, was so nettled at the reception she had met with, as to say, 'I think your mistress is the rudest woman I ever saw in my life.' 'No, madam,' replied she, 'I am bold enough to say, you are the rudest woman I ever saw in my life, for I overheard all your conversation.'[38]

The Enchantress's sudden, and surprising, submission to the Doating Lover is said to have followed the gift of a 'pair of valuable diamond ear-rings'.

These and the other jewels could only have come from the Prince of Wales (who was without money, but there are ways and means for an heir to the throne). Mary says that she refused many gifts, accepting only 'a few trifling ornaments' afterwards returned, and whose value did not exceed a hundred guineas (probably £10,000 today, so not such trifles). She also received a miniature portrait of the Prince by Jeremiah Meyer, the Kew-based artist who was official miniaturist to Queen Charlotte. It was in a diamond setting and inside the case she found a small heart cut out of paper, on one side of which was written 'Je ne change qu'en mourant' [I only change in death], and on the other, 'Unalterable to my Perdita through life'. Such a gift was of great emotional significance; many women wore miniatures of their husbands on ribbons round their necks or, as the Queen did, as bracelets on their arms.[39] In giving Mary his image, the Prince was giving himself and declaring that it was for ever, not only in his paper messages but in the diamond setting. The Duchess of Devonshire later wrote that Mary had the portrait set in diamonds herself, but this is unlikely; when the Prince made a romantic gesture he did it completely.[40] Mary recognised the miniature as such, and through all the troubles of her life would never part with it.

The Prince made another grand gesture; in one of his letters he enclosed no mere bank-note for £100, but a signed and sealed bond promising to pay Mrs Robinson the sum of £20,000 on his coming of age.[41] When she opened the letter, Mary wrote that she responded with astonishment and tears, but she did not tear the document up. She must have secreted it with the letters and jewels as, embarking on a journey with no certain destination, she prepared to meet her wooer face to face.

5

Florizel and Perdita

The thing which is most talk'd of at present is the Prince of Wales, who keeps Mrs Robinson en maîtresse déclosée, c'est tout à fait un établissement; *she wears his picture about her neck, and drives about with four nag-tailed horses & two servants behind her.*
(Lady Harriet Spencer to Miss Georgiana Shipley)

Just at the point when Mrs Robinson's *Memoirs* moves towards its climax, when seduction by letter and amorous glance becomes a mingling of bodies, the narrative comes to an abrupt stop. The last two sentences before it breaks off read:

> The unbounded assurances of lasting affection which I received from his Royal Highness in many scores of the most eloquent letters, the contempt which I experienced from my husband, and the perpetual labour which I underwent for his support, at length began to weary my fortitude. Still I was reluctant to become the theme of public animadversion, and still I remonstrated with my husband on the unkindness of his conduct.[1]

'The narrative of Mrs Robinson closes here', the published version declares; what follows is claimed to be a 'Continuation by a friend', but incorporating a lengthy quotation from a letter to another 'friend' in America, dated 1783. The manuscript shows, however, that Mary did not break off mid-page; the 'last' sentence ends at the far right-hand corner of the very bottom of page 201 and there is no indication whatsoever that she did not continue on to another sheet.

The *Memoirs* are written on loose sheets of paper, many of them 'envelopes' which originally wrapped letters to her (usefully providing a number of her addresses); the sheets vary in size but each is carefully numbered on the top right-hand corner. They appear to have been copied from an earlier draft since at one point Mary writes that she 'transcribe[s]' a passage on 29 March 1800. Something therefore must have followed page 201, perhaps to do with the Prince, which so worried Maria that when preparing the memoirs for publication she felt the need for more drastic action than simple deletion. Moreover there was probably much which followed in the text to alarm her. It was one thing to publish damning remarks about Lyttelton and Fitzgerald, who were dead, another to print comments on the living; her effacement of innocuous remarks about the More sisters reveals her anxiety. Mary had parted acrimoniously from her last lover, Banastre Tarleton, but Maria herself had no reason to quarrel with him, and although her mother is likely to have been judicious in what she said about the Prince, it was still a delicate matter.

It can be guessed that in a panic Maria turned for advice to one of her mother's literary friends, probably Samuel Jackson Pratt who wrote one of the elegies inscribed on the tomb. (It was not William Godwin, as to him she wrote: 'Though I am not guilty of so much vanity – as to call *myself Biographer*, yet I am going to be *accessory* to something like it' [her italics], a revealing sentence in its phraseology.)[2] It is likely that she and her accomplice concocted a plan to pretend that Mrs Robinson had broken off her writing, to select from what came later and present it impersonally, while also relating what happened at the end of her life. If a reader changes 'she' and 'her' to 'I' and 'my', many later passages become Mary-language, for example this sentence describing her perplexity about leaving the stage for the Prince: 'A laborious though captivating profession, the profits of which were unequal to the expenses of her establishment, and the assiduities of her illustrious lover, to whom she naturally looked for protection, combined to divide her attention and bewilder her inexperienced mind'.[3]

The royal romance, however, could not be treated in this way, and the conspirators would have known that publishers would not be interested in the memoirs at all unless there was a first-person account. So they created an American 'friend', conveniently deceased, to whom she was supposed to have written a long account in 1783. Many commentators have felt uneasy about this 'letter' since its whole feel is of the *Memoirs* written in 1798–1800. But in any case it can be shown to be a fabrication, despite artful asides to 'my friend': it refers to Prince

Frederick as the Duke of York, but he did not receive his dukedom till 1784, and to the Prince's equerry General Lake, who was still Colonel Lake in 1783. The 'letter' must be part of Mary's original text, with who knows what changes and excisions. It is also quite likely that the memoirs *were* completed, though Mrs Robinson is quoted as expressing regret that she had not continued them 'up to the present time': she could have meant beyond 1798, when she wrote the draft. But even if she did break off at some point, it would have been at a stage well beyond the end of the affair with the Prince. It had not even begun when she is supposed to have laid down her pen.

For Florizel the early months of 1780 must have been frustrating. At some time he planned an assignation with Perdita at Lord Malden's London house, but was unable to escape his supervisors. Even beyond the supposed age of maturity, eighteen, the Prince's life remained rigidly time-tabled. A newspaper account of his day's routine – at a time when the Florizel/Perdita affair was supposedly in full flow – revealed that he spent two hours of study before breakfast, then the rest of the day with his tutors, when

> politics or history, agriculture, arts, manufactures, commerce, fisheries, colonies, companies, finances, credit and taxes, are all discussed, in order that the Prince may be acquainted with their rise, progress and present state, and fully comprehend the maxims which ought to guide them. Always before dinner the Prince pays his devotions to their Majesties, upon which occasion it is that the King mentions any circumstances in the stile of explanation, or advice. His Royal Highness does not allow more than an hour at table; he is very temperate [*sic!*] like all the family . . .[4]

Part of Florizel's determined pursuit of Perdita must have been rebellion against this regime and a desire to outwit his gaolers. A suggestion that she be smuggled into the Queen's House disguised as a boy was rejected by Mary as too risky, a decision which 'threw his Royal Highness into the most distressing agitation'; it was to be a feature of his pursuit of women that he would work himself up to the point of hysteria when thwarted.[5]

It was probably early spring when Mary and the Prince at last met outside the public eye. The plan was for Malden to bring her to Kew after the household had retired to bed; the Prince would escape and meet Perdita and her chaperone outside the grounds. On the chosen evening, therefore, Mary and Malden travelled to Kew and crossed to the willow-fringed island in the Thames known as Brentford or Kew Ait, just downstream of the Dutch House. On the island there was a tavern, the Three Swans, famous for its dishes of eel, and for music and revelry. There the pair dined, though Mary was much agitated. At the appointed hour, with a boat ready to take them across, she waited with her escort for the signal:

> The handkerchief was waved on the opposite shore; but the signal was, by the dusk of the evening, rendered almost imperceptible. Lord Malden took my hand, I stepped into the boat, and in a few minutes we landed before the iron gates of old Kew palace. This interview was but of a moment. The Prince of Wales and the Duke of York (then Bishop of Osnaburg) were walking down the avenue. They hastened to meet us. A few words, and those scarcely articulate, were uttered by the Prince, when a noise of people approaching from the palace startled us. The moon was now rising; and the idea of being overheard, or of his Royal Highness being seen out at so unusual an hour terrified the whole group. After a few more words of the most affectionate nature uttered by the Prince, we parted, and Lord Malden and myself returned to the island.[6]

Despite the brevity of the meeting, Mary declares that if her mind 'was before influenced by esteem, it was now awakened to the most enthusiastic admiration', and she enthuses about 'the graces of his person, the irresistible sweetness of his smile, [and the] tenderness of his melodious yet manly voice'. 'How would my soul have idolised such a *husband*', she declares.

Meantime her actual husband was probably in a drunken stupor. According to Huish, some man ('we will not affix the epithet of noble before that word') had been deputed to carouse with Thomas Robinson to prevent him from following Mary.[7] (He must have recognised what was happening, but may have thought that any liaison of his wife would have side benefits for himself.) Meetings at Kew continued, Huish claiming that the Prince once disguised himself as a watchman before climbing over the gate. All were fearful of discovery; Mary, the Prince and Lord Malden camouflaged themselves in dark colours, but were made uneasy by Prince Frederick whose coat was a visible buff. Nevertheless, 'nothing could be more delightful than our midnight perambulations', as if nothing of a sexual nature was in transaction.[8] As they strolled in this 'romantic spot' the conversation was, if we believe her, almost a continuation of the daily tutorials, composed of talk about 'the busy world, its manners and pursuits, characters and scenery'. To enliven the occasion the Prince of Wales would sing, to such effect that 'the tones of his voice, breaking on the silence of the night . . . appeared to my entranced senses like more than mortal melody'. How surprising that this otherworldly music did not attract attention faster than a buff coat.

During this part of their narratives, some early chroniclers of Mary's life reach for the purple ink to evoke the Thames-side scene. The meetings are described as taking place 'at that hour of milkmaids, when every hedgerow offers its milky couch for lovers' raptures, the palace shows its chimney-pots against the violet sky, the black-mottled water holds yet the yellow primrose, and the ear is caught by the splash of a water-rat or the plaintive cry of a lone waterfowl'.[9] But it may have been elsewhere than on a milkmaid's couch that the Prince at last found himself 'in Elyssium' (as he misspelt it about a later entanglement), Perdita giving herself to Florizel in body as well as soul. Local legend, recorded a hundred years or so later by a Richmond antiquarian, was that Mrs Robinson and the Prince of Wales met in a brick house close to the corner of the main Kew road, and that 'it was quite the usual thing to see the lights all over the house, and to hear sounds of revelry until 3 and 4 in the morning'.[10] The building was nicknamed 'Hell House', and there was said to be an entrance into it from the back of Kew Gardens. But there is also an account of another meeting-place, pre-dating the *Memoirs*, and apparently in Mary's own words.

In 1787 a biography of Sophia Baddeley was published by her friend and companion, Elizabeth Steele. Mrs Baddeley, eleven years older than Mary and an actress and singer, had also been notorious for her love affairs. But by 1780 she had fallen on hard times and was sending begging letters to former admirers. One day Mrs Robinson arrived at her house in Pimlico in an 'elegant phaeton, with four beautiful poneys [*sic*], and two little post-boys, in blue and silver jackets', bringing with her a contribution of 10 guineas from the Duke of Cumberland.[11] Mrs Baddeley had recently been brought to bed and Mary congratulated her on her child's birth, but Miss Steele saw her privately 'shed a few tears' over the state of the former beauty, whom in earlier years she had much admired. Mary told them of her own presently favoured circumstances, with the astonishing claim that she had known the Prince since he was 'but fourteen years of age':

> 'Many a time,' continued she, 'has the poor dear boy got out of his bed when he was at Kew, and come to me in the middle of the night at the inn, at Kew-bridge.' 'How do you mean?' said I [Miss Steele], 'got out of bed?' 'Yes,' replied she, 'their Majesties always paid such attention to their children, as to go and see them every night, after they were in bed; and often has the dear Prince got up after this, dressed himself, and with the assistance of his brother, the Duke of York, climbed over the garden-wall, after mid-night, and come to me; staid some hours, and returned home over the wall again, before day-light; unknown to any one, but his brother; so that his affection for me, is of no short duration'.[12]

Here we have Mary's words reported by someone other than herself, and only seven years after the event (at the time of publication she was out of the country), though she could not then have named the 'Duke of York', and at Kew the Prince did not live in the same building as his parents. No credence can be given to the boast of a four-year relationship which, if accurately remembered by Miss Steele, perhaps reveals Mary's underlying fear that it would *not* be long-lasting. But the climb over the wall for assignations at a nearby inn may well be true. Did Mary really refer to the Prince as the 'poor dear boy'?

All such trysting with the Prince during April and May had to be fitted not only around the court schedule, but Mary's theatrical engagements. She had been on stage only once during March, partly because of Holy Week when the theatres closed, but also because, as was reported, in early March she was 'dangerously ill', an illness perhaps exacerbated by stress.[13] Previously she had continued to play Perdita, and on 28 January for the first time Rosalind in *As You Like*

It. The next day she was on stage again as the speaker of a new Prologue for a comedy by Elizabeth Richardson, *The Double Deception.*[14] Perhaps Mary herself was the author of this one, trying her hand at turning out the pithy rhyming couplets which were their hallmark. Speaking the couplets was an art too, with players such as Thomas King and Frances Abington renowned for their delivery. It was a very exposed solo role; a bell would ring to signal the end of the music, then the Prologue (dressed in black) moved onto the forestage in front of the green curtain. No quiet mumbling was possible: voice and manner had to be incisive, pointing the wit of the piece.

For Mary as Rosalind there is a portrait, thought to be by Zoffany, displaying her bare-headed, with a mass of swept-back hair; unfortunately it is only half length, so we see no breeches.[15] The most curious aspect is the expression, showing not the gay teasing Rosalind but the reflective girl of 'No, no, Orlando: men are April when they woo, December when they wed; maids are May when they are maids, but the sky changes when they are wives'. Of her performance the *Morning Chronicle*'s critic wrote:

> Mrs Robinson last night acquitted herself very respectably in the character of Rosalind . . . Her figure was perfectly proper, and her deportment graceful. She will, however, improve her performance in the part, if in future she uses less labour in her oratory, and does not aim at the emphatic so much. The language is most elegantly simple, and the actress, to do Rosalind justice, should speak with all the ease imaginable, and not affect to be more marking and expressive, than she would be, if holding a conversation in real life, and talking to those before whom she felt no manner of restraint.[16]

Over-emphasis was still a fault, but Mrs Robinson fared better than John Palmer, famed for his Joseph Surface in *The School for Scandal*, who was 'not by any means equal to Jaques'. When she chose *As You Like It* for her benefit night on 7 April, Mary ensured a good Jaques by inviting John Henderson from Covent Garden to take the part; a musical afterpiece, *The Quaker*, followed.

By this date the wheels of the scandal machine were turning, and it may be that Sheridan capitalised by asking her to perform more often in her last two months than at any other time. Mary speaks of her theatrical career as one she loved but found 'laborious'; a modern actress might not think so since she was on stage only half a dozen times a month, sometimes less. But the schedule was demanding in terms of lines to be learnt or revised: in April 1780 Mary played eight roles on ten nights, and in May another eight roles on eleven nights, on two of which she acted in both mainpiece and afterpiece. Four of the parts, all breeches roles, were new to her: Oriana in Farquhar's *The Inconstant*, Imogen in *Cymbeline*, the Widow Brady in Garrick's lively afterpiece *The Irish Widow*, and Eliza Camply in a new afterpiece, *The Miniature Picture* by Elizabeth Craven (who was shortly to cause a scandal by leaving her husband).

Nothing shows more clearly how competent an actress she had become than her appearance as the Widow Brady. This part requires versatility, the actress first adopting a slight Irish brogue for the Widow's modest self, then a heavy one as she disenchants an elderly suitor by hoydenish behaviour; she next transforms herself into her fire-breathing brother who threatens to run the old man through, and finally brings the play to a bravura end with a four-stanza song (in an Irish accent). In her final role, as the 'sentimental grave Miss Camply', she dresses herself as her cousin, Sir Harry Bevel, in order to discover whether the man she loves is courting another young woman since he has lent her Eliza's portrait in miniature (Mary must have thought of the Prince's picture and its message of everlasting love). A comic Scot, Lord McGrinnon, adds to the confusion.

Lady Craven, a society beauty, had written the play for a charity performance with her friends at Newbury, near the family seat; Sheridan, having asked to borrow the script, outraged her by staging it publicly without her permission. Nevertheless she attended the second performance, bringing with her a party which included the Duchess of Richmond and the Duchess of Devonshire. A devoted admirer, Horace Walpole, described how Lady Craven sat in 'the front row of the stage-box, much dressed, with a profusion of white bugles and plumes, to receive the public homage due to her sex and loveliness'.[17] But he condemned the performers as 'wretched indeed . . . [William] Parsons murdered the Scotch lord, and Mrs Robinson (who is supposed to be the favourite of the Prince of Wales) thought on nothing but her own charms, or him'. It is a cheap gibe, and is belied by next day's report in the *London Courant*:

> Mrs Robinson . . . never appeared to more advantage: she was all ease, spirit, and expression; and we could see from the animated satisfaction visible in Lady Craven's looks . . . that the character was played entirely to her approbation. When we reflect that this was the author's favourite part, and that which she herself played at Newberry, it must be allowed that Mrs Robinson must have conceived and executed it with truth and propriety.[18]

Moreover the critic of the *Morning Chronicle*, who had found fault with Mary's performance as Rosalind earlier in the year, now offered warm praise:

> Mrs Robinson's Eliza does her infinite credit; she displays a degree of acting merit in the breeches scenes of the character, infinitely superior to any sample of professional talent she had before shewn, and stands eminently distinguished from the other performers.[19]

Ironically it seems that, having determined to leave the stage, Mary threw off self-consciousness and produced her best performances. Anxious to keep her, Sheridan offered much better terms for the following season, but she was not to be persuaded. On 31 May, the last night of the season, she ended her career with Eliza Camply, telling one of the actors as she entered the Green Room for the final time that she would appear no more. 'Endeavouring to smile', she repeated the last words of the song which ends *The Irish Widow*:

> Oh Joy to you all in full measure,
> So wishes and prays Widow Brady!

Then she burst into tears. The prompt book carries the note: 'This was Mrs Robinson's last appearance on the stage'.[20]

It has been claimed, nevertheless, that Mrs Robinson did return to the stage in 1783, and possibly also 1787.[21] This was not so, however. After the break-up of her royal relationship Mary contemplated a return, but says that friends whom she consulted 'dreaded that the public would not suffer my reappearance on the stage', and she took their advice.[22] Belief in her reappearance results from a mistaken linking of separate newspaper reports about different Mrs Robinsons. On 31 March 1783 the *Morning Herald* published in its gossip column the comment: 'The *Perdita* is so much improved within these last two years, that she scarcely retains a resemblance of her *former self*; chiefly to her appearing more *en bonne point*, than she formerly did'. On the same page there is a quite unrelated review of Hannah Cowley's new comedy *A Bold Stroke for a Husband*, at Covent Garden, in which a Mrs Robinson played Victoria. This Mrs Robinson, who performed at the Haymarket over several seasons, has been identified as Hannah Henrietta Robinson, from the Theatre Royal Bath.[23] She also appeared in Edinburgh in 1787, at which time Mrs Mary Robinson could scarcely walk into a theatre, let alone onto a stage. Moreover, had she indeed returned to acting in 1783 it would have been sensational and attracted much comment.

In a biographical anthology of 1801, written though not published before her death, an anonymous writer declares of Mrs Robinson's theatrical career that

> In the parts of Rosalind, Imogen, and Viola, we have not been happy enough to see her equal in any successor, taking form and face into the comparison . . . In Juliet and Perdita, Mrs Robinson will probably remain for ever unrivalled.[24]

This is a large claim, especially given the small number of occasions on which she played the parts; either Mary had a very partial admirer, or she had a hand in writing the account herself. A more sober assessment was made soon after she left the stage in the *Town and Country Magazine*:

> If she was not remarkably excellent as an actress, she was at least so happy as never to be remarkably deficient, in any part she attempted; she seldom played without applause'.[25]

The truth is that she was not an actress long enough to secure an enduring reputation. Could she have done so if she had continued on the stage?

There would have been two more seasons in which to establish herself at Drury Lane before Sarah Siddons became its star; but the grand heroic roles in which Mrs Siddons excelled, such as Lady Macbeth and Jane Shore, were not those that suited Mrs Robinson. Dorothy Jordan's advent in 1785 would have been a greater challenge, for she shone in those parts such as Rosalind and Viola which Mary claimed for herself. It is unlikely that Mary could have matched either woman in stage presence, though she was better-looking than both, elegant and graceful in her movements, with an expressive face and 'a remarkable sweetness of voice'. She could, however, have continued in comedy and breeches roles, and made the 'lighter' tragic roles such as Ophelia, Cordelia and Desdemona (which she never played) her own. Moreover, though Mrs Siddons and Mrs Jordan were overnight successes at Drury Lane, they by no means burst upon the scene as novices. Both women had spent years developing their skills in Dublin and provincial theatres, while Mrs Robinson might be said only to have completed an apprenticeship by the time she left the stage. Her departure was mourned by at least one play-goer as the loss of one of Drury Lane's 'most promising ornaments', and in 1794, years after she had left the stage, the critic of the *Morning Chronicle* recalled the 'graceful éclat that used to accompany her personal appearance on the Boards'.[26] Mary lacked the vivacity which made Mrs Jordan so brilliant in hoyden roles, but she possessed dramatic qualities enough to have made 'unrivalled' not too outlandish a claim had she persisted with her career.

The event which Mary would have been anticipating when she said good-bye to Drury Lane on 31 May was the celebration of the King's birthday on 5 June (his actual birthday was 4 June, but because this fell on a Sunday in 1780 the usual afternoon levée and evening ball at St James's Palace were postponed a day). Mary could not participate in the ball itself, but the Prince had invited her to come and watch from the spectators' box. However, the inauspicious happenings surrounding the birthday this year were not a happy omen, since from 2 June London experienced terrifying mob violence, with 300 deaths and much destruction of property.

The so-called Gordon Riots had been threatening all year, with newspapers regularly carrying advertisements for Lord George Gordon's Protestant Association. This had been formed to petition for the repeal of legislation two years earlier which had allowed Roman Catholics a few minority rights, such as attendance at mass.[27] On 2 June, when the petition with 100,000 signatures was to be delivered to Parliament, inflammatory notices were posted thoughout Westminster and the City of London; members arriving at the House found themselves pulled and pushed about by a mob waving banners demanding 'No Popery'. Over the following week the property of anyone believed to be Catholic or sympathetic to Catholics was attacked. First targets were Catholic chapels attached to foreign embassies, and several were burnt to the ground. Then the mob turned to private property; the Bloomsbury home of Lord Mansfield, the Lord Chief Justice, was destroyed and he lost books and papers of a lifetime.[28] When four rioters were arrested and taken to Newgate the mob forced their release and that of all other inmates; then they torched the building. The King's Bench prison and the Fleet were likewise fired, and the Bank of England had to be defended against rioters.[29] Only when the King proclaimed martial law on 8 June was order restored.

A rumour that the mob was preparing to storm St James's Palace on 5 June, led many of the nobility to stay away from the birthday celebrations. Lord Malden is listed as attending however, and he probably escorted Mary to the Lord Chamberlain's box. It must have been galling to have to watch as the Prince of Wales, splendidly attired in a 'sky-coloured blue silk coat, beautifully embroidered with silver', opened the ball with Lady Augusta Campbell, daughter of the Duke of Argyll.[30] For once Mary does not describe her own dress, though she would have made sure that it was of high fashion, nor does she appear to remember the frightening background to the occasion. Her self-absorbed concern is with how the Prince behaved; if he could not dance with his Perdita, Florizel did not forget her, embarrassing her by his 'marked and injudicious attentions'. She watched as Lady Augusta drew from her bouquet two rose-buds and presented them as '"emblematical of herself and him"', as the Prince later told Mary. But far from gallantly placing them on his bosom, the Prince called to a friend, the Earl of Cholmondeley, and indicated that the flowers were to be given to Mary. She displayed them on her own bosom, 'proud of the power by which I thus publicly mortified an exalted rival'.[31] But to humiliate a woman of the nobility was unwise; Perdita might triumph now, but when social ranks closed against her she would reap the penalty of ostracism.

At the birthday ball the Prince distinguished her as mistress of his heart, but the occasion exemplifies how marginal was Mary's public role, and this was to be the pattern of the relationship. Actual meetings were still clandestine affairs, though she says that the Prince openly indicated his preference for her in public places of entertainment such as the theatre, military reviews and the royal hunts at Windsor. But she was never at his side; the Prince was still under his father's control and, even after his eighteenth birthday in August, the King laid down rules for his behaviour: he was not to attend masquerades, for example, nor to lounge around Hyde Park. At the theatre he was to sit formally in his own box with his regular attendants only, so Mary would have had to sit on her own and communicate only with yearning looks. She would have received no invitation to the private ball held at Windsor Castle for his coming of royal age (at eighteen he became old enough to rule in person), though she probably witnessed the parade of soldiers in the Great Park at midday, the firing of a 21-gun salute, and the regatta on the river by Eton scholars, which the Prince watched from a barge – but not with her. Nor was the Prince, as expected, immediately given his own establishment. Instead he was to have a 'half-establishment', with his own household, but with neither his own London house nor an independent income. Having learned of his son's very improper attachment to an actress, the King may have determined to put an obstacle in the way of greater disgrace by preventing money being squandered on a mistress; his birthday letter to his son reproved him for his 'love of dissipation [which] has for some months been with enough ill nature trumpeted in the public papers'.[32]

There must nevertheless have been a time of fulfilment, pride for Mary, happiness and gaiety for both; of all the Prince's mistresses Mary was surely the one who would have been most ready to discuss choice of fabric for a waistcoat, as he had asked of Mary Hamilton. The Prince is said to have given Mary a ball at Weltje's club, with the Duchess of Devonshire and many society notables present (Louis Weltje was the Westphalian cook who became the Prince's Comptroller and Clerk of the Kitchens and Cellars).[33] She herself threw supper parties at her Covent Garden home for the Prince and friends, where he was no doubt, as he could be, the most charming of guests, with delightful conversation, a gift for music, and a talent for mimicry which, it was said, could have made him the 'best comic actor in Europe'.[34] Only the Prince could have commissioned the miniature of Mary of 1780 by Meyer, presumably intended as a companion piece to the one he had given her of him; it shows a delicate-featured face, with hair falling in ringlets onto her shoulders, and stands as testimony to his short-lived love.[35]

But there are no eye-witness accounts of the pair together. The nearest to a record of amorous partnership is found in Rowlandson's famous watercolour of Vauxhall Gardens, where among the crowd strolling under the trees while listening to a singer serenading from a balcony can be found Florizel and Perdita; he whispers in her ear as she inclines towards him. This picture is an imaginary image; in reality it was not possible for Mary to appear with Prince Charming by her side, and the romance became, in its public manifestations, a very one-sided affair. For the Prince it could only be a matter of stolen occasions; for Mary however it was a full-time occupation, and she played the role of Prince's mistress as she thought it should be played – ostentatiously. Lady Harriet Spencer, the Duchess of Devonshire's sister, watched with amazement as Mrs Robinson drove dashingly round town with the Prince's miniature round her neck, her badge of office, sign of her possession of his heart. As an anonymous writer noted, everything about her appearance was designed to be eye-catching:

> Perdita was now the envy of every female heart: her chariot, her phaeton, her dress, her every thing, was equally the subject of censure and imitation; and every new gown set the giddy circle in an uproar. She sometimes flaunted in a cabriole, drawn by milk white ponies, and seemed like the Cyprian goddess, descended from the celestial regions to visit this favourite isle.[36]

Forty years on, Miss Laetitia-Matilda Hawkins could recall not only the spectacle, but a remarkable and theatrical feature of it, that Perdita adapted her 'deportment' to her dress, creating a new persona to match each outfit, and alternating rustic innocence with the knowingness of sophisticated beauty:

> When she was to be seen daily in St James's Street and Pall Mall, even in her chariot this variation was striking. Today she was a *paysanne*, with her straw hat, tied at the back of her head, looking

> as if too new to what she passed, to know what she looked at. Yesterday, she, perhaps, had been the dressed *belle* of Hyde Park, trimmed, powdered, patched, painted to the utmost power of rouge and white lead [for a white skin]; tomorrow she would be the cravatted Amazon of the riding house: but be she what she might, the hats of the fashionable promenaders swept the ground as she passed.[37]

The ornamentation of this chariot also drew the eye; it was the one in which she drove to see Sophia Baddeley, in blue and silver, with a 'pretty basket of five round flowers' above a rose-wreath, and the initials MR painted on the panels, the design deceiving onlookers into thinking it a 'five-pearled coronet'.[38] But she was giving a solo performance: the irony of Mrs Robinson's great liaison was that it made its effect from individual showmanship rather than partnership.

Even so, after years of a worthy but rather dull monarchy the emergence of a beautiful mistress of a handsome prince had appeal, and drew the crowds:

> Whenever I appeared in public, I was overwhelmed by the gazing of the multitude. I was frequently obliged to quit Ranelagh, owing to the crowd which staring curiosity had assembled round my box; and, even in the streets of the metropolis, I scarcely ventured to enter a shop without experiencing the greatest inconvenience. Many hours have I waited till the crowd dispersed, which surrounded my carriage, in expectation of my quitting the shop.[39]

This press of anonymous faces could have been disturbing, but Mary was used to audiences and found it only an 'inconvenience'. The attentions of the scandal-hungry press were, however, to become distressing.

In 1780 Londoners had a choice of eight morning newspapers, or prints, costing 3*d* (threepence) each, with 1½*d* going to the Treasury in tax; this high cost ensured that most reading was done not at home but in the coffee-houses to which men daily thronged and where newspapers were delivered in bulk.[40] The four-sided prints gained most of their revenue from advertising, and the front pages carried notices for the evening's entertainment at the theatres, for exhibitions and special shows, forthcoming masquerades and ridottos, just-published books, sales of houses and goods (on 7 March 1780 the 'superb, elegant and genuine Household Furniture' of the Right Hon. Lord Lyttelton), miracle medicines, transforming cosmetics, coachbuilders, millinery and mantua-makers and many more, including the occasional oddity such as a patent coffin for defeating grave-robbers. Inner pages were used principally for reporting parliamentary debates, each paper having loyalty to (and being subsidised by) a political faction. There were theatre reviews, news from abroad and the provinces, and letters to the editor. But from 1772, when the *Morning Post* was launched, there had also been entertainment in the form of gossipy 'paragraphs' about personalities of the day, which proved so popular that other papers followed suit. It is in such columns that much of the later history of 'The Perdita' is found. How much came from the pens of the journalists, how much was supplied by the subjects themselves, and how much was inspired by personal malice or genuine outrage, is not clear, not least because these insertions were paid for but not entered into ledgers, to avoid being taxed as 'advertising'; it has been claimed that by 1780 'there was hardly a "paragraph" in the [*Morning Post*] that was not paid for by someone'; the terms 'puff', 'suppression fee', 'insertion fee' and 'contradiction fee' became part of journalistic language.[41]

The 'personality' of the newspaper world itself was the pugnacious Reverend Henry Bate, founding editor of the *Morning Post*. Bate had been chaplain to Lord Lyttelton, and had gained the title 'The Fighting Parson' after a fracas in 1773 in Vauxhall Gardens, when he challenged a group of men harassing Mrs Elizabeth Hartley (Mary's first Hermione); a complicated series of events developed, involving both Lord Lyttelton and George Robert Fitzgerald on opposite sides, and ending with Bate in a bare-knuckle duel in which he beat his adversary's face to a 'perfect jelly'.[42] In the spring of 1780 he was in worse trouble, having been found guilty of libelling the Duke of Richmond, though his prison sentence had to be postponed because the gaols had been destroyed. Accusing his fellow-proprietors on the *Post* of cowardice, he left the paper, and on 1 November founded a rival, the *Morning Herald*. The point of this history is that Bate's wife Mary, Elizabeth Hartley's sister and another actress, was a friend of Mary Robinson; after the *Herald*'s birth it became the print in which to find news (rather than malicious comment) about her. But because of its antagonism to Bate, the *Post* was the more ready to print abuse.

On 18 July the *Post* published a letter signed 'Ovid', supposedly written from Windsor:

> And so the Theatrical *Perdita* of Drury Lane is labouring night and day to insinuate to the world, that an *amour* either has taken, or is to take place, between her and a certain young illustrious character. If such a report, may, in the smallest degree contribute to the fair lady, in her other pursuits and designs, it would be a pity to contradict the report; but otherwise, Mr. Editor, it may be friendly in you to whisper into her ear, that if the young gentleman had really any *penchant* for her, which, however, is not the case, her present system of *vain-boasting* must give his heart a very speedy *quietus*.[43]

Two days later the paper told how a 'certain young actress . . . appeared in the side-box of the Haymarket Theatre a few evenings since, with all the grace and splendour of a Duchess'.[44] A scurrilous attack came on 3 August from 'Crop', making comparison with Nell Gwyn, in the assumption that 'our *quondam* Princess' was after wealth and a title, and following it by a lengthy account of her performance of Rosalind in terms of sexual innuendo.[45] On 9 August a laboured piece of writing presented a series of 'raree shews', one of them being of

> the famous Perdita of Drury-lane, sitting at the play-house in the sidebox opposite the P— of W—. Look how wantonly she looks, thinking, Gracious Sir! Please to bestow one —— upon a poor woman! Ho! Ho! Fine raree shew!

Placing herself in the side-boxes, preserve of the nobility and the righteous, was seen as a presumption, and 'Dramaticus' (a regular commentator on theatrical matters) attacked 'the audacity of Mrs R—', her husband and a companion, in occupying a side-box:

> I know no rank of prostitution that can either lessen the crime or the disgrace of it; and, however profligate the age may be, I believe that the greatest libertine of our sex would revolt at the idea of handing his wife, sister, or daughter, into a box where they were certain of being surrounded by public prostitutes.[46]

Either Mary or a supporter responded immediately, expressing bafflement at the identity of Mrs R—, the initial of a 'very amiable, modest and accomplished woman, whose character and conduct entitles her to rank with any woman in this kingdom'.[47] A day later there appeared a biography of the 'celebrated Theatrical PERDITA', a hagiographic account of Mary's life, no doubt written by herself and without reference to the Prince, which concludes:

> Her amiable conduct towards her friends and relations evinces the goodness of her heart; she is the most *affectionate of mothers*, the most *faithful of friends*: the perfections of her *person* are trifling in comparison with the virtues of her *mind*; if the slanderous part of the world would for once weigh the little follies she may be guilty of with the merit she possesses, the tongue of calumny would be silent.[48]

Throughout her life Mary would in verbal portraiture try to portray the real Mrs Robinson as a serious-minded, domestically devoted woman. But what could be observed was the flamboyant Perdita, a visual creation not unlike the dazzling scenic illusions of de Loutherbourg. Dramaticus hit back, and a correspondent calling himself 'No Flatterer' condemned the 'most fulsome panegyric which ever disgraced a newspaper', and sneered at 'that most virtuous, *most* innocent, *most* amiable, *most* poetic, and *most* beautiful of her sex, the *most* renowned *Perdita*'.[49]

The correspondence was unpleasant, but it is nevertheless startling a month later to find a letter claiming that so much of a scandalous nature had been relayed in the papers that 'the unhappy woman is now almost in a state of insanity'.[50] The writer warns that if editors continue in this way 'they will have her blood to answer for'. Mary was also receiving anonymous letters, and there had just been published, price 6*d*, some doggerel and offensive verses entitled *Florizel and Perdita*, presenting her as a painted whore of the stage:

Sometimes she'd play the Tragic Queen,
Sometimes the Peasant poor,
Sometimes she'd step behind the Scenes,
And there she'd play the W—.

Two Thousand Pounds, a princely Sight
For doing just no more,
Than what is acted every Night,
By every Sister W—.[51]

Accompanying them is a crude illustration showing a décolletée Perdita, a Welsh hat perched on top of her head-dress and surrounded by boxes of cosmetics; the Prince in Roman costume raises his hands in apparent admiration, and behind Perdita stands the horned figure of Thomas Robinson. He features in the last verse:

Her Husband too, a puny Imp,
Will often guard the Door,
And humbly play Sir Peter Pimp,
While she performs the W—.

Robinson was widely seen as promoting his wife's liaisons, the 'sniffing and carrying animal' of her sexual encounters.[52]

But Thomas had sexual appetites of his own. On 7 October the *Post* gleefully reported an 'awkward accident' at Covent Garden Theatre, when he had been found by his wife in one of the green [upper] boxes in the company of a fillette:

> Her jealousy instantly became ungovernable, and the first efforts of her fury made her forgetful of her *character* and *station* – She flew to the box – seized the unhappy husband – dragged him by the hair of his head into the lobby, and there spent her violence in blows and reproaches to the complete entertainment of a numerous auditory.[53]

'Poor penitent *Tommy*' was carried off home, the story illustrating both Mary's fiery temper and that he could still arouse her jealousy. It may have been this incident, however, which determined her to leave him, although it was customary, even regarded as an 'absolute necessity', that a demi-rep be married in order to preserve an appearance of virtue.[54] But, apart from his resort to prostitutes, Mary had discovered that the world was *not* tolerant of his complaisancy, scoffing derisively both at the cuckold and 'the most despicable *pander* that ever disgraced the married state'.[55] In that guise he is also present in Rowlandson's *Vauxhall Gardens*. Florizel and Perdita dally, but while she touches her chin coyly with her left hand, her right arm is locked in her husband's. Robinson is caricatured as an old and shrivelled pander, in a painting which combines idyll with incubus. A motive for Mary's freeing herself from Thomas may have been that he had become an encumbrance.

What did the Prince himself make of the furore? It could be that Mary's appetite for display, surpassing his own, became distasteful to him. It may be that they quarrelled: it has been suggested that he was angered when Mrs Robinson was rude to a friend of his.[56] For long before Rowlandson set brush to paper, the bonds of Perdita's relationship with Florizel were abruptly severed when, in mid-December, she received a 'cold and unkind letter' briefly informing her that '*we must meet no more*!'[57] In scarcely more than a year the Prince had passed from infatuation to anticipation to consummation, to satiation. As Rosalind might have quipped: princes are April when they woo, December when they bed. The most significant event of Mary's life, the one which shaped all her history to come, was over. For the Prince however, it had been just a rehearsal.

6

'Ye Old Infernal Cause Robinson'

I think myself authorised to declare that the treatment I receive from the Prince of Wales is so ungenerous and illiberal that I am sufficiently justified in any step my necessities may urge me to take.

(Mary Robinson to Lord Malden, 29 August 1781)

The silken cords with which it was said that Perdita had bound up Florizel's heart snapped with bewildering speed. Only Miss Hamilton could have told Mrs Robinson how rapidly the Prince could fall out of as well as into love. The cold letter of dismissal to Mary was the first such he sent, though Mrs Fitzherbert would be dealt with similarly after nine years of discreet devotion as his unacknowledged wife. Incomprehension was Mary's immediate reaction; she claims that only two days previously when they had met at Kew his affection had 'appeared to be [as] boundless as it was undiminished'.[1] She wrote demanding an explanation, but received no reply, nor to a second letter.

The Prince was at Windsor and Mary determined to seek an audience, an impulsive and, as it turned out, foolhardy and pointless decision. She raced out of London in a pony carriage as night was falling with only a nine-year-old 'postillion' in attendance, though when a footpad tried to seize the reins on Hounslow Heath the boy proved equal to the situation, spurring the pony beyond his reach. But the journey was in vain, as when they reached Windsor the Prince would not see her. On the way, however, she had caught sight of Elizabeth Armistead, a woman in whom she knew the Prince had expressed interest, and she drew the inevitable conclusion. 'Mrs' Armistead, a few years older than Mary, was a notorious demi-rep; although, as the saying went, she had been born in a cellar, by her mid-twenties it was thought she could claim the conquest of 'two ducal coronets, a marquess, four earls, and a viscount'.[2] At this time she was theoretically the mistress of Lord George Cavendish, but his sister-in-law the Duchess of Devonshire relates how one night he had gone to Mrs Armistead's house, only to find the Prince of Wales trying to hide behind her bedroom door; he made a low bow and retreated.[3]

Mary consulted with Lord Malden and the Duke of Dorset (of libertine reputation, though described by Mary as someone of 'honourable mind and disinterested friendship'). Both expressed themselves baffled by the sudden change, and Malden offered himself as a go-between, this time on Mary's behalf. The Prince was affable, and a meeting took place at Malden's house. There he greeted Mary with what seemed like a return of the old affection, and they spent some hours 'in the most friendly and delightful conversation'.[4] But next day the Prince cut her dead in Hyde Park.

The earliest notice of a rupture is found in the *Morning Herald* on 13 December 1780, where the reason given is a 'little jealousy' because of over-familiarity between the lady and 'her guardian noble *inamorato*'. It took some time, however, for full realisation that the affair was over. In January the *Town and Country Magazine* got events wrong again when it published its *tête-à-tête* of 'The Fair Ophelia' and 'The Illustrious Heir', claiming that it was as Ophelia that 'her beauty, her seeming innocence, her soft distress' and, ironically, her 'unkind treatment from the prince of Denmark' that attracted the Heir.[5] By April, however, the magazine was telling a reader that '*The History of Florizel and Perdita* is quite out of date'. Nevertheless, the story did not go away; the romance of the pretty shepherdess and her prince, however tarnished, had caught the imagination, and writers and artists were to keep it alive; *Florizel and Perdita*, a satirical print combining the pair in a single heart-shaped head was published in 1783, Rowlandson's *Vauxhall Gardens* in 1784, Richard Cosway painted miniatures of the Prince in the 1790s as 'Florizel', and satirical images of the Prince which make reference to Mary were produced throughout the rest of the century.

The main reasons for Florizel's breaking his 'eternal' vows must have been his wandering eye combined with his youth, but at the end of 1780 other events were making him unhappy, restless and reckless. His own household, based in a wing of Buckingham House, had at last been established, but he was deeply distressed when his brother Frederick was sent to Hanover to complete his military education. The brothers had been inseparable; at their parting on 30 December the Prince of Wales 'stood in a state of entire insensibility, totally unable to speak'.[6] In January he also lost his 'best friend', Lieutenant Colonel Gerard Lake, on whom he could always rely for disinterested advice. The King wanted to sweep away all those who had surrounded the Prince, and Lake was packed off to the American war. But Lake was not a corrupting influence, and before he left England he wrote to the Prince thanking him warmly for his friendship, and warning him about difficulties he might face; he urged the young prince not to attach himself to any political party, and added another wish, 'which is to beg that you will not write any more letters to a certain sort of ladies', in the hope that 'what you have already suffer'd will be a sufficient warning'.[7]

Mary had not taken her dismissal lightly. To be replaced so quickly, and by Mrs Armistead, a practised courtesan, was humiliating. Over the next months the papers enjoyed chronicling the rivalry of the two women, sitting in splendour at the theatre with others of the sisterhood, while keeping sharp watch for the direction of His Royal Highness's lorgnette, or trying to outdo each other in the smartness of their equipages in Hyde Park. Brimstone yellow was the 'high ton' colour for the spring of 1781, and both appeared in spanking new chariots; it was said that they would pull down the windows, grimace and spit at each other like alley-cats.[8] Oddly, it was also suggested that each represented a political faction with the Prince, Mrs A—d the Foxite opposition, and Mrs R—n the government and court.[9] This was particularly absurd given that at the end of December Mary had sent the Prince an ultimatum, feeding the information to the *Morning Herald*:

> A certain *amour royal* is now totally at an end; a separation has taken place a *thoro* for more than three weeks, and a settlement worthy such a *sultana* is the only thing now wanting to break off all intercourse whatever. Mrs R—n thinking the adjustment of this part of the *divorce* too essential to be trifled with, has written roundly to her once *ardent lover*, 'that if her establishment is not duly arranged within the space of fourteen days commencement of the new year, his —— —— must not be surprized, if he sees a full publication of all those *seductory epistles* which alone estranged her from *virtue*, and the *marriage vow*!'[10]

Mary's threat was taken seriously, and negotiations to buy back the letters begun, though this was not what she wanted: she expected her debts to be paid, and to be given an annuity, as men customarily provided for their mistresses. Her only bargaining tool was the correspondence, for which she was labelled a mercenary trollop; but as she was to point out, she had incurred debts in expectation of a settlement, and though she was a spendthrift (something the pair had in common) she had believed that the position in which the Prince had placed her demanded show.

As a gesture of good will, Mary returned jewellery and a few letters through Colonel Lake, and in an unpublished continuation of the passage in his letter to the Prince in which he wrote of 'a certain sort of ladies', Lake showed that he had formed a favourable impression of Mrs Robinson:

> I really believe by what I can learn, that your lady in my street [?] means to behave in every particular with propriety & attention to you, as to myself you well know I am scarcely acquainted with her therefore can say no more, than to wish she may and so as to please you & merit your protection.[11]

(Cutting lines which modify the damning effect of the previous phrase from an otherwise fully quoted letter suggests a rather churlish reluctance on the part of the editor of the Prince's correspondence to allow redeeming features in Mary's behaviour.) Nothing was settled at this time, and shortly afterwards the Prince himself fell seriously ill. It was insinuated in the press that he was suffering from venereal disease, caught because, apart from Mrs Armistead, he was also partaking of 'nothing but *fallen fruit*, and that of the *rather common* kind'.[12] The Prince told his brother that for a fortnight he had been cooped up in his bedchamber 'without ever tasting anything but barley water or some damned wishy washy stuff of that sort'.[13] Frederick assumed that Uncle Cumberland had been leading him on in 'raking & rioting' but the Prince assured him that the Duke had been acting as his firmest, staunchest friend in an affair where he needed advice, 'ye old infernal cause Robinson'.[14] Whatever its origin, his illness was probably exacerbated by fear of public revelation of his letters; in May Walpole noted in his journal a rumour that in them the Prince had described the Princess Royal as '*that bandy-legged bitch*, my sister', and there may have been imprudent references to the King as well.[15]

Mary had not, however, published the correspondence; had she done so all hope of getting her debts paid would have disappeared. Ironically, she then developed letter problems of her own. Newspapers announced publication on 24 March of 'GENUINE LETTERS from Perdita to a JEW with the Jew's Answer'; these were the mixture of genuine and forged letters concocted by the money-lender John King on the pretext of exposing the Robinsons as swindlers. He cites instances unsupported by any evidence, yet as with the intimacy with Lord Lyttelton there is some independent backing for his accusation of sharp practice. The newspaper *The World*, in its edition for 25 October 1787, carried a story of a recently deceased man called Grady from whom, it was said, Perdita's husband (the name Robinson does not appear) attempted to extort money on the grounds that he had seduced his wife; luckily for Grady, his hair-dresser had noticed that it was the husband himself who brought Perdita to the house. It is an unpleasant little tale, but may simply indicate belief that any such story could be linked to the Perdita.[16] Press advertisements for the *Letters from Perdita* declared that specimens of the originals were to be found at the publisher's, so Mary went with Lord Malden (whom she had accepted as her protector in place of the Prince as soon as she realised the permanency of his abandonment) to try to retrieve them, as recounted in the *Morning Post*:

> The *noble paramour* of the celebrated *Perditta* and the fair dame herself . . . made a bold push to recover *certain letters*, upon the originality of which a *certain book* has lately been published; but the attempt was abortive; the publisher would not surrender, but challenged the demandant to the *Chapter coffee-house*, there to decide his right. The *attic regions of Pater-noster Row* were in an uproar, but, the amorous pair were obliged to retreat without the objects of their wishes.[17]

The publisher might have accepted a pay-off, but since the Prince had not paid for his letters Mary had nothing to offer for hers.

It was at this time, in her need for income, that Mary thought of returning to the stage, a rumour printed by the *Herald* with the suggestion that 'finding all arts and devices fail in attempting the recovery of the *inconstant Florizel*' she hoped for 'another *princely heart*, on its first enlargement from the *royal nursery*!'[18] Yet despite her financial troubles Mary did not stop decking herself out in elaborate finery, or ordering a whole series of expensive new carriages (a 1794 treatise on carriages gives the price of an 'elegant chariot' as £277 12*s*).[19] That she could still obtain credit must have been on the assumption that ultimately there would be a settlement with the Prince, though there were surely trade-ins. '*Coach, Vis-à-Vis, Chariot, Gig, Cabriole, Phaetons of every complexion* have alternately swelled her *transient* equipage', reported the *Herald* on 13 June, the day after she had '*dashed* into town through Hyde-park turnpike' in a new phaeton drawn by four chestnut-coloured ponies, her postillion and servant fitted out with blue and silver liveries while she herself was 'dressed in a blue great coat [a one-piece dress] prettily trimmed with silver'. And this was only two days after she had been seen in Hyde Park in a 'new *brimstone car*, drawn by six well-accoutred foresters'. Another expense was the rental of an '*elegant* villa' at Old Windsor; this Thames-side village, once the seat of Saxon kings, was small enough for an envelope (used for writing the *Memoirs*) addressed simply to 'Mrs Robinson Old Windsor' to reach her there.

Mary had by now broken completely with her husband and was living in Cork Street in the West End, although she says that in meetings and letters he professed 'agony' at the separation and urged their reunion (the only address known for Thomas in the years that followed is Stafford Street in the parish of Saint Mary le Bow near Cheapside).[20] Lord Malden lived nearby in Berkeley Square, and will have been paying the rent for Mary's London home. Cork Street was a place of intrigue; another kept woman living there and likewise sporting a brimstone chariot was the bewitching Emily Warren, mistress of an East India Company grandee. She had been trained for her profession by a madam, so was exactly the sort of woman with whom Mrs Robinson hated to be coupled. But Reynolds painted both of them, and they remain neighbours of a sort as their portraits hang today in adjacent rooms at Waddesdon Manor.[21] Mary's actual next-door neighbour was a Polish countess being pursued by the King's brother, the Duke of Gloucester. This became an embarrassment to the Prince of Wales when, as he told Prince Frederick while relating summer trysts with his latest passion, the 'angelick' Countess of

Hardenburg, 'an unfortunate article in ye. *Morning Herald* appeared, saying yt. ye. German Baroness . . . had taken a house next door to Perdita's in Cork Street, & yt. my carriage was seen constantly at her door'.[22] The Count was alerted, and letters and lies flew to and fro until the Prince confessed all to the Queen; she told the King, and he sent the Count and Countess packing. The whole business must have infuriated King George for only in May he had been reproving his son for the 'shameful transaction' in which he was having to engage on his behalf. He meant the recovery of the Prince's love letters from Mrs Robinson.

The King had put the business in the charge of Lord Southampton, the head of the Prince's household. The functionary principally involved, however, was Colonel George Hotham, the Prince's Treasurer – the perfect civil servant, discreet, clear-headed, ramrod efficient. At the end of July he went to see Mrs Robinson to learn the extent of her debts (if she tried to charm him, he remained impervious). She named a sum between £4,000 and £5,000; this was a rough calculation and the true figure was later assessed as £5,600, though the Colonel suspected a ploy to obtain more money. The ensuing correspondence can be read in full as Malden, acting for Mary, kept the letters received and the drafts of the replies. The first of the series is Colonel Hotham's, setting out an offer of £5,000 in his precise, impeccable hand-writing. Only the flavour of the bureaucratic, supercilious language can be conveyed in print:

> My Lord,
>
> In obedience to Your Commands, I take the earliest Opportunity in My Power of informing Your Lordship, that I have Authority to say that in consideration of a past Connexion, which never more can be renewed, Mrs Robinson has it in Her Power to receive the Sum of Five Thousand Pounds; which, on Her Restitution of such Papers as passed during its continuance, will instantly be paid Her.
>
> This Sum, on a strict Retrospect into every Part of Mrs Robinson's conduct during the Time the Attachment subsisted, is deemed as proper & Sufficient Reward; & I am commanded to acquaint Your Lordship, (as I will beg the favour of You to inform

Mrs Robinson,) that nothing farther will be offer'd; that this Proposal is Final; & in case of that Lady's Non-Acceptance of this Sum, Your Lordship will receive no farther Trouble on this Unpleasant Subject.

I have the Honour to be,

My Lord,

Your Lordship's most obedient

& most humble Servant

G. Hotham[23]

Mary hated the idea that she was engaged in a piece of cold marketing over 'Papers'. Moreover she believed it was her right not only to have her debts paid, but to receive an annuity, and she was not being unreasonable. It was normal for a man to pay his mistress such a sum, even after the affair had ended. In March an actress called Ann Brown was said to have given up three such annuities on her marriage, including one from Malden.[24] The Prince knew the rules, but was not in a position to authorise any such payments. Only the King could do so and undoubtedly, for all his defiance, the Prince had some fear of his father.

Aware of the negotiations taking place, enemies and supporters of Mrs Robinson sparred in the press. On 3 August the *Morning Post* published a virulent and misinformed paragraph declaring that the Perdita had received an offer of £600 a year plus a 'douceur' of £6,000 in return for the letters, 'but the avaricious Thais is determined to hold fast the r— *amorous budget*, unless she is granted double the above annuity, as well as a douceur'. The writer warned that even if such a sum were paid 'she would certainly preserve copies, and every use might be made of them that can possibly be made of the originals', and advised the royal family to 'treat her menaces with a silent contempt'. Next day two paragraphs of rebuttal appeared in the *Herald* (one from Mary, the other Lord Malden?) declaring 'Shame on such scribblers!'; both pieces argued that the effect of the 'illiberal and groundless paragraph' was to reflect badly on '*an admired and amiable young personnage*' even by hinting that he might possibly break 'engagements of *honor* he has entered into in the most *solemn* manner'.

Following receipt of Colonel Hotham's letter a discussion was held between the Prince and the two lords, and another when the Colonel was also present; Mrs Robinson, though the principal concerned, was as a woman excluded. Lord Malden was convinced that on the first occasion the Prince had not closed the door on the possibility of an annuity, and further letters to that effect were sent to the Prince and to Colonel Hotham, the one to the Prince drafted in Mary's handwriting (the only way she could participate). But they met the stonewall response that 'no Alteration or Addition in any Manner, implied by conversation or otherwise (as Your Lordship seems to Wish,) is ever, at any time, intended to be made'.[25] Malden appealed to Lord Southampton for his recollection of the meeting with the Prince, but Southampton would go no further than to report what he believed to be the Prince's actual words: 'I will not say, what I will, or will not do in the future. I will make no promises, I will not bind myself. I owe it to the K—g not to do it'.[26] Mary vented her frustration in a scrawled, angry note to the Prince:

> I will quit England instantly but no earthly power shall make me ever receive the smallest support from you. Your indelicacy in insulting me by such a proposal was totally unexpected I confess. My conduct has been *towards you* irreproachable. I hope you will feel every degree of satisfaction in your own mind when you reflect how you have treated me. I have nothing further to say but that you shall never be troubled by any further application from me neither will I receive the smallest favour from you –[27]

It was as well that the letter broke off there and was never sent: she would solicit for favours from the Prince for the rest of her life.

In the end Mrs Robinson capitulated, handing over the letters to Malden for delivery. But the flurry of correspondence was not over for, as the Colonel reported and perhaps prompted by the paragraph in the *Post*, the Prince still had a fear:

> H.R.H. thinks it not only proper, but *absolutely necessary*, that I should receive from Your Lordship, (on the part of Mrs Robinson,) what may be thought a sufficient Assurance & Security, that the Restitution of these Letters is, bonâ fide, compleat [*sic*]; that no Originals or Copies are retained; in order that not only no Publication of them or any part of them shall take place, but that no Eye, except that of the Writer & of the Person they were

> written to, should look into Papers, which certainly never were intended for the Inspection of any third Person whatever.[28]

Malden forwarded this insulting letter to her for comment; in her reply to him Mary not only expressed resentment, but gave back their human, emotional value to the documents she held:

> . . . I do not know what answer may be thought sufficient, the only one I can or *ever will be* induced to give, is that I am willing to return every letter I have ever received from his RH bona fide. Had HRH honorably fulfilld *every* promise he has heretofore made me – I never could or would have made ampler restitution, as I have Ever Valued those letters as dearly as my existance & nothing but my distressed situation ever should have tempted me to give them up at all – [29]

Underneath is a little doodle, a crown which has been blotted over by a finger: Mary deleting His Royal Highness as she felt she herself was being obliterated. No further guarantees were demanded and Malden indicated to the Colonel that he would wait on his convenience with the letters on 27 August; when Hotham came without the money it was Malden's turn to be suspicious and refuse to part with the letters. Finally, on 10 September, the Colonel brought the warrant for the money to Berkeley Square and wiped his fastidious fingers of the 'disagreeable business'.

King George III deplored it all likewise; he had not wished to open the subject with his First Minister, Lord North, but found himself obliged to give him an account of the affair:

> My Eldest Son got last Year into a very improper connection with an Actress and woman of indifferent Character through the *friendly* assistance of Ld. Malden a Multitude of letters past which she has threatened to publish unless He in short bought them of Her; He has made Her very foolish promises which undoubtedly by Her conduct to him she entirely cancelled; I have thought it right to authorize the getting them from Her and have employed Lieut. Col. Hotham on whose discretion I could depend to manage this business; He has now brought it to a conclusion, and has Her

> consent to get these letters on Her receiving 5000 £ undoubtedly an enormous sum; but I wish to get my son out of this shameful scrape; I desire you will therefore see Lieut. Col. Hotham and settle this with Him.[30]

It was as well that Mrs Robinson never knew that, far from the letters never being seen by anybody else, they were passed over to Lord North who had no compunction about reading them. They were, he told his son-in-law, 'remarkably well written'.[31]

Negotiations and money worries over, Mary decided 'to amuse her mind and beguile her thoughts from the recollection of past scenes' by taking herself to Paris. During the summer she will have read of the path already carved out to the style capital of the world by other demi-reps, including Mrs Armistead and Grace Dalrymple Elliot (known as Dally the Tall, she was the errant wife of society doctor Dr John Elliot, who later became Mary's own physician). All were said to be seeking diversion among the 'feathered fops of France'.[32] As in carriages so in foreign travel, the Perdita was not to be outdone and she could now afford the trip. After satisfying the most clamorous of her creditors, she must have kept back as much of her £5,000 as she dared, and had indeed very soon made her mark by appearing in Hyde Park in a brand new 'Bouë de Paris' Coach (the fashion colour of the moment, whatever it meant).

It was perhaps surprising, however, that the voyage across the Channel was so popular, given that England and France were at war. The French had smarted from defeat in North America in the so-called Seven Years War which ended in 1763, and despite their rejection of a monarchy Louis XVI had been persuaded to support the Yankee rebels, recognising the new nation in 1778. For a time it was feared that the French would invade on the south coast, but plans were abandoned in favour of direct intervention in America. A force of 3,000 men was assembled, including cavalry; evading the British navy it had reached America in 1780.

The war had been a bitter affair, not least for the many loyalists who wished to maintain the link with the mother country. It was not a popular war at home either, particularly in a city like Mary's home town of Bristol where merchants had suffered loss of trade. Both armies had had their triumphs and reverses; there had been heroism and atrocity on both sides. But by 1781 it had become clear that it was a war the British could not win; it had proved extremely difficult to conduct in unknown, vast and difficult terrain, heavily forested and with few roads, and with supply lines stretching back over 3,000 miles of ocean. At the same time war was also being waged against the Spaniards who were trying to capture Minorca (in which they succeeeded) and Gibraltar (in which they did not). Conflict in the Mediterranean tied up English naval forces and left the fleet in America dangerously vulnerable to superior French numbers of ships. Pleas for more naval support from New York, where the English commander Sir Henry Clinton was based, were grudgingly answered, which in turn made him cautious that autumn about sending any of his own ships to the relief of his second-in-command, Lord Cornwallis, under siege by the combined forces of George Washington and his French allies further south in Yorktown. When a French fleet reached Yorktown and took command of the waters the English garrison was completely cut off, bombarded from all sides. On 17 October Cornwallis was forced to capitulate, though his men marched out proudly in surrender to a band reported to be playing 'The World Turned Upside Down' – which many of them felt it had been. A French nobleman, the Duc de Lauzun, was ordered to carry the news back to France (when it reached England it precipitated Lord North's resignation and caused the King to contemplate abdication).

Just two days after hostilities on the other side of the Atlantic effectively ceased, the *Morning Herald* announced that the Perdita would be crossing from Margate to Ostend en route for Paris, taking her daughter and some servants with her (but leaving Lord Malden at home, possibly from some resentment that he had not managed to obtain for her the deal she thought her right). Maria had celebrated her seventh birthday only the previous day. Mary had never left England before, but as the daughter of an Arctic venturer and sister of merchants in Italy, she would not have allowed herself to be nervous of the crossing. She had secured letters of introduction, notably to the resident English banker in Paris, Sir John Lambert. Perhaps some of these introductions were obtained from her father, who it was reported at the beginning of the year had taken command of a 'stout privateer' on the Thames, so he was back in England again and looking for war-time employment by the Admiralty.[33] Sir John found her 'commodious apartments' and just as important, secured her a box at the opera.

The fame of Mrs Robinson had gone before her and attracted the attention of the libertine anglophile, the Duc de Chartres. He was descended from Louis XIII and became Duc d'Orléans in 1785, but is best-known to history as Philippe-Égalité, the name he adopted when titles were abolished in the Revolution. In 1800 Mrs Robinson wrote three short articles about those she had known in pre-Revolutionary France, one of them about the Duc d'Orléans (remembered then with abhorrence for the vote he had cast for the death of his cousin Louis XVI); while acknowledging that he was a stylish and witty man, she described him as a compound of 'ambition and degradation, vanity and folly, courage and audacity'.[34] He often featured in the English gossip columns; only in September it had been reported that he had, to general annoyance, cut down the trees in the park of his Palais Royal in order to build arcades of shops, theatres and coffee houses (these were to become centres of the Revolution). It was also said that he had presented his English mistress, Grace Dalrymple Elliot, with a miniature of himself, set in diamonds.[35] Possession of one English mistress did not restrain his appetite for another, and he obtained an introduction to Mary from Sir John Lambert.

But notwithstanding his immense wealth, Perdita was not attracted. All the attentions he showered upon her, inviting her to races or to fêtes at his villa at Monceau, failed to lure her into his embraces. One invitation only she accepted; the Duc staged a fête in honour of her birthday on 27 November, as it happened the day on which Louis XVI had ordered all Parisians to illuminate their dwellings to celebrate victory (the expense of the war, and the egalitarian, republican ideals absorbed by his soldiers in America, were to cost the King dear). Mary went to the fête, chaperoned by Sir John Lambert and an unnamed German lady. At Monceau the Duc had created some extraordinary gardens, 'La Folie de Chartres', where serpentining paths wound among streams, fountains, cascades and buildings representing all ages and cultures, with a Greek temple, Chinese pagoda, Dutch windmill, Egyptian pyramid, Venetian bridge and other wonders. To add to the magic, on this evening 'every tree displayed the initials of *la belle Angloise*, composed of coloured lamps, interwoven with wreaths of artificial flowers'.[36] But Mary did not respond to the invitation underlying these compliments.

To the Duc de Chartres she was, however, indebted for the highlight of her Parisian stay: the opportunity to visit Versailles to see and be seen by Marie Antoinette. The Queen, who had recently given birth to the Dauphin, asked the Duc to bring the Englishwoman to a *grand couvert*, the daily meal held in public. Anybody could attend if decently dressed, but Mary wanted to be eye-catching; who better to consult over her attire than Marie Antoinette's own milliner, Rose Bertin? Milliners were not mere makers of hats, but modistes; the Queen ran up enormous bills with the brilliant Mlle Bertin who held court in her shop in the Rue de Saint-Honoré, where she 'sat upon a sort of Throne', herself splendidly dressed, her hands covered with rings and with 'Watch, and Chains, and Trinkets of infinite Value spread all over her'.[37] She was undoubtedly the right person to go to if money was no object (which with Mary it rarely was), and the so-called 'Minister of Fashion' would herself have responded to Mrs Robinson's looks and figure. Thus she created for Mary perhaps her finest costume ever, a dress of 'a pale green lustring [crisp glossy silk] with a tiffany petticoat [of a diaphanous gauze], festooned with bunches of the most delicate lilac'; when she wore the dress at the English opera the following year its colour was described as 'a beautiful rainbow green of the slightest shade'. For her head Mlle Bertin designed a creation with white feathers, probably the cap described as 'ornamented with feathers and a wave of artificial roses, interspersed with various flowers, on a ground of sea green', fastened on with brilliants.[38] To complete her appearance she had to pomade and powder her hair, and apply two circles of bright rouge to her cheeks; this custom was ridiculed by foreigners for making the women look like painted dolls.[39]

When, thus bedecked, she found herself in the Palace of Versailles, Mary must have marvelled; how homely and insignificant would St James's Palace in its huddle of Tudor red-brick have seemed in comparison. But the way of life at Versailles was a mixture of order and disorder; along with the unvarying royal rituals, the gilt and mirrored regularity of the palace's architecture, Mary would have found the ante-rooms she passed through seething with crowds of all classes and conditions, and have noticed the dirt and even dog turds that lay unattended on the marble floors. The only scene recorded in the *Memoirs*, however, is of the *grand couvert* itself, where Mary was struck by the contrast between the 'royal epicures' and the 'gazing plebeians' on either side of a narrow crimson cord which alone separated the great from the gawpers. She watched the King wolf down his food, while the Queen ate almost nothing; since the Queen disliked eating in public this was usual. But on this day Marie Antoinette had something to occupy her attention; after inspecting Mrs Robinson she whispered commendations which 'most oppressively flattered' though seemingly did not offend. Mary returned flattery by showing her admiration for the Queen's white arms as she drew on her gloves; obligingly the Queen uncovered and displayed them again. It was, in its way, flirtation of the kind Mary excelled in. The miniature of the Prince lay on her breast and, according to the *Memoirs*, the Queen asked Chartres to request its loan. It was returned with the gift of a purse netted by the Queen herself. This is a more dramatic version of the story told by Mary in another of her journal articles, where she says that the request was conveyed next day by the Duc de Lauzun, who also brought it back with the purse.[40]

The Duc de Lauzun (later Biron), who had brought the good news back from America, was like Chartres both a libertine and, despite his support for the rebels, an anglophile; his memoirs (unpublished in Mary's lifetime) tell of a string of mistresses, of whom he claims Perdita as one.[41] In contrast to Chartres, Mary liked Lauzun, describing him in the third of her magazine articles published in 1800 as 'manly and prepossessing . . . lively and well-informed', of 'a temper so irresistibly fascinating, that he seldom was known to lose the affections of those with whom he had once lived on terms of sociability'.[42] She may therefore have admitted his advances. Lauzun further says that Mary insisted that he accompany her to Calais on her return to England for more dalliance; he paid tribute to her as 'gay, lively, open, and a good creature' as translated into English, or more piquantly in French that 'elle était gaie, vive, franche et bon enfant'.[43]

Undoubtedly what Mary would have wanted from Lauzun, however, was to hear his tales of the American war. He was proud of having raised, equipped, and trained a body of dragoons (mounted infantrymen) known as 'Lauzun's Legion' which, in the summer of 1781, tipped the balance in favour of the Americans at Yorktown.

One of the stories he must have told her was of his encounter with his controversial English counterpart, Lieutenant-Colonel Banastre Tarleton of the Green Dragoons. For the American south Tarleton is still a bogeyman, but for the English he had been a hero, while for Lauzun he was a worthy opponent, with whom he had sought active engagement:

> I saw as I approached that the English cavalry outnumbered mine by three to one; I charged them without drawing rein; our lines met. Tarleton caught sight of me, and came towards me with raised pistol. We were about to fight a duel between our lines, when his horse was overthrown by one of his dragoons pursued by one of my lancers. I dashed upon him, to take him prisoner; a troop of English dragoons thrust themselves between us, and covered his retreat: his horse remained in my hands.[44]

Had Lauzun killed Tarleton that day Mary's future would have been very different.

The newspapers had frequently recounted the exploits of Lieutenant-Colonel Tarleton, and Mary would have read them with patriotic pride. Cornwallis's letter of commendation to Clinton, after Tarleton had undertaken a forced ride of 105 miles in 54 hours and then won a decisive victory, was printed in every paper, though this engagement at Waxhaws in North Carolina also established his American reputation as 'Bloody' or 'Butcher' Tarleton; he was accused of the massacre of a defeated enemy seeking to surrender (he was unhorsed when the white flag was raised and it has never been proved that he saw it and ignored it). 'Tarleton's quarter'– meaning no quarter – became a rebel cry of outrage. Yet on meeting him, one French nobleman discovered him to have a 'most gentle and genteel face as well as elegance, a certain air of ease and French manners'.[45]

At the end of the year Mary returned to London with her luggage full of French fashions, and perhaps in a corner of her heart a curiosity, a question mark, about the bold, handsome green dragoon.

7

Interlude: At the Portrait Painter's

The Perdita *has been particularly successful in the Commerce of this Year. How immense must have been her* Imports *and* Exports *is cognisable from this one Circumstance; she has sate for her Picture four Times, viz. twice to* Romney, *once to* Gainsborough, *and once to* Sir Joshua Reynolds!

(*Public Advertiser*, 19 April 1782)

'This seems to be a *Portrait-painting* Age,' wrote William Combe in the Introduction to A *Poetical Epistle to Sir Joshua Reynolds* (1777). Sir Joshua would have nodded in gloomy agreement; he aspired to history painting, considered the highest form of art, while his chief rival Thomas Gainsborough, contemptuous of 'the curs'd Face business', prized landscape painting.[1] Yet for both men portraiture proved lucrative. Whatever their reservations, the artists established themselves in smart studios with galleries to show off examples of their work. For this purpose actresses and women of the town were useful: they were handsome, famous, and did not immediately carry their portraits off to their own walls. Reynolds, in any case, had a fascination with painting actresses and women of dubious reputation.[2] Portrait collecting in the form of engravings had become a fashionable pastime, so advertisement and profit were taken further; for sums ranging from a few shillings to a guinea or so the public could obtain likenesses of the personalities of the day, or at least gaze at them in the windows of the many print-selling shops. The combination of Mary's looks, notoriety, and willingness to sit, meant that at the height of her beauty and fame, images of Mrs Robinson in one form or another were of an abundance rivalled only by royalty. Three out of the four major oil paintings of her were produced in little more than a year, from the spring of 1781 to the spring of the following year.

On 8 September 1781, an engraving by John Raphael Smith of a portrait of Mrs Robinson was advertised in the *Herald*, claiming to be the 'only genuine' portrait yet 'of that celebrated Beauty . . . from a capital painting by Romney', although a painting of her by James Roberts (who had been responsible for the portrait as Amanda for *Bell's British Theatre*) had been included in the Royal Academy exhibition earlier that year.[3] Mary's sitting to George Romney in his premises in Cavendish Square must have been too late for that year's exhibition, though it appeared in the next. In fact Romney painted two portraits, a head and a half-length, but the first of these is lost. The art-historian John Ingamells calls Romney's portraits at this time 'the equivalent of well-written essays' for their careful exactitude, but his portrait of Mary must have surprised anyone seeking to discover in it the notorious demi-rep.[4] The sitter does not vaunt her charms; her powdered hair, muff and double head-covering (linen cap tied under the chin with a bonnet on top) are fashionable, but she wears sober colours, while neck and bosom are modestly hidden beneath a gauzy neckerchief. Her colour looks fresh and natural, and her gaze, while directed towards the viewer, is not wanton: this serious-seeming woman might be on her way to a meeting of the occasionally advertised women's debating society.

The purpose of portrait-painting was itself a subject of debate: should the artist's primary concern be with likeness, or character? Gainsborough ranked likeness as the most important aspect of portraiture, but Reynolds, aware that his illustrious sitters had their long-term reputations in mind, thought that character and its ennoblement could be expressed at the expense of individual features.[5] For women sitters enhancement of looks was commonplace; capturing exceptional beauty such as Mary Robinson's was harder to achieve. Moreover, Romney's painting shows how its nature could be affected by the sitter's costume and demeanour. Hazlitt described having one's portrait painted as 'like the creation of another self', and indeed portraiture gave Mary the chance to present herself in a variety of guises, just as she did when riding out in her chariots.[6]

On 25 August 1781 the *Herald* told its readers that Mrs Robinson was sitting for Gainsborough. It seems extraordinary that in the month of her bitter negotiations with the Prince, and after she had declared that nothing would induce her to accept the 'smallest favour' from him, Mary would sit for a portrait commissioned by none other than the Prince of Wales. M.J. Levy suggests that the purpose of the painting, a purpose in which the artist must have colluded, is 'to rebuke the Prince for his failure to honour his obligations': she looks out mournfully if not balefully from the canvas, holding a miniature open in her right hand which, while too small for the features to be identifiable, is of a man in a scarlet uniform on which there seems to be a Garter Star.[7] Yet the Prince had placed the order and was himself sitting to Gainsborough at this time. Was it a gesture of good will? The Prince had said that he did not bear grudges. Was it fulfilment of a promise which in this case he could easily carry out, especially since he did not pay for this or other canvases, and was in debt to the artist at his death in 1788 for the sum of £1,228 10s?[8] Or should it be seen in the context of that strange, amoral world in which mistresses passed from one man to another without apparent rancour? To add to the moral uncertainties, the *Herald* also reported that Gainsborough was engaged in a portrait of Grace Dalrymple Elliot, another whose favours the Prince had recently sampled; the resulting daughter was named Georgiana, though the father could just as well have been the Earl of Cholmondeley.

Gainsborough's large, full-length painting of Mrs Robinson has been described as 'a marvel of technical accomplishment', distinguished by its 'silvery radiance of tone'.[9] Mary wears a gauzy robe 'of a warm diaphanous white' with matching petticoat, and set off with a few blue ribbons; the costume's very simplicity can be seen as another reproach to the Prince, and the choice of colour as conveying the 'purity' of *her* faithfulness. Gainsborough liked to add dogs to his portraits and, with its alert look contrasting with the sitter's forlornness, this faithful dog (linked in colour to the woman) underlines the painting's message to the man who commissioned it. His infidelity is conveyed by his image, held rather than worn as it would be if the relationship flourished. Posed seated on a bank in a rural landscape of trees and twining convolvulus, Mary is to be seen here as 'Perdita'. However, this is not Shakespeare's innocent shepherdess; her dress is low-cut, the neck covered with only the thinnest of gauze veils, lips and cheeks are artificially coloured, and she sits with legs crossed, a posture not adopted by respectable women in portraits. The painter makes her sexuality apparent, though surely not so crudely as one critic argues, who believes that the 'fluffy, fuzzy' handkerchief in her 'right' hand (actually the left) is 'a simulacrum for the pubic hair which it strategically covers': the artist's sense of anatomy has gone astray if so.[10]

For the third of the group of oil portraits Mary sat to Reynolds after her return from France; in his 'Sitter Book' the artist records Mrs Robinson in attendance on eleven occasions between 25 January and 5 April 1782, all except one of these appointments being at two o'clock (maintaining the same light level was important).[11] The number of sittings indicates the care he took: to another sitter Sir Joshua once wrote that three appointments of an hour and a half would suffice.[12] We have a clear idea of what those sittings would have been like through the recollections of his pupil, James Northcote. Mary would have been posed on a chair with castors mounted on a dais, in a room that was lit only by a small high window from which initially almost all light was excluded. The shape and main features of the face were then captured; similarly Gainsborough would first sketch out the main outline of his composition in near darkness. Both artists set up their easels close to the sitters. Gainsborough used very long brushes to achieve his filmy effects, where the details dissolve the closer the viewer gets to the picture. Reynolds used normal brushes but was constantly on the move, peering closely into his sitter's face then moving back to look at the effect from the distance. Lady Burlington described his procedure as somewhat alarming:

> He continually walked back and forward. His plan was to walk away several feet, then take a long look at me and the picture as we stood side by side, then rush up to the portrait and dash at it in a kind of fury. I sometimes thought he would paint on me instead of the picture.[13]

Sir Joshua did not discourage an audience at his studio in Leicester Fields, today's Leicester Square, so friends of the sitter could look in to observe progress. There is an undated pen-and-wash drawing by Rowlandson of an animated scene labelled 'Mrs R— sitting for her picture', where a gallant bends over her while another young man and woman look over an artist's shoulder at his drawing; another Rowlandson titled 'At the Portrait Painter's', where a couple are in secret dalliance while a gouty old man has his likeness taken (and improved), likewise conveys the sexual frisson which could attach to portrait painting.

Reynolds had the previous summer been travelling in the Low

Countries to study Rubens, and his portrait is influenced in pose and costume by two Rubens paintings – one of his wife Helen Fourment, the other of her sister Susanna (the latter picture, *Le Chapeau de Paille*, is in the National Gallery).[14] In Reynolds's half-length Mary is pictured in a square-necked black dress of a kind known, confusingly, as a Vandyke dress, with a plumed black hat; elements of contemporary fashion are seen in the black ribbon round her neck and her powdered hair (it is a pity that in all the portraits Mary's auburn hair is hidden by powder). Mary did not necessarily come to the studio dressed up in this way. Though important clients' wishes were taken into account, artists adjusted costume to suit the picture, and Reynolds had a wardrobe of clothes which he would invite his sitters to try on. Reynolds (though not Gainsborough) nevertheless often deputed the painting of the clothes to an assistant in the sitter's absence; perhaps the number of Mary's sittings means that he undertook it himself, setting the black-clad figure dramatically against a dark red curtain. This is drawn aside to reveal a small landscape, an exotic scene quite different from the muted colours of the pastoral Gainsborough background. Here a mountain peak catches the light beneath an otherwise louring sky; it may represent Mount Parnassus, home of Apollo and the Muses, in compliment to Mrs Robinson as poet. Such a personal reference can be found in other of Reynolds's works, for example in a portrait of her namesake Archbishop Robinson, where a distant church spire is incorporated into the background. This portrait can also be seen as a riposte to Romney's, since Reynolds has chosen to paint Mary in the same three-quarter profile, but with the eyes challengingly swivelled to the viewer.

Which of the three portraitists wins the laurels is a matter of personal preference. A contemporary critic thought the Reynolds 'beyond comparison the best, not only, as usual, outdoing his Brother Artists, but perhaps in this Instance excelling himself'; the Romney was runner-up, 'deserving of praise', while the Gainsborough was, purely on grounds of likeness, 'one of his Few Failures'.[15] Gainsborough had intended his painting for the 1782 Royal Academy exhibition but withdrew it at the last moment, perhaps because it was not thought a good likeness, or more likely because he had become George III's principal portraitist and did not want to offend with a public display of his son's ex-mistress. In comparison with other portraits it can be seen that Gainsborough's Perdita has too elongated and thin a face, but even the Reynolds and

Romney do not show quite the same features. James Northcote was damning about the Reynolds, judging it, and his subsequent portrait, 'complete failures' in terms of likeness, as Reynolds had been unable to capture the essence of the sitter's remarkable beauty.[16]

In his first portrait of Mrs Robinson, Reynolds presents the confident extrovert, but in the second he turns the coin to reveal the reflective, melancholy introvert. It was produced in the early months of 1783, though the artist's sitter-book is missing for this period, so the exact dates are unknown. Some art-historians think that the painting was still in hand in 1784, which has the attraction of reading later events into it, but a report in the *Herald* of 21 March 1783 that the picture had been taken to be engraved appears to rule that out. It is a profile portrait, in which the sitter gazes down in reverie, unconscious of any audience. Despite powdered hair and lips touched with colour, she is not presented as a society belle; the impressionistic, unfinished painting of the clothing denies it importance, while the hard black line of the ribbon which slashes across the throat makes her seem very vulnerable. The figure is set against a dark background of rocks, sea and sky, and these sombre surroundings, relieved only by a line of light at the horizon, create a melancholy narrative feel. Why is she sitting in lonely meditation as day darkens into night? Is this the abandoned Ariadne, pining for Prince Theseus?[17] The painting haunts the imagination, teasing the viewer to complete its story.

If beauty is difficult to catch, charm is even more fleeting, but an anecdote of a painter's studio manages to capture something of what made Mrs Robinson beguiling. As a boy John Thomas Smith, who became Keeper of Prints at the British Museum, was a pupil of John Keyse Sherwin (as was Angelo Albanesi, who had engraved the frontispieces for her volumes of poetry). Sherwin produced two portrait engravings of Mary, one of them influenced by the Gainsborough, though in it she holds a letter rather than the miniature. Smith narrates how one morning, when it was his turn to attend to the visitors, Mrs Robinson arrived with her mother in her light-blue carriage with basket of flowers motif, which had been designed by Sherwin. She came into the room singing:

> She asked to see a drawing which Mr. Sherwin had made of her, which he had placed in an upper room. When I assured her that Mr.

> Sherwin was not at home, 'Do try to find the drawing of me, and I will reward you, my little fellow,' said she. I, who had seen *Rosetta*, in 'Love in a Village', the preceding evening, hummed to myself, as I went upstairs, 'with a kiss, a kiss, and I'll reward you with a kiss.'
>
> I had no sooner entered the room with the drawing in my hand, than she imprinted a kiss on my cheek, and said, 'There, you little rogue.'[18]

The anecdote can possibly be dated. *Love in a Village* (1762) was a popular operetta by Isaac Bickerstaffe, with music by Thomas Arne (it included the song of the Miller of Dee); it was regularly performed, but a likely performance is the one at Drury Lane on Saturday 15 September 1781. If this date is right, then Mary's cheerfulness would be explained by her recent receipt of the Prince's money, and the consequent easing of her financial worries.

Another tale of Sherwin's studio comes from that righteous spinster Laetitia-Matilda Hawkins. History painting combined with portraiture when in 1789 the Princess Royal posed as Pharaoh's daughter in his *Finding of Moses*, and society women flocked to have their likenesses included too; no place was found for Mrs Robinson, but the artist suggested a painting in which she should be Abra ['slave girl' in old Greek and a word used for a maid in eighteenth-century opera], kneeling to Solomon. But when the Prince of Wales's features were proposed for Solomon, Perdita flashed out: 'Kneel to *him*? I will die first.'[19] Miss Hawkins's tale may be apocryphal, but the sentiment rings true.

Mary was at ease in the portrait painters' studios. She had warm feelings for Sir Joshua; she commemorated him in verse after his death, and also wrote a poem during his lifetime. 'To Sir Joshua Reynolds' (1789) commends him not only for capturing likeness and conveying texture and light with his paints ('the iv'ry shoulder's polish'd fall to shade'), but also praises him for communicating the characters of his sitters:

> The *Statesman's* thought, the *Infant's cherub mien*,
> The *Poet's fire*, the *Matron's eye serene*,
> Alike with animated colours shine
> Beneath thy glowing Pencil's touch divine . . .[20]

It would have been remarkable if Sir Joshua had not found her poem to his taste; in a letter he returned compliments, congratulating her in turn on 'the wonderful facility (or handling, as we painters call it) which you have acquired in writing verse'.[21]

The initial three oil paintings were followed by more portraits and many spin-offs. Gainsborough made a smaller copy of the full-length, and a half-length for Mary herself, perhaps paid for with the Prince's money; another paler version, almost a ghost image, was found without explanation during Queen Victoria's reign in an upper room of Windsor Castle. (It is a pity that Gainsborough did not seek to paint her again and in Mlle Bertin's rainbow green dress; no artist could better have captured its shimmer and sheen.) A copy of Reynolds's first portrait was sent to Russia for Catherine the Great, and John Hazlitt produced an attractive, if rather softened, miniature version on ivory (Wallace Collection). Another miniature painting of a later date, by the amateur artist John Chubb who was a Bridgwater relation of Hester Darby, adopts the same iconography of betrayed love and ensuing poverty as the Gainsborough.[22] Mary gazes at the miniature in her hand in a room bare of all effects except for a pen and inkstand, perhaps signifying the writing through which she sustained herself in later life. Numerous works by lesser-known artists copy or adapt either the Gainsborough or Reynolds paintings; of better-known artists, John Hoppner produced several studies of her, the miniaturist Richard Cosway painted some pretty, if saccharine, watercolours on ivory, Angelica Kauffmann and George Engleheart also painted miniatures.[23]

In the last decade of her life portraits were still being produced, mostly showing too youthful-looking a woman for belief. But George Dance the architect, respected for his lifelike if unflattering portraits in pencil and red chalk, produced profile drawings in 1793 which do portray an older woman, her nose sharper than in the Reynolds profile and heavier around the jaw.[24] To the end of her life Mary sought images of herself, sending a note on 18 July 1800 to the sculptor John Flaxman:

> Mrs Robinson presents her compliments to Mr Flaxman; and wishes to know if he would do her the Honor to arrange her Bust, as she is very earnestly requested by many literary friends, to have one

> completed. There is a Mask at Mr Flaxman's, in the Strand, which was some years ago modelled on her face, and which is consequently a perfect resemblance . . .[25]

Clearly nothing came of it; perhaps the wax mask had already been melted down, or perhaps Flaxman doubted Mrs Robinson's ability to pay for the work. So there is no 'perfect resemblance' to compare with the painted portraits.

The four principal oil paintings ultimately came together in the collection of the 2nd Marquess of Hertford, and were among those paintings which formed the basis of the Wallace Collection, housed in what had been his home in Manchester Square (the first of the Reynolds portraits was sold out of the collection by a later Marquess, and became part of the Rothschild Collection at Waddesdon Manor, where it joined the Gainsborough which Mary had owned). The Hertfords were her friends and supporters, appearing in the list of subscribers for her 1791 volume of poetry, which uses an engraving of Reynolds's second portrait as its frontispiece. The 2nd Marquess bought all the pictures except for the Gainsborough, hanging the sea-coast Reynolds in his bedroom. Gainsborough's large painting joined the other three as a present from the Prince Regent in 1818, and might be called part-payment for his wife's services as Prince's mistress at the time. But after Lady Hertford's death in 1834 the sitter's name was lost, and for half a century the painting was known simply as 'A Lady with a dog'; only in 1894 was Mrs Robinson's identity restored to her image.[26]

Despite her praise for Sir Joshua and her readiness to sit for her portrait, Mary herself seems to have thought individual personality better conveyed in words than paint. In 'Stanzas to a Friend, who desired to have my portrait', she speaks slightingly of portraiture as producing 'looks eternally the SAME/And lips that NEVER move'.[27] Nevertheless Mary was well served by the artists; it is as much through her portraits as her words and history that she is known today, while in her own time the many engravings, if not the actual paintings, allowed people to assess her for themselves, to note the discrepancy between the refined face of the real woman and the coarse image peddled by pamphleteers. Never was that contrast more glaring than in the years of Mary's greatest notoriety, after her return from France.

8

Reluctant Cyprian

> Herald, *wherefore thus proclaim*
> *Nought of woman but the* shame?
> *Quit, oh quit, at least awhile*
> *Perdita's too luscious smile . . .*
> (Anon, but Dr Charles Burney, *Morning Herald*, 12 March 1782)

Harlotry as a profession was in the late eighteenth century given a glamour and social prominence through newspaper publicity as at no other time; members of the Cyprian circle, the votaries of Venus, the Paphian priestesses, the impure sisterhood, the amorous phalanx, the Cythereans, received what we would call star billing. These were not the common prostitutes with which London swarmed, but of the station to which they all aspired, the demi-reps kept for their exclusive pleasure by the titled and the wealthy. The *Herald* led the way in reportage, but most dailies regularly carried stories of the fair frails, another title. After her affair with the Prince of Wales, Perdita shot to the head of their ranks, maintaining her position because her flair for fashion and her reckless extravagance enabled her to out-dress and out-chariot her closest rivals, the Armistead, Dally the Tall and the Bird of Paradise. All of these women's doings were followed as assiduously as Perdita's; copy writers had a particular liking for the diminutive Bird of Paradise, Gertrude Mahon, who earned her sobriquet because of her love of bright colours ('The Bird of Paradise having lately *moulted*, is now in *finer feather* than ever', and so on). Though Perdita outdid them in conspicuous consumption it was a virtual obligation of their position; a demi-rep was expected to dress superbly, to sport at least two carriages, and to maintain a well-run household in a fashionable part of town.[1] The expenses of the role were borne by the protector, and it was Mary's misfortune that all her lovers were unable to furnish her with establishments lavish enough to meet all her outgoings. The Prince's £5,000 to pay her debts got her temporarily out of difficulties, and credit continued in anticipation of his coming of age, for which she still held his signed bond for £20,000. Lord Malden, who had now become her protector, inherited his grandmother's money in 1781 and rented a house on the west side of Berkeley Square, into which she moved on her return from Paris. He also settled an annuity of £200 on her, but in relation to Mary's level of spending this was a modest figure.

But Mary was a reluctant member of the Cyprian corps, believing that her superior sensibility lifted her above their level. This she argued in an autobiographical piece published in the *Post* at the end of August 1782. It is titled 'Hasty Sketch of Perdita by a Gentleman over HEAD and EARS in Love', but the reader soon realises that it has been neither hastily written nor by a man in love. Although it is anonymous and in the third person, its language and sentiments mark it out as being by Mary herself. The theme of the passage is of nature thwarted:

> Formed by the bond of nature for almost every opposite pursuit to that in which the whirl of life has engaged her, Perdita but half enjoys her present situation, yet she gives to it every grace and embellishment of which it is susceptible.[2]

Public display is a duty, not a desire, 'the meteor which dazzles for a moment' but whose bright illusion soon fades to 'the gloom of profound despondency'. Her true nature possesses the 'soft dejections of a pathetic spirit, a tender friendship with the Muse' and 'a soul that aches for the softness of unstraying love', but these blossoms of her nature have been desolated, 'beaten off by the weather of the world'. She will not concede that she has shaped her own destiny, concluding on the contrary that she should be given 'the highest praise, who in a difficult situation shews, by her sensibility, that she deserves a better'. Her acquired status depressed her, but claims of superiority would have infuriated the rest of the sisterhood; even a year earlier there was an occasion at the opera when the Armistead, Dally, and a French Cyprian known as the Du Thé, linked arms and bore down so determinedly on Perdita that she had to be rescued by onlookers.[3]

These women were not therefore likely to have been among those said by the *Herald* to be agog to see what fashions Perdita had brought back from Paris. But on 8 January 1782 the Perdita side of Mary Robinson, which did enjoy such moments, duly made a goddess-like appearance:

> Last night the divine *Perdita* visited the opera, for the first time since her return from Paris . . . She was dressed in white satin, with *purple* breast-bows, and looked *supremely* beautiful. – Her *head-dress* was in a stile that may be called the *standard* of *taste*; her *cap*, composed of white and purple feathers *entwined* with flowers, was fastened on with *diamond* pins.[4]

The audience, it was said, lingered on to watch her select a theatre-box to rent. For another appearance she wore Mlle Bertin's pale green creation; the *Herald* enthused about the dress and Perdita's hair adornment of 'braided *wheat-ears*, fastened on with *diamond* pins' (the braiding was done with silver and gold wire).[5]

From then on, everything the *lovely*, the *elegant*, the *sprightly* Perdita introduced was scrutinised and copied. When she carried a 'cataract' muff (a French creation of long-haired fur which hung down like a waterfall) every woman of fashion followed suit. Next spring the '*lark-heeled* Perdita' helped fill the columns of the prints when she was seen in gold-clocked stockings ('clocks' were patterned figures worked into the stockings, but gold thread was a novelty). The biggest fashion sensation, however, was created in the autumn of 1782 when she wore a *Chemise de la Reine* to the Opera. This simple muslin dress had been adopted by Marie Antoinette in the 1770s but had not been seen in England before. A painting by Louise-Élizabeth Vigée Le Brun shows the French Queen wearing the chemise: it has three-quarter length puffed sleeves and frills around the neck, and falls simply and gracefully. That was what made it so startling, that it clung to the figure without the support of pads or hoops. As the *Chronicle* pointed out, it was an unbecoming garment for 'ill-made women'; however, all the fashion-conscious wanted to follow suit whatever their shape.[6]

More column inches were devoted to the 'operatical uproar' which followed Perdita's fitting-up of her opera box according to Parisian taste, the chairs upholstered in pink satin and the walls lined with mirrors. Rude jokes followed about what might be seen. Nevertheless the *Herald* declared that 'there is a *neatness* and *decency* in the dress of the *Perdita*, that challenges universal admiration' and women were advised to copy her (it is impossible to know if this is Perdita puffing herself).[7] The string of new carriages continued too. One first seen in December 1782 was lined with white silk with scarlet trimmings, with the MR cypher in a wreath of flowers displayed on the sides; attendant footmen sported green liveries faced with yellow and trimmed with silver lace. When she appeared in this carriage to watch the cavalcade of coaches descending on St James's Palace for the Queen's birthday reception on 18 January 1783, she drew such crowds that she could not continue and 'was obliged to make a farewell bow, and drive home'.[8] The point was made that, cast-off mistress and uninvited guest though she might be, Perdita was of as much fascination as any grandee of the English aristocracy.

The most spectacular of all her carriages was a vis-à-vis 'launched' in time for the King's birthday on 4 June that year:

> In the centre of the door pannel, on a *mantle* of pink and silver, lined with ermine, her cypher is painted . . . The sun appears rising on one side; a coronet of flowers is placed over the cypher, and at the foot a lion couchant . . . The lining is of a rich straw-coloured silk, the fringe and lace of which is pink and silver. The wheels and carriage are pale yellow and silver, with silver springs. The harness furniture is ornamented with silver buckles, joints, &c. The hammer-cloth [material over the driver's seat] is so superb, that it alone amounts to *one hundred pounds*; and the vis-à-vis, including every expence, upwards of *nine hundred guineas*![9]

Such regal pretensions provoked satiric verses dedicated to the 'Matchless Phryne [courtesan] Perdita', mocking 'the Great, the Gay, the Good, & Gallant Florizel' whose ill-directed munificence was supposed to have funded the folly. The use of the English lion, 'peeping out his disgraced head from the place where the Jordan [chamber-pot] should be', was especially resented:

> Hence all Competitors, away!
> Phryne's bright chariot of the day
> On brimstone wheels doth run;

With ducal coronet of Flowers,
Gather'd in *Cambria*'s fertile Bowers,
Rais'd by the *Rising Sun*.

The *Rising Sun* its influence shed,
The *Curtain* shades the crimson bed,
Thro' which he longs to peep;
The *Lion*, like the *piss-pot* plac'd!
Sneaks out his head, as if disgrac'd,
Couchant, & dead asleep.[10]

In fact it was neither Florizel's nor Perdita's money which had financed this fantastic beast. The chariot was the product of another social vice, gambling, being the 'aggregate of a few stakes' during play one night at the club known as Brooks's.[11] The politician and man-about-town, Charles James Fox, had proposed to his fellow gamblers that a certain unclaimed sum could not be put to better use. Put another way, Fox had been Perdita's lover during the previous summer, had had no money with which to effect a conventional 'settlement', and had produced instead this spectacular gesture. For as with fashions and carriages so with lovers; in 1782 Mary Robinson had shifted from one man's bed to another's, moving from a scion of the English aristocracy to a soldier and then to a politician.

Mary had tired of Lord Malden, who had probably only ever been a port in the storm of her abandonment by the Prince. He had been her loyal supporter in the financial negotiations with the Prince, but he did not have enough soul and spirit for her, and is the likely model for Lord Melcomb in *The False Friend*, who is described as 'one of those mortals who are born neither to degrade nor benefit society'.[12] The men who attracted Mary differed, but had one thing in common. They were all pre-eminent in their fields. The Prince was the leader of society, Tarleton its hero, Fox the outstanding orator and politician. If to them are added the dramatist Sheridan, who may have been a lover, and men such as Godwin the philosopher and Coleridge the poet who were not lovers but whose friendship she later cultivated, then it can be seen that in male admirers Mary Robinson sought out the best. There is a letter which Mary wrote in the last year of her life to Godwin, in which she says that since she 'first felt the power of discrimination, since I adored the excellent part of mankind . . . I have been a wanderer in search of something, approaching to *my idea* of a perfect being'.[13] Needless to say, she never did find her 'perfect being'.

Mary may have met Banastre Tarleton first at Sir Joshua Reynolds's studios, where both were sitting for their portraits in early 1782. Tarleton's first three appointments, in the mornings of 28 and 30 January, and 1 February, coincide with three of Mary's, though hers were in the afternoon. But given the likelihood that Mary wanted to meet the dashing dragoon, she could have engineered matters. Tarleton would have known of Perdita by reputation too; while he had been too long away to have seen her on stage, knowledge of the scandal with the Prince of Wales went to America. Legend even has it that a bordello in Charleston, the British army base after its capture in 1780, was christened 'Perdita's'.[14] The war was not yet officially over, but all those who surrendered at Yorktown had returned on parole to England, and in Tarleton's case to a hero's welcome. The Prince of Wales, overjoyed to be reunited with Gerard Lake, also wanted to listen to Tarleton's tales of war and quickly admitted him to his circle of gambling and drinking partners. This cannot have been entirely welcome news to his family in Liverpool.

Mary Robinson and Ban Tarleton came from similar backgrounds. Like her, Tarleton had been born and brought up in a trading port, Liverpool (never losing the accent).[15] His father was likewise a business man with shipping interests, but whereas Mary's father had lost money in his disastrous Arctic trading ventures, John Tarleton had made a fortune from his West Indian plantations and slave-trafficking; however morally dubious such trading seems today, he was highly respected in his native city. With his wife Jane he had six sons and a daughter (two sons dying young); Banastre, the second son, was born in 1754 and intended for the law. He went to school in Liverpool and then to University College Oxford, where he made his reputation as a sportsman; though of small build he was tough and fit, excelling at cricket, tennis, boxing and riding. When his father died in 1773, leaving him £5,000, he abandoned his degree course and set off for London, where he enrolled at the Middle Temple. But like Thomas Robinson he neglected his studies, engaging instead in 'all the gaieties of a man of pleasure', until gambling debts became such that 'he judged it expedient to go abroad to avoid disagreeable consequences'.[16] His mother purchased him a commission as a Cornet in the Dragoon Guards, by coincidence just the day after the first shots were fired at Lexington in the War of Independence.[17] He was sent to America where he was quickly posted to the rank of Lieutenant-Colonel in the newly raised British Legion in 1778, known as Tarleton's Green Dragoons. He became famed for the speed and daring of his raids, and the rebels, armed with slow-firing muskets, learned to fear the onrush of his sabre-wielding force. For his military exploits Tarleton has had a hostile press, but he continues to fascinate Americans, one commentator recognising that 'he is often not given credit for his genius in strategy'.[18] Off the battle-field he earned an equal reputation for whoring, gambling and, more respectably, amateur theatricals – a love of the theatre was something else he and Mary had in common. Tarleton wrote home proudly of his military achievements and the commendations of his commander, Lord Cornwallis; unfortunately, his 'cursed Itch for Play' continually got him into trouble, and appeals for funds from his mother had to be made, accompanied by abject promises not to do it again.[19] She bailed out her wayward son, but he was aware that his brothers feared the family fortune being eaten up by his gaming debts. Nevertheless it must have been a day of rejoicing for the family when on Sunday 17 February 1782, to the ringing of church bells, Liverpool's famous son returned to the city of his birth through cheering crowds. It was proudly reported that he cried out, 'Don't be afraid of taking hold of my hand! Though I have lost two fingers, I can use my pen, and will draw my sword when I can be of service to my country'.[20] (He was self-conscious about his mutilated hand, however, generally concealing it in a pocket.)

By this date he had already had several sittings to Reynolds, who portrayed him as military hero. The figure is posed cool but purposeful, reaching for his sword amid the confusion of war. He wears his uniform of tan-coloured boots, white breeches, short green jacket and shako with black swan's feathers; nervous horses, captured cannon, flags and the smoke of battle form the background. When exhibited at the Academy Exhibition (along with *Mrs Robinson*), the portrait was widely praised, the *Public Advertiser* thinking it 'among the chef d'oeuvres of Portrait Painting whether the modern or ancient'.[21] Only the satirist Peter Pindar (pen-name of Dr John

Wolcot) sounded a more sceptical note, ridiculing the pose in his *Lyric Odes to the Royal Academicians*:

> Lo! Tarleton dragging on his boot so tight!
> His horses feel a god-like rage,
> And long with Yankees to engage –
> I think I hear them snorting for the fight.

Gainsborough also exhibited an immense canvas showing Tarleton mounted, but it was not well received and afterwards disappeared; Reynolds's painting cost the Tarletons £250 and remained in the family till 1951, when it was given to the National Gallery.[22]

It has been plausibly suggested that the placing of one of the cannons is a laddish reference to prowess in the bedroom as well as on the battlefield.[23] After his return, and despite rumours of marriage, Tarleton was soon cutting a swathe through the boudoirs of the demi-reps, and is supposed to have boasted that he had 'killed more men, and lain with more women than anybody'. This grossness was exaggerated into 'butchered more men' by Horace Walpole, who delighted in Sheridan's riposte: '*Lain with* . . . what a weak expression; – he should have said, *ravished* – rapes are the relaxation of murder'.[24] However, if the story is to be believed, it was not as a rape that Tarleton's affair with Mary Robinson began, but as a piece of cold-blooded seduction for a wager.

The anonymous *Memoirs of Perdita* of 1784, in which the account is found, mixes fact and fiction. This work may well be a compilation by several hands, possibly a jest concocted in a club, since the quality of the writing varies. Some of it is adolescent smut and very silly smut too, as when Perdita is supposed to have relished her ravishment by a swarm of ants. Other passages are fair-minded:

> You, who doubtless have seen her person, know that her deportment is elegant, and to sprightliness of wit, she joins a share of levity, that attracts, rather than disgusts, because it is not carried to the excess that constitutes the affectation of wantonness.[25]

The tale told here is that Lord Malden, Tarleton and others were in a tavern when the former began to boast about Perdita and her devotion to him. He offered 'to confirm this opinion, with a bet of a thousand guineas'. Tarleton jumped at the chance, promising to win her and jilt her too. The terms agreed, Tarleton wooed the unsuspecting Perdita, like Othello softening her heart with 'all the strange adventures which fill a soldier's life'.[26] She agreed to go with him to an inn near Epsom, and there after a fortnight's love-making he left her, while he returned to London to claim his money. The furious Perdita appealed in vain to Malden to pay the inn-keeper's bill. Eventually Lord Cholmondeley took pity and rescued her, in return for which she 'blessed him with joys he had long solicited'. This story comes from a suspect source, though the notion that the affair began with a bet is true to Tarleton's character.

Whatever its beginning, the affair and the split with Malden came to the attention of the press in dramatic fashion in June. Perdita was taking an airing in Hyde Park when she was in collision with a furiously driven phaeton; her coach overturned and she was left in a 'state of insensibility'. She was carried to the house in Berkeley Square where, 'after orders were given for the necessary attentions to be paid to the *fair invalid*, his Lordship is said to have quitted the house, and to have taken up his residence ever since in St James's-street'.[27] His action was thought to have been prompted by the discovery that Mrs Robinson's companion on her outing had been Lieutentant-Colonel Tarleton. However, the newspaper was behind with the news: his Lordship had already moved out. He must have taken his departure prior to 30 May 1782, on which date he made the house over to Mrs Robinson, with the promise that he would continue to pay the rent, so the rift had occurred before the accident.[28] Malden's action appears magnanimous, but he took his revenge by paying neither the rent nor the promised annuity thereafter.

If the story of seduction and abandonment is true, Ban must have wooed and won Mary for a second time. Even so, it seemed that the Robinson/Tarleton relationship would be one of passing ships, since by the end of July Ban was writing ruefully to his elder brother that he had been displaced in Perdita's affections by Charles Fox. But he was not resentful, declaring that 'I shall ever applaud the Perdita as the most generous woman on earth', though he does not explain in what her generosity consisted.[29]

Mary's new lover, Charles James Fox, was an extraordinary man, greatly gifted yet seemingly indifferent to cultivating those talents fully. Of brilliant intellect and conversation, a dominating presence in the House of Commons since first entering it at the age of nineteen, it was nevertheless in the opinion of many not politics to which he gave his primary attention, but gaming and whoring. In the second of these pursuits the blood of his great-great-grandfather Charles II (through Louise de Kérouālle) flowed freely, and with his dark hair and jowl he resembled the Stuart king too. When he began his affair with Mary, in July 1782, he was in deep political trouble, having resigned as Foreign Secretary, a position he had held since Lord North's government fell over the crisis in America and was replaced by a Whig partnership headed by Lord Rockingham. Fox, who had opposed the American war from the outset, had been made responsible for the peace negotiations. He wanted to grant the Americans independence on their terms in order to break their tie with the French, but he found himself opposed by the leader of another Whig faction, Lord Shelburne; Fox suspected Shelburne of dealing covertly with the King and thus undermining the authority of Parliament. Between Fox and George III was mutual loathing; Foxites nick-named the King 'Satan', while the King hated Fox not just for the populist, reformist views which had earned him the title 'Man of the People', but for his pernicious influence (as the King saw it) over the Prince of Wales, for whom Fox was both elder brother and preferred father-figure.

Although in his youth a dandy, by the 1780s Fox affected an appearance of slovenliness, famously described by Walpole:

> His bristly, black person, and shagged breast quite open, and rarely purified by any ablutions, was wrapped in a foul linen night-gown, and his bushy hair dishevelled. In these cynic weeds and with epicurean good humour, did he dictate his politics – and in this school did the heir of the Crown attend his lessons and imbibe them.[30]

The word 'imbibe' was well chosen, as excessive drinking was another well-cultivated vice. The schoolrooms in which the heir received his tuition were the drawing-rooms of Whig grandees such as the Duke of Devonshire, and the gambling clubs, particularly Brooks's. This exclusive club (members were elected) was housed in a newly built 'country house in St James's Street' designed by Henry Holland, where members could dine and lose their money in elegant surroundings.[31] On the day of his resignation, 4 July, Walpole recorded that Fox dined with the Prince of Wales before going to Brooks's, where he stayed till four in the morning, and 'it being so early, finished the evening at White's [opposite] with Lord Weymouth'.[32] The resignation had been precipitated by the death in a virulent flu epidemic of Lord Rockingham (Mary had been 'alarmingly' ill in the same outbreak); the King, determined to keep Fox from office, appointed Lord Shelburne as First Minister.

Mary was already a Foxite politically; at the opera in January she had worn 'an image of the *Royal martyr*' (his friends nicknamed Fox 'Charles the Martyr' for his misfortunes).[33] This reference was hinting at a liaison, so a sporadic one may already have taken place, but following his resignation Fox made Perdita his full-time occupation. As his friend James Hare expressed it crudely in a letter to Fox's brother-in-law, Richard Fitzpatrick:

> Charles passes his whole day with Mrs Robinson, to the utter Exclusion and Indignation of the gallant Col. Tarleton, but not, I believe, of Capt. Craddock, for it is supposed that she has bad Taste enough to like fucking with him almost as well as the late Secretary, whom I never see but at Mrs R's window, unless he comes to Brooks's after she is gone to bed, and gets drunk with Stanhope and Jack Townshend.[34]

Captain Craddock does not otherwise feature on Mary's list of lovers, and the letter must be seen in its context of bad-tempered grumbling following a heavy gambling loss.

Standing at a window was hardly engaging in sexual congress, and Fox claimed that he stayed so long in Mrs Robinson's house because it had a good view of Shelburne's, so he could keep an eye on him. Perdita too responded quickly when the *Herald* reported that she was taking the ex-Secretary for daily outings in her pony-phaeton, denying that the relationship was anything other than 'perfectly *political*'.[35] However, the reputation of neither lent much credibility to a claim that politics was their only concern. Gossip proliferated, Horace Walpole telling a correspondent that 'Charles Fox is languishing at the feet of Mrs Robinson', and adding George Selwyn's quip: 'Who should the *man of the people* live with, but with the *woman of the people*?'[36] There was also much political invective against Fox both in the government-financed newspapers and in caricatures. Since the pair had been observed driving out together on 3 September, the *Herald* (in which the King now held a controlling interest) printed 'The Second Lesson of Politicians', an anti-Fox piece using Perdita in order to discredit him:

1. Now *Charles F-x* being dismissed from the Secretaryship of State, returned again to Gaming and Dissipation.
2. And he resumed his Pharaoh Bank at Brookes's, and sojourned with Mrs. *Rob-s-n*, the Harlot of the Day, and he drived her about in a Phaeton.
3. The rattling of the wheels filled the air of the streets, and the neighing, and trampling of the horses was heard afar off.
4. And the People turned, and gazed upon him, and said, He driveth like *Jehu*, though not to the confusion of *Jezebel*![37]

There are 22 verses in all. Less vicious but still satirical was the cartoon, *Perdito and Perdita*, which showed Perdita as whip driving a sheepish Fox past St James's Palace; she is in control and he is the 'lost one'.

She was similarly used to condemn Tarleton, whose achievements in America were likewise coming under attack. In early August two damning anonymous letters appeared on the front pages of the *Chronicle*, aimed at destroying his military reputation.[38] The first, merely a skirmishing manoeuvre, reproved him for failing to reward a soldier who had saved his life; the second carried the main offensive, accusing him both of the slaughter of unarmed men at Waxhaws, and of such gross misjudgement at the Battle of Cowpens that the force under his command was utterly destroyed. Cowpens was indeed a disaster; in the 'finest American tactical demonstration in the war' General Morgan had lured the over-confident British into the midst of his force, raked them with devastating fire, then unleashed his own cavalry and put them to ignominious flight.[39] Shocked and demoralised, Tarleton sent in his resignation, though Cornwallis would not accept it. But Lieutenant Roderick MacKenzie, afterwards identified as author of the letters, had been badly wounded

Right: *Mrs Robinson* by Thomas Gainsborough, 1781, commissioned by the Prince of Wales. *Below left*: Miniature of the Prince by Jeremiah Meyer, thought to be similar to the one held in Mary's hand in the Gainsborough portrait. *Below right*: *Mrs Robinson* by George Romney, 1781.

The front of the Drury Lane Theatre, as designed in 1775 by the Adam brothers.

David Garrick by Thomas Gainsborough.

Richard Brinsley Sheridan by John Hoppner.

Mrs Robinson as Amanda from *Bell's British Theatre*, 1777.

Play-bill for Mrs Robinson's Benefit night, 30 April 1778.

For the Benefit of Mrs. ROBINSON.
At the Theatre Royal in DruryLane,
This preſent Thurſday, the 30th of April, 1778,

M A C B E T H.

Macbeth by Mr. S M I T H,
Macduff by Mr. B R E R E T O N.
Duncanby Mr. CHAMBERS, Roſs Mr. AICKIN,
Malcolm Mr. DAVIES, Banquo Mr. PACKER,
Lenox by Mr. NORRIS, Donalbain by Mr. R. PALMER,
Captain Mr. Farren, Angus Mr. Chaplin, Seward Mr. Hurſt, Doctor Mr. Wright,
Hecate by Mr. B A N N I S T E R,
Witches by Mr. Parſons, Mr. Moody & Mr. Baddeley,
Lady Macduff by Miſs S H E R R Y,
Lady Macbeth by Mrs. R O B I N S O N,
(Being her Firſt Appearance in that Character,)
The original Muſic compoſed by MATTHEW LOCKE,
Will be performed, with full CHORUSSES and Additional ACCOMPANIMENTS, by
Mr. B A N N I S T E R, Mr. G A U D R Y.
Mr. Legg, Mr. Chaplin, Mr. Carpenter, Mr. Holcroft, Mr. Philimore,
Miſs Abrams, Mrs. Love, Mrs. Pitt, Mrs. Smith, Miſs Collett, Mrs. Gaudry,
And Mrs. W R I G H T E N.
To which will be added a new Muſical Farce, call'd

The LUCKY ESCAPE.

The M U S I C chiefly compiled.
The P R I N C I P A L C H A R A C T E R S by
Mr. V E R N O N,
Mr. W A L D R O N,
And Mr. D O D D.
Miſs C O L L E T T,
And Mrs. W R I G H T E N.
Tickets delivered for K I N G L E A R will be taken.
The Doors will be opened at a Quarter after Five, to begin exactly at a Quarter after Six o'Clock
Books of the Performances to be had at the Theatre.
To-morrow, The Comedy of The C L A N D E S T I N E M A R R I A G E,
With a new Comic Opera, (never performed) call'd The C R I S I S, or Love and Fear
For the Benefit of the Miſs H O P K I N S's.

Drury Lane stage, showing the royal boxes immediately left and right of the stage. The play is *The School for Scandal*, 1777, when the screen in Joseph Surface's library falls to reveal Lady Teazle. With Mrs Abington as Lady Teazle, Thomas King as Sir Peter Teazle, William Smith as Charles Surface and John Palmer as Joseph Surface.

Nº XIII.

Nº XIV.

The Dramatic Enchantress.

The Doating Lover.

Publish'd by A. Hamilton Junr. near St John's Gate June 1st 1780.

Tête-à-tête from the *Town and Country Magazine*, May 1780, showing Mary Robinson and Lord Malden as *The Dramatic Enchantress* and *The Doating Lover*.

Scene of a Masquerade at the Pantheon on Oxford Street, by Charles White, 1773.

Florizel and Perdita, published 16 October 1783. Ranged on a shelf are the trophy-heads of real or supposed lovers, Tarleton, Fox and Lord North. Robinson is 'King of Cuckolds', while the King, bereft of half his crown, cries 'Oh! My Son My Son'.

Vauxhall Gardens, by Thomas Rowlandson, watercolour of 1784. On the right the Prince of Wales whispers in Mary's ear, while Thomas Robinson hangs on to her other side. The two women in the centre are the Duchess of Devonshire and her sister, who leans against a tree around which peers Henry Bate.

Lieutenant Banastre Tarleton by Sir Joshua Reynolds, 1782.

Below left: *The Thunderer*, by James Gillray, a satirical attack on Tarleton, published 20 August 1782. Perdita, sign of The Whirligig inn, cries 'This is the Lad'll Kiss most Sweet. Who'd not love a Soldier?' *Right*: *Perdita on her Last Legs*, artist unknown, published August 1784. A destitute Perdita begs from the Prince of Wales. On the wall play-bills advertise *Florizel and Perdita* and *Jane Shore*, drama of a repentant royal whore.

Perdito & Perdita, published 17 December 1782. Mary drives Fox in a phaeton with her cypher past St James's Palace, in supposed illustration of her power over him.

Thomas Rowlandson: *'Mrs. R – sitting for her picture'*, believed to be Mrs Robinson (pen and grey wash).

Engraving by Thomas Burke from Reynolds' portrait, used as frontispiece for Mary Robinson's 1791 *Poems*.

Dr Awsiter's Hot and Cold Baths, Brighton, by John Nixon (1803). Mary tried these baths in the summer of 1783 when first afflicted by illness. She returned to Brighton on other occasions, and the beach scene would have been familiar to her.

at Cowpens and burned with resentment; now he had his revenge. A few days later the deadly satirical artist James Gillray published a cartoon almost certainly commissioned by MacKenzie.[40] *The Thunderer* features Tarleton as Bobadil, the boastful, cowardly captain of Jonson's *Every Man in his Humour*, and the figure copies that of the Reynolds portrait except that he flourishes his sword, boasting in a word bubble of the 'Three, Four, Five, Six . . . Twenty of them, kill'd them . . . Twenty more, kill'd them too . . . two hundred a day, five days a thousand . . .' and so on. Behind stands his gull, the Prince of Wales, who with his badge of three feathers for a head is literally feather-brained; both are posed (with genitalia emphasised) in front of a tavern whose sign is a bare-breasted Perdita, sexually impaled on a spike. The tavern is called 'The Whirligig', a device used by the army to punish prostitutes.

Ironically Perdita was not then Tarleton's mistress, but sometime during September she returned to him. Newspapers regularly carried shipping bulletins, but the *Morning Post*'s 'Ship News' of 21 September was a clever spoof, with much double-entendre:

> Yesterday a messenger arrived in town with the very *interesting* and *pleasing* intelligence of the *Tarleton armed ship*, after a *chace* of *some months*, captured the *Perdita frigate*, and brought her safe into *Egham* port. The *Perdita* is a prodigious fine *clean bottomed* vessel, and had taken many prizes during her cruize, particularly the *Florizel*, a most valuable ship belonging to the *crown*, but which was immediately released after taking out the *cargo*. The *Perdita* was captured some time ago by the *Fox*, but was afterwards retaken by the *Malden*, and had a complete suit of new rigging when she fell in with the *Tarleton*. Her manoeuvring to escape was admirable: but the *Tarleton* fully determined to take her or perish, would not give up the chace, and at length, *coming along side* of the *Perdita*, fully determined to board her *sword in hand*, she instantly surrendered *at discretion*.

The sequence of lovers may not be correctly ordered, but the swiftly changing nature of her relationships is conveyed. This time, however, Perdita had found her home port and was never to seek another.

It is likely that, as the anonymous *Memoirs of Perdita* suggested, Mary did come to love Tarleton for the dangers he had passed, and she expressed her intense admiration in her 'Ode to Valour', inscribed to Colonel Banastre Tarleton. Its ten stanzas are of stratospherically elevated sentiment, from its opening trumpet blast which apostrophises 'TRANSCENDANT VALOUR! – godlike Pow'r'. The poem proclaims that man is the creator's sublime achievement, valour man's greatest attribute and, with a nod at General Wolfe, INTREPID TARLETON its supreme exponent:

> TARLETON, thy mind, above the POET's praise
> Asks not the labour'd task of flatt'ring lays!
> As the rare GEM with innate lustre glows,
> As round the OAK the gadding Ivy grows,
> So shall THY WORTH, in native radiance live!
> So shall the MUSE spontaneous incense give!
> Th' HISTORIC page shall prove a lasting shrine,
> Where Truth and Valour shall THY laurels twine;
> Where, with thy name, recording FAME shall blend
> The ZEALOUS PATRIOT, and the FAITHFUL FRIEND![41]

Mary was often accused of vanity; if she was vain it extended to pride in her lover. But there was more than admiration in the relationship, and it must have been a sexually satisfying partnership too, perhaps for Mary the first that she had known.

The press report said that the lovers were at Egham, between Staines and Windsor, which means that Mary had taken Ban to her house in Old Windsor; he would have found good riding in Windsor Forest, and no doubt as a friend of the Prince he joined the royal hunts. Mary rode too, and it was while she was riding through Windsor at Christmas-time, that reconciliation with the Prince of Wales took place:

> *Perdita* and her Colonel have taken up their residence at Old Windsor, and are perpetually on horseback. The beautiful fair one was coming from her morning exercise of riding, at the time his R.H. came thro' this town from the chace; his R.H. stopt when he came near her, and pulling off his glove, shook her by the hand; the blushing *Perdita*, holding one of her hands at the same time across her face. – Oh, modesty in the extreme![42]

This impulsive gesture by the Prince ended the feud, and it was far better for Mary to be on good terms with him. The benefit of better relations was felt in 1783 when he came of age and Fox persuaded him to exchange the £20,000 promissory note for an annual allowance of £500, with £200 to continue for Maria if she outlived her mother. Unfortunately some of the Prince's accounts are missing and it is not possible to tell when payments began, but from what remain it can be seen that the annuity was paid quarterly, on 5 January, 5 April, 5 July and 10 October. Though Mary complained of irregularity in later years, at least from January 1791 to January 1796 it was paid on time. In a sense therefore, because of this annuity, she remained the Prince's mistress for the rest of her life.

While Mary never thought the money enough, it was nevertheless essential to her, and she had reason to be grateful to Fox who, at the time when the annuity was negotiated, was in a strong position. Lord Shelburne's administration had fallen, and the King found himself obliged to accept a coalition led by his former First Minister, the Tory Lord North, and Charles Fox for the Whigs. It was an uncomfortable partnership, but for the moment it held. The torrent of anti-Fox abuse continued however, and Perdita's settlement formed a subject for further satire. A cartoon showed her in a coach drawn by goats and driven by the Prince of Wales, Fox as postillion handing her the 'Grant of £60,000' which Parliament had awarded the Prince on his coming of age. Lord North lies supinely on the carriage roof. Even when his relationship with Mrs Robinson was over she was, as with the Prince, a useful rod with which Fox's enemies could beat his back.

In the early 1780s, scandal and Perdita were inextricably linked, and where there were no facts they were made up. It was inevitable that she would be portrayed as an adherent of Dr James Graham's notorious Temple of Health and Hymen, from 1780 to 1783 one of the shows of London. No European capital had more to offer in the way of exotic entertainments, though most were innocuous, even educational. In the spring of 1782, for example, it was possible to see a dromedary from Grand Cairo at Astley's Circus, or the City of Rome in miniature, or to attend a lecture on the heavens at the Haymarket theatre featuring a comet which descended from the top of the auditorium in parabolic orbit round the sun. At the *Eidophusikon* [natural forms], an exhibition of moving pictures created by Philippe de Loutherbourg, customers could (for five shillings) watch the sun rise through fog over an Italian sea-port and set after a rainy day by the cliffs of Dover, see Niagara's cataracts falling, the moon rising above a rocky shore on the coast of Japan and, as grand finale, 'Satan arraying his Troops on the banks of the Fiery Lake'. Gainsborough visited again and again. Since Mary was a friend of de Loutherbourg she would certainly have attended, perhaps taking Maria. The *Eidophusikon* was said to be a show which any woman could safely visit on her own.

Not so the Temple of Health and Hymen, to which women often went veiled or even disguised as men.[43] James Graham was a mixture of showman, charlatan and eccentric medical theorist; his nightly lectures offered some sensible advice on sexual health, but with much mumbo-jumbo as he enthused over the 'genial invigorating tide of the celestial fire, combined with the powerful influences of music, magnets, and the balmy odours of aromatic aetherial essences'.[44] Only curiosity could have impelled so many to part with six guineas to enter Graham's 'Temple', an Aladdin's cave of glass and glitter where music played and perfumes scented the air. For further sensual stimulation conductors, placed under the seat cushions, delivered an electric shock, and a semi-naked woman appeared as 'Goddess of Health'.[45] But by 1783 the market was running dry, and Graham was forced to cut his prices. A caricature *The Docter* [sic] *Himself Pouring out His Whole Soul for 1s* [shilling] shows him preaching – with a suggestively placed upright scroll in his hand – to an audience which includes Fox and a simpering Perdita.

Dr Graham's other money-spinner was his giant 'Celestial Bed', on hire for £50 a night. The huge bed, set on 'forty pillars of brilliant glass of the most exquisite workmanship' beneath a canopy which exhaled 'odiferous, balmy and etherial spices', was supposedly for the purpose of conception. Cynics assumed that the bed was the territory of voluptuaries, and the anonymous satirist of *The Celestial Beds* placed Perdita on it, luring Florizel there in hope of a royal bastard:

And shall not she, his joy and pride,
Be for a pledge electrify'd?
Yes, Graham shall exert his art,
And give a bantling to her heart!
The Muses' darling it shall be,
The flow'r of royal progeny![46]

Mrs Robinson was to satirise Dr Graham as Dr Pimpernel (with a pun on the first syllable) in her novel *Walsingham*, but at the time *The Celestial Beds* added to the smut and smirk which vulgarised the Perdita.

A new and titillating journal, the *Rambler's Magazine*, was launched in January 1783, lengthily subtitled *The Annals of Gallantry, Glee, Pleasure, and the Bon Ton; calculated for the entertainment of The Polite World; and to Furnish The Man of Pleasure with a most delicious banquet of Amorous, Bacchanalian, Whimsical, Humorous, Theatrical and Polite entertainment.* Who else to serve up at the feast but Perdita? Both illustrations in the first edition feature her, one with Dally the Tall and the Bird of Paradise as they dress to receive their lovers; in the other, *Florizel granting Independancy to Perdita*, she lies on a couch, a picture of a nude Danaë enjoying a shower of gold on the wall behind. It accompanies an obscene spoof of legal language as 'certain premises' are granted to Florizel in return for his both 'yielding and paying' weekly. Thereafter not a month goes by without jokes, innuendos and cartoons featuring Perdita's voracious appetite for sex and money.

From time to time newspapers printed denunciations of their own scandal-mongering. 'A Lover of Decency' wanted to know 'of what use it can be to society to know that a prostitute has got a new gown from Paris', while another wrote in disgust at 'whole columns of [scandal], filled with Mrs R—'s green carriage, Mrs M's flower-pots, Mrs A—'s bouquet . . .'.[47] A versifier thought the *Herald* should devote less space to Perdita's 'too luscious smile' and more to celebrating 'Such as shine their sex's glory', intellectual, literary women like Hannah More, Elizabeth Carter, Frances Burney, Hannah Cowley, Hester Chapone, Frances Boscawen and Hester Thrale.[48] Ironically it was with these women that Mrs Robinson wanted to be bracketed and which she was to spend much of her later life trying to achieve; the 'Hasty Sketch of Perdita' quoted earlier, published in the summer of 1782 when Fox's mistress, shows how weary she became of the Perdita stereotype. Nevertheless there was no falling off in her leadership of fashion; the spring of 1783 was the time of the mirrored opera-box and the gold-clocked stockings, and she and Tarleton were observed together at all reported social occasions. They made a handsome couple: at a Pantheon masquerade where they spent the evening arm in arm, Tarleton wore the uniform of a hussar with a blue jacket, a waistcoat and breeches embroidered in silver, and a pair of leather boots which 'fitted as tight as a silk stocking'.[49]

But problems were looming for Tarleton. Once he had been paired off with an American prisoner he was free for active service and had hopes of going to India with Lord Cornwallis, who had been nominated by Lord Shelburne to become Governor General and Commander-in-Chief. However, when Shelburne fell so did the plan for Cornwallis. Tarleton was only on half pay but had been living extravagantly; immediately on his return from America he had become a part of the racing set including the Prince, Fox, Sir John Lade, and Sir Harry Featherstonhaugh, who held race meetings at his country house Uppark in Sussex. But while Sir Harry had an income of £10,000 a year, Tarleton's was less than £350. Moreover he had not conquered his gambling habit and had borrowed money both from Drummond's Bank and Louis Weltje, owner of a club and the Prince's right-hand man. Ban sold off his horses and planned to sell his commissions, and he also appealed to his mother and brothers for the £1,000 he still owed. But they were determined not to pay off any more gambling debts.

Correspondence between London and Liverpool became increasingly desperate.[50] Ban tried emotional blackmail, telling of a rumour that he had committed suicide and reminding them that it would not be pleasant for them if he were sent to a debtors' prison. A more effective move was the enlistment in his cause of Lord Cornwallis, who wrote to Thomas Tarleton regretting his brother's folly but assuring them of his own 'very sincere regard' for the young man and his certainty that he had 'much goodness of heart at bottom'. His intervention brought the family round and they produced a scheme to satisfy creditors, Cornwallis himself signing Weltje's bond, in return for Ban's promise to leave the country and live quietly and economically in France. His mother wanted him to make a further sacrifice; she concluded a letter urging him to 'See your follies in their real light, and become a New Man', by saying that

> it will give me real pleasure & satisfaction to hear that your connection with Mrs Robinson is at an end [for] without that necessary step all my endeavers [*sic*] to save you from impending destruction will be ineffectual.[51]

To her irritation he did not reply at once; when he did, on 25 July, he had left London and was waiting to cross into France:

> You desire me to write more fully about Mrs Robinson – the connection is closed – She is too proud to follow [illegible] and she has long been too generous, always I should have said to have encreasd the poverty of any man – I most solemnly assure you she has not been the occasion of my bankruptcy – Play alone which I abjure has.[52]

When he wrote this defence of the woman he loved, but whom he had left two days beforehand without saying good-bye, he was quite unaware that she was lying dangerously ill.

The previous weeks must have been distressing for Mary. Having found a measure of happiness she did not wish to lose it, but neither did she wish to live in obscurity in provincial France. Perhaps she never knew that Ban had dangled before his mother the possibility that he might marry to solve his problems, or that Mrs Tarleton believed her to be their root cause. In early May she was reported ill and, though it was in June that she made her appearance in the splendid vis-à-vis paid for by the gamblers at Brooks's, this was also a time when the rareness of her appearances was causing comment. There was perhaps a reason: on 13 June the *Herald* reported her 'in a state of pregnancy' and she did not correct the report, something she was usually quick to do when stories about her were inaccurate.

There is little reliable information about what exactly happened after Tarleton left London on 23 July, though an account of the first part of the evening written anonymously after Mary's death is so circumstantial as to ring true. She apparently tried to forestall his departure by asking Fox for a loan of £800:

> Her messenger returned with 300L. and a note, saying, Mrs Robinson might depend on receiving the remainder on the following morning. This was at night. Mrs Robinson had been at the opera; and the Duke de Biron [Lauzun], and an English nobleman of the highest rank had returned with her from that place to supper. Not having seen [Tarleton] at the opera, where he had promised to join her, nor finding him at her house, she sent to every quarter in search of him;

> and as no intelligence of him arrived, she concluded he had departed without taking his leave . . .[53]

Late though it was, Mary determined to go after Ban with what money she had obtained, and set out in a coach. But during the journey she became ill and, if she was pregnant, miscarried. On her return to London she continued extremely ill, or developed some other medical condition precipitated by a miscarriage. Unsurprisingly the *Memoirs* merely refer to 'that unfortunate journey, the consequences of which proved so fatal to her health'.[54] What is certain is that, whatever the nature of the illness, it caused such irreversible physical damage that she was never to walk normally again. She was twenty-six years old.

9

Ill Health and Bad Debts

The Perdita, *who was once a planet, and shone with such a lustre, as dazzled the eyes of a Prince, is now, alas! quite on the decline, and scarcely to be distinguished among the group of lesser stars that crowd the* milky way.

(*Morning Post*, 7 January 1785)

The first reference to Mary's illness occurs on 31 July, when the *Herald* reported that 'Mrs Robinson lies dangerously ill at her house at Berkeley Square'. Two days later she was 'not so bad as was reported, but is still very unwell'. On 7 August she was 'recovering', her carriage noticed outside a haberdasher's where it was ignored by an unfeeling Florizel. Then on 22 August readers learned that 'with the velocity of a comet' Perdita had flown off some days previously to Southampton or Brighthelmstone, as Brighton was then called. The choice of phrase suggests the eager socialite, but Mary had gone to Brighton on medical advice to try sea-water bathing for her ravaged body. At this stage journalistic comment was light-hearted, in expectation of recovery; the *Herald* even suggested that the illness was a mere fit of the sulks because of the 'declining influence of her charms'. What it was actually to mean is best conveyed by Miss Hawkins, who describes what she saw some years later at the Opera House, where Perdita had once reigned supreme:

> On a table in one of the waiting-rooms . . . was seated a woman of fashionable appearance, still beautiful, but not 'in the bloom of beauty's pride'; she was not noticed, except by the eye of pity. In a few minutes, two liveried servants came to her, they took from their pockets long white sleeves, which they drew on their arms, they then lifted her up and conveyed her to her carriage; – it was the then helpless paralytic Perdita![1]

Even the acid Miss Hawkins recognises the wretchedness of Mrs Robinson's dependent state, while naming the affliction for what she saw: paralysis. Mary never uses this word, over the years maintaining that she was suffering from a 'severe rheumatism', or a 'rheumatic gout'. The official version (which may be her own words, rendered impersonally) is told in the *Memoirs*:

> An imprudent exposure to the night air in travelling, when, exhausted by fatigue and mental anxiety, she slept in a chaise with the windows open, brought on a fever, which confined her to her bed during six months. The disorder terminated . . . *in a violent rheumatism, which progressively deprived her of the use of her limbs.*[2]

The anonymous author of the 1803 account gives the same story with more detail but with one telling inaccuracy:

> With the passion and zeal of generous minds, Mrs Robinson, between one and two o'clock in the morning, threw herself into a post chaise to follow him [Tarleton], without sufficient precaution of dress against the cold, although it was the depth of winter, and the weather was very severe. She was agitated, and heated, by her apprehensions; and let down the glasses of the chaise; and, in that situation fell asleep. At the first stage, she was obliged to be carried into the inn, almost frozen; and from that hour, never recovered the entire use of her limbs.[3]

Frozen limbs from a freezing journey – but it took place mid-summer, not mid-winter, providing powerful evidence that Mary was covering something up when explaining the circumstances of her illness in later life to friends. The writer then describes another consequence of the illness:

> For a long time the joints of her fingers were contracted; but they were afterwards partially restored, and she could even write with facility.[4]

On the basis of this very limited evidence, diagnosis can only be speculative. Even assuming a miscarriage we cannot know at what stage the pregnancy was; it is unlikely that news would have appeared in a newspaper before at least three months, though it could not have been so far advanced that the condition was generally observable. Four to six months pregnant in late July may be guessed. But after twenty weeks miscarriage can be very threatening to the mother: *Abruptio placentae*, for example, where the placenta breaks away from the wall of the uterus, may lead to death from loss of blood. A precipitating factor in this condition is thought to be hypertension, and it is easy to believe that Mary, who had been under stress for weeks, could have developed it; high blood pressure can also from five months result in eclampsia, which leads rapidly to a fit, unconsciousness, loss of the baby and possibly a stroke. Rumours of a '*stroke* of the palsy' were reported in the *Rambler's Magazine* in November.[5] However, a stroke would more commonly have produced a one-sided paralysis, not both, and eclampsia then might well have proved fatal. It is impossible to know what caused Mary's miscarriage, if indeed she had one.

There is one eye-witness account which provides supporting evidence. The Earl of Pembroke, the lord who had offered to take her on as mistress, sight unseen, when she was in the Fleet prison, and who could have been the 'English nobleman of the highest rank' with her at the opera on 23 July, saw Mrs Robinson in Brighthelmstone. At the end of a letter to his son, Lord Herbert, he describes her wretched appearance:

> Adieu, my dear George; no considerable event has taken place here since you went away, except the arrival of Mrs Robinson. Her face is still very pretty, but illness has brought on a disadvantageous, additional scowl to it; & as to her body, she is quite défaite [undone], se trainant à peine [barely dragging herself along], a perfect Sciondalona. She may possibly come about again, but she must not go to an Opera on the day of miscarriage.[6]

It is a tantalisingly brief comment (the reference to an 'additional scowl' suggesting Mary's state of distress and discontent even prior to her illness), but the Earl sounds in no doubt that a miscarriage had taken place.

We do know that, either as the sole or as a secondary condition, Mary suffered an acute illness of some weeks with long-term lower limb paralysis accompanied by severe pain, though because she survived for seventeen years conditions such as malignancy can be ruled out. One tentative diagnosis is rheumatoid arthritis, whose onset can be associated with stress or a viral infection; the contractures in her hands would be explained by this condition. Another possibility is Guillain-Barré Syndrome, likewise virus-induced and which can follow childbirth; it too has an acute onset and causes symmetrical nerve-damage, beginning in the patient's legs, with resulting pain and difficulty in walking, and it may extend to the arms, but if it reaches heart and lungs death is likely. Most sufferers today make at least a partial recovery, but some 10 per cent may suffer more profound disability.[7]

If Lord Pembroke's comments sound jokily unfeeling it was perhaps because he had little sympathy to spare; he had come to Brighton on the advice of his physician to enable his nine-year-old daughter Charlotte, dying of consumption, to try the warm water baths. Sea water, drunk or ducked in, was the great panacea of the second half of the eighteenth century, especially following publication of Dr Richard Russell's *A Dissertation on the Use of Sea Water in the Diseases of the Glands* (1750), which argued the curative and rejuvenating qualities of sea water, and included case histories which are not limited to the cure of glandular disorders (it was, however, for the swollen glands of his neck that the Prince of Wales was prescribed sea-bathing in 1784). Dr Russell established himself in a practice at Brighton, society flocked to consult him, and the little fishing village developed into the foremost south-coast resort. Dipping for health became a serious business with its own rituals of bathing-machines and bathing-women who ensured that the bather was pushed right under; the shock of sudden immersion in cold water was thought beneficial in stimulating the circulation. However, one of Dr Russell's successors, Dr John Awitser, recognising that Brighton's stiff breezes, dashing waves and chilly waters might prove more fatal than revivifying to invalids, created warm as well as cold sea-water baths in a temple-like building just below the cliffs. This would no doubt have been where Mary went, along with Charlotte Herbert; the warm waters will have soothed if they could not heal her affliction.

For her short stay Mary probably lodged in the Old Ship Hotel on the sea front, since it was there that she stayed during the following summer. Brighton had developed rapidly over the thirty years since Dr Russell's arrival, but it was still quite small, bounded east and west by cornfields, to the south by a long shingle beach and boisterous sea, and to the north by the rolling Downs, a little piece of which flowed down to the area of green known as the Steine. This was the social centre of the resort, a place to see and to be seen. On this occasion however Mary's condition would have caused her to shun public places, and she left town before the arrival of the Prince of Wales on 7 September; of all men she would not have wished to encounter him when looking so ill.

For the Prince, however, all was pleasure. His uncle Cumberland had taken the house on the Steine which had once been Dr Russell's, to which he had invited his nephew before, but until his twenty-first birthday the Prince was bound by the King's prohibition on travelling further than 50 miles from London. Now, less than four weeks after his independence day, he made the trip, and on a Sunday too to annoy his father more. Bells rang out to greet him, and a salute was fired from the guns at the battery, though unfortunately 'thro' some indiscretion in reloading one of the pieces, it went off, and wounded the under-gunner so mortally, that he died in a very short time afterwards'.[8] Despite the tragedy, the Prince was soon enjoying a stroll on the Steine with his uncle; he might change his mistresses, but between George, Prince of Wales and Brighton an indissoluble union was being formed.

In late November 1783 Mary was back in Berkeley Square, her reappearance in her chariot celebrated in the *Herald* with a flourish:

> The *Lybian lions*, that lie *couchant* under the burning sun on the *vis-à-vis* of the *all-subduing* Perdita, after having been concealed from the public eye for some time, again range abroad with a fierceness equal to that of *tygers*, which drew, of old, the chariot of Cupid!
>
> Now winter surrounds us, and chills with frost those feelings which depend upon the blood; *the Perdita* comes forth to cheer us, and with the potent rays of beauty counteracts the severity of the season.[9]

But the news did not continue cheerful. She now had two problems, illness, which confined her to bed again in January, and a return of financial worries. Malden was paying neither rent nor allowance, and she had built up debts which the Prince's £500 a year could not cover.

In January a flurry of press paragraphs both declared and denied seizure of her goods. Several (inserted by Mary?) not only suggested that the Prince should come to her rescue, but insinuated that it would be an insult to his generosity to suppose that he would not:

> The paragraph mentioning the seizure of Mrs *Robinson*'s effects was totally *void of foundation*, and only calculated to injure the character of a certain *young gentleman* by casting a reflection of the grossest nature on his honor and liberality in the bare supposition that *he* would suffer a calamity of such weight to approach a person who has ever been honored with his esteem and partiality![10]

His Royal Highness was deaf to the hints, and for the moment Mary struggled on.

And where was Tarleton all this while? He had not been oblivious to Mary's plight; somehow he had learned what had happened and had slipped back across the Channel to her (there was a regular service to Brighton from Dieppe). On 25 August, answering some remark of his son's, Lord Pembroke wrote that 'Tarleton is at this instant with Mrs Robinson. Why do ye suppose him on the Continent?'[11] But Ban would not have dared to stay long or openly, and thereafter moved restlessly around northern France. He was miserable about Mary, writing to his brother Thomas and disingenuously concealing that he had been with her:

> I reveal to you everything. I have not forgot M^rs^ R— n — Oh God such a conflict I hope never again to encounter. I hear she is dangerously ill – But no more. I shall grow distracted.[12]

He was also bitter at the failure of the British authorities to make some gesture of reward for the years of service in America of himself and his men. The tattered remnants of his legion reached England in January 1784, apart from a few who had taken up the offer of land to cultivate in Nova Scotia, 'an uneven, barren place, not fit for mankind to dwell in' as the *Herald* described it; of the rest, those permanently crippled were admitted to Chelsea Hospital while the others were discharged, unprovided for.[13] Tarleton brooded on the injustice. He assured his mother that he was working diligently at perfecting his French and studying his profession, though he had not taken himself down to Tours as Lord Cornwallis had urged, but hung about those places where he could find other Englishmen, engaging in just those activities of which both of them disapproved. So he fretted, and frittered time away, conscious that any change in fortune would have to be initiated by him. One idea was that he would write his memoirs of the American campaign, and waiting for the delivery of documents and maps provided an excuse to linger near the Channel. Rumours of a general election then offered another opportunity, since he was ambitious to become an MP for his home town of Liverpool. So he crossed back to England and made for London and Mary.

The Fox/North coalition had collapsed in December over Fox's India Bill; this sought to control the power of the East India Company by investing it in a Board of Commissioners, a reasonable proposal in itself, but all the nominees were Foxites. When the House of Lords rejected the bill, the King jubilantly reclaimed the seals of office, and to general amusement appointed the 24-year-old William Pitt, seen as scarcely more than a schoolboy, as the new First Minister. Fox's majority in the Commons slowly disappeared, and on 25 March 1784 the King dissolved parliament, an action no monarch had undertaken since Stuart times. But far from a public outcry, the money which poured from royal coffers into buying votes ensured that in the ensuing election the Foxite Whigs were soundly beaten. Fox's one rather hollow victory was his re-election as an MP for Westminster during the famous six-week campaign when the Duchess of Devonshire canvassed among the Covent Garden alleys, supposedly exchanging kisses for votes.[14] Though much was made of this in the scandal sheets, kisses were innocent trading-counters among all the mud-slinging, back-handing, stone-throwing and rabble-rousing which were the stock accompaniments of electioneering. The Tarleton family greased palms in Liverpool, but by nine votes Ban failed to be elected.

In a letter of 9 April Lord Cornwallis names Mrs Robinson as one of the women who helped Fox, though she was hardly in a condition to canvass the streets (and had she done so the daily prints would have had their teeth into her).[15] One thing she may have done was to turn out some of the reams of satirical verse which accompanied the election, and she may also have been seen in her carriage wearing Fox's colours of buff and blue and sporting a jaunty red brush in her hat. In the crowing over the Foxite defeat which followed in the government-sponsored *Post*, one spiteful paragraph links her with his campaign:

> The *Cyprian divinity* of Berkley-square, is said to be *on her last legs*. Thus the fate of the *Buff* and the *Blue* extends through all their connexions; famine and disgrace bringing up the rear.[16]

This is also a reference to a return of her financial problems. The paper had already sneered that she could no longer afford to advertise herself in the press, but the choice of expression, 'on her last legs', was a cruel jest. It was taken up in visual form by the *Rambler's Magazine* in their August issue. Perdita is seen in rags soliciting money from the Prince of Wales; on a wall behind is an advertisement for a performance of *Florizel and Perdita*.

Ironically, Mary was planning just such an appeal, taking herself to Brighton again when he was there. The Prince had not responded to proddings in the press, so now Mary tried direct appeal. The tenor of her letter can be gauged by the Prince's reply, addressed to her at the Ship Inn:

> I have receiv'd your Letter, & it really quite overcomes me, the scenes of distress you so pathetically paint. I will certainly wait upon you, but I am afraid it will be late before I can come to the Ship, as I have company with me. Should it be within the *compass* of *my means* to rescue you from the Abyss you apprehend that is before you . . . I need not say that the temptation of gratifying others, & at the same time & by the same means making one's self happy, is too alluring to be neglected a single moment; however you must allow me to be thus explicit & candid, that it must in great measure depend upon the extent of what will be necessary to be done for your service, & how far my funds may be adequate, as well as my [having ?] equal to attain that object. In the mean time only rest assured of my good wishes and good intentions. I am, dear Mrs Robinson, very sincerely yours, George P[17]

This is the only surviving letter from the Prince to his one-time Perdita, sympathetic, emotionally self-indulgent, and in contrast to all those former ones, promising nothing. Nor did he come to her rescue. It is true that he was always in debt himself, but that did not prevent him helping the Duchess of Devonshire when she was in difficulties through her addiction to gambling; Christopher Hibbert, George IV's biographer, reveals that he would, discreetly, put money into her bank account.[18] Mary was unlikely to have learnt about these acts of generosity, but for the rest of her life she was to see the Prince of Wales indulging himself in expensive projects such as Carlton House, and feel bitter that he would do nothing for her beyond the agreed allowance.

Mary had carried portable property (like the Prince's miniature) away from London in anticipation of creditors seizing her Berkeley Square effects. When these were eventually put up for sale in January 1785, the auctioneer offered to return the goods if anyone would stand surety of £250 for them; no one replied. The Gainsborough half-portrait was knocked down for 32 guineas.[19] Not everything was put up for auction; furniture to the value of £116 4s was taken in lieu of the unpaid rent. A list of what was seized gives some idea of the elegant life Mary had led; for example, from the Front Room were taken:

> A Steel Stove Fender Poker Tongs and Shovell, A Wilton Carpet, Two large Pier Glasses in gilt Frames, One chimney Glass to match, Two double-branched gilt Gerondoles, Two gilt Pier Tables with marble Tops, three Green Lustring window curtains with gilt Cornices, six Cabriole Elbow Chairs white and gold to match, leather Cushions filled with Feathers and green Manchester striped Cases Two Elbow Chairs and Stool to match a Sofa and Squab to correspond a three Leaf folding Fire Screen covered with Silk japaned Frame.[20]

It was a repeat of Nicholas Darby's debacle in Bristol.

At the time of the sale Mary was no longer in England to be humiliated; on 13 August previously the *Post* had announced her departure for France, not unsympathetically:

> *Mrs Robinson* has been obliged within these few days to leave England for the Continent for the recovery of her health. She has lost almost the use of her limbs, and upon her journey was lifted in and out of her carriage. Her disorder is of a rheumatic gout of so obstinate a nature that her recovery is doubtful.

Three days later a paragraph of moral reflection was more brutal:

> The example of the *Perdita*, which two or three years ago was of the most dangerous kind to the beautiful and the thoughtless of her sex, is now as salutary; a life of wanton dissipation has reduced her to penury and distress; poverty, with all its horrors surrounds her; her constitution and the use of her limbs are done; death stares her in the face . . . To view the Perdita *now*, would be a lesson indeed![21]

Tarleton did not leave immediately with Mary but with the Prince took part in a three-day race meeting at Uppark. There on both 17 and 18 August he beat his friend George Hanger, a companion in the American war, on a horse called *Speranza* – hope.[22] Perhaps he carried that thought with him as he then joined Mary in France.

She was, as the *Post* intimated, now in a pitiful condition. When John Tarleton saw her with Ban in October he wrote to his mother:

> Mrs Robinson is in a bad state of health & cannot in my opinion survive the Winter, as she is most dreadfully afflicted with the Rheumatism – I had the satisfaction of dining with him [Ban] on Friday last & was informed that she intended to reside here the whole season – if her health would permit her.[23]

Her wealth too, he might have added, as 'here' was not an obscure little country cottage but the Hotel de Russie in the Rue de Richelieu, Paris. All she had to live on was the Prince's annuity; disagreeable as it must have been Mary had had to write to Colonel Hotham for her quarterly allowance, as she explains in another letter to the Prince (which also reveals her real motive for staying on the continent):

> My dear Sir,
>
> Colonel Hotham will perhaps inform your Royal Highness of my having apply'd for the last quarter of my annuity, if it is more convenient to you to pay it half yearly, I will with pleasure wait till that time, wishing in every respect to do what is most agreeable to your Royal Highness.
>
> I should not have made any application to Colonel Hotham, but being in want of money (on account of Lord Maldens neglecting to

pay his annuity these *fifteen months* past,) – will I trust be deem'd a sufficient apology. –

As I fear I shall not dare to return to England for some time, I shall be infinitely happy in executing any order your Royal Highness will honor me with during my residence in Paris. I have the honor of subscribing myself

Your Royal Highness's affectionate and faithful servant

Mary Robinson[24]

Mary was not a hypocrite, and would not have subscribed herself 'affectionate' if she had not meant it; the letters to and from the Prince show that past animosity was over.

After she left England, Mary's precise movements are not easy to trace. On 15 December the *Herald* reported that 'The lovely, though ill-fated Robinson, the now too-verified *Perdita*, winters it in the south of France, upon the scanty pittance gleaned from her amorous treasure'. Her letter to the Prince from Paris was written mid-January, then another report in the *Herald* of 11 February claimed that she was with the Duc de Lauzun at his chateau in the south of France. She thought of taking up the invitation of her merchant brother, John Darby, to make her home with him in Leghorn (Livorno); that she did not do so is explained in the *Memoirs* as a consequence of a letter from her physician, Sir John Elliot, urging her to try the spa waters of Aix-la-Chapelle. But her decision was probably not quite so clear-cut; her relationship with Tarleton complicated matters, and living with a brother would have cost her her independence. Italy remained a pipe-dream as she headed north to the spa towns in the border areas of France and Germany.

Spa itself (in modern Belgium), its name synonymous with all hydropathic resorts, was the foremost of such towns in terms of social cachet; the London daily papers frequently printed news of its eminent arrivals and in July 1785 the *Herald* claimed Mrs Robinson as a visitor. But we know more of her stays in 1786 and '87 in Aix-la-Chapelle and St Amand. The baths at Aix, or Aachen, have a long history going back to Roman times, and later the Emperor Charlemagne. But it was in the late seventeenth century that Aix developed into a fashionable resort, when the town bought land outside the gates and erected bath houses, drinking fountains, an assembly hall, covered promenade, guest houses and a casino; famous visitors included Handel, Mozart, Voltaire and Casanova.[25] The bathing facilities were sophisticated, with steam baths and pumps which directed jets of water 'on the whole body, or any particular part, and from different heights and directions'.[26] The water could also be drunk, though it had a 'singular and disagreeable taste' and an unpleasant smell. Perhaps that was why the vapour baths were 'impregnated with aromatic odours' and the waters of the Bains de la Rose, which Mary used, strewn with rose leaves. She found friends in Aix of intellectual and social standing, the Duc and Duchesse du Châtelet. The Duc had been French Ambassador to London, though before Mary's years of notoriety, where he had formed a friendship with Lord Mansfield, the Lord Chief Justice; his mother was the remarkable *femme savante*, the Marquise du Châtelet, who had been the mistress of Voltaire and who translated Newton's *Principia* into French. The Duc had married her god-daughter, who had also been a pupil of Voltaire. Unbiassed by Mrs Robinson's English reputation as Perdita, they entertained her with 'balls, concerts and rural breakfasts', while younger members of the family beguiled nights when pain kept her awake by 'singing her favourite airs to the accompaniment of the mandolin' beneath her windows.[27] If no cure could be effected, the treatments and the kindness she experienced were restorative.

But at the end of the year there was further cause of distress: the death of Nicholas Darby. Whatever his faults as a father she was proud of what he had achieved and she shared his resentment at his treatment by the British authorities both over Lapland and more recently. In 1783 Darby had distinguished himself at the siege of Gibraltar, where as master of his own small fighting ship he had engaged the enemy till his rigging was almost shot away; afterwards he saved many Spanish sailors from drowning, or perishing in the flaming wrecks. For his gallantry he was commended by the Admiralty, but that was as far as the Board's gratitude went. He therefore offered his services to the Empress Catherine of Russia who had made it known that Russia was seeking British officers (England had been supplying naval personnel since the time of Peter the Great). Despite being over sixty years old Darby obtained a commission and departed for St Petersburg, leaving behind his aging wife and sick daughter. After two years in the Russian Imperial Service he expected to be made an admiral, but on 5 December 1785 death 'put a stop to his career', an appropriate phrase in the *Memoirs* for a man who had always put his own advancement before his family's well-being.[28] But Mary seems not to have blamed him for neglect, giving expression to her grief in an 'Ode to the Memory of My Lamented Father'. It is a panegyric to her father's courage not unlike the 'Ode to Valour' which she dedicated to Tarleton in the first flush of their relationship. She celebrates Captain Darby's spirit in the face of adversity, when

> . . . with a soul sublimely brave,
> Didst thou endure the dashing wave;
> Still buffeting the billows rude,
> By all the shafts of woe, undaunted, unsubdued![29]

His misfortunes in life she ascribes to 'the wily SNAKE – INGRATITUDE'; unspoken but surely part of the feeling of the poem is her sense that she too has been its victim.

She may also have been victim the following summer of a cruel joke. It was with considerable shock that she read in a copy of the *Post* dated 14 July 1786 that 'Mrs Robinson, the once famous *Perdita*, died a few days ago at Paris'. Mary found her 'death' attributed to a despondency brought on by straitened circumstances and the loss of her reputation as a 'Cyprian devotee'; she was enraged with her description as 'the natural daughter of a Gentleman, who held a commission in the army', born in Ilminster in Somersetshire of a mother called 'Derby [who] formerly kept the George Inn in that town'. The paper reflected on a woman who 'would have been an ornament to her sex' had she not succumbed to flattery, folly and vice, though there was some more generous assessment of her career and character:

> She was possessed of literary abilities. A Farce of her own writing was brought out for her benefit at Drury-Lane Theatre; and several other practical productions have at different times appeared in the public prints, of which she was the author. Her abilities, as an

> actress, was [*sic*] above mediocrity, but did not place her as the first of her profession. She was genteel in her manners, delicate in her person, and beautiful in her features. Her heart was open to the feelings of humanity, of which the late Mrs Baddeley was a striking example;– Mr[s]. R— relieved her when in Chelsea, in the most deplorable and wretched situation that the helpless woman could be in.[30]

Three weeks later, but without apology, the paper published Mary's rebuttal:

> Sir,
> With astonishment I read in a *Morning Post* . . . a long account of my *death*, and a variety of circumstances respecting *my life*, equally void of the smallest foundation.
>
> I have the satisfaction of informing you, that so far from being *dead*, I am in the most perfect state of health; except for a trifling lameness, of which, by the use of the baths at this place, I have every reason to hope, I shall recover in a month or six weeks.[31]

She wrote of her pride in 'Captain Darby, whose *legitimate* daughter I had the happiness of being' and who had died commander of a ship of seventy-four guns in the Russian service, 'beloved and regretted by all his connections and acquaintance'. The slur on her mother was corrected with the tart addition that 'Ilminster is a place to which I am a total stranger'. Her mother had known the area, but she was not going to admit that.

Despite its gravity of tone the 'death' announcement is probably a spoof. Two weeks before there had been a notice in the *Post* saying that 'of Mrs Robinson, once so famed, the world hears nothing', a remark which could have set someone to plan a good jest.[32] One clue is the facetious cause of death: no one dies of loss of reputation as a courtesan (in Paris too: Oscar Wilde would have rumbled the jokester at once). Another is the degrading of Mary's parentage, of which she was proud and therefore easy to catch on the quick. The reference to Sophia Baddeley is also illuminating. In the years following Mary's visit in her phaeton in all her glory, Mrs Baddeley had suffered from a nervous disorder that affected her walking, and she had to be supported by charity in her last years; her fate, like Mary's, was taken as a moral lesson. If the death notice is indeed a hoax, a likely candidate for perpetrator is Tarleton's friend the incorrigible rogue George Hanger, who had been a supporter of Mrs Baddeley; once when she was debarred from the Pantheon he led a group which physically forced her entry. To the King's disgust Hanger, whose witty memoirs, *The Life Adventures and Opinions of Col. George Hanger*, are prefaced with a woodcut of himself on the gallows, was one of the Prince's set, men who apart from drinking, gambling and whoring loved horse-play and practical jokes. Possibly the reference to the George Inn is a clue to his identity. Certainly, if the death notice was designed to draw Mrs Robinson into response, she rose to the bait.

But the lameness was more than 'trifling', and in the following summer Mary made trial of the mud baths of St Amand. There is a simple drawing, perhaps by twelve-year-old Maria, of the cottage she rented, and it looks attractive, with a thatched roof, roses round the walls, and set in a garden surrounded by trees.[33] But the spa itself was unpleasant, its smell described by Dr John Ash in 1788 as 'more disagreeable than usual'.[34] The *Memoirs* refer in disgust to the 'receptacles of loathsome mud' and the 'distasteful ditches' of St Amand; according to Dr Ash there were more than a hundred baths within a building resembling a greenhouse, separated from each other by wooden frames. Patients were immersed partially or up to the armpits, according to their affliction, 'either in an erect posture, or resting on the surface of the boue [mud], with blankets or a sheet interposed, for some hours'.[35] Afterwards they were carried to a hot bath to be cleansed of the clinging black mud and noisome 'reptiles' – presumably leeches – which, according to the *Memoirs*, fastened to them. A register was kept of cases and signed by the patients, detailing their states before and after treatment; Dr Ash could have read Mary's notes, but for her there was no miraculous cure.

The years of continental wandering were spent in more than a vain search for health, however. No longer engaged in a hectic social round she had leisure to devote to writing and study, in conjunction with the tuition of her daughter. We know from a footnote in Maria's own novel, *The Shrine of Bertha*, that a 'Language-Master' was engaged for her who had been tutor also of Charlotte Buff, immortalised by Goethe in *The Sorrows of Werther*, and Mary herself may have shared the tutoring, perfecting the German which she later used in translation work.[36] But Mary probably undertook much of Maria's education herself; the success of her instruction is seen in the effectiveness of her daughter's own writing, not least in her overseeing of the publication of her mother's complete poetical works following her death. Though Mary had always written poems, from this time onwards their composition became a natural recourse. She also thought further of writing for the theatre; on 23 November 1785 the *Herald* announced that 'Mrs Robinson has lately written a comic opera: the scene lies at Villa Franca [Villefranche], and the principal character is a pretended experimental philosopher, who is visited by ladies of all nations to learn the effects of animal magnetism'. It sounds a promising subject for a farce, drawing on memories of Dr Graham, but a month later the paper reported that none of Drury Lane's players knew of any plans for its production.

The principal literary preoccupation of these years, however, was for Tarleton, in helping him to write his *Campaigns of 1780 and 1781 in the Southern Provinces of North America.* When military commanders lay down their swords they tend to pick up their pens, especially when self-justification is an imperative. The overall commander in America, Sir Henry Clinton, and Lord Cornwallis his second-in-command, had already sparred over responsibility for defeat, but had agreed on one thing; as Robert D. Bass puts it, it appeared to them that on 17 January 1781, 'Lieutenant Colonel Banastre Tarleton lost the battle [Cowpens] that lost the campaign that lost the war that lost the American colonies'.[37] Tarleton naturally wanted to exculpate himself. The book, published on 17 March 1787 at £1 6*s* a copy, is a handsome quarto volume which includes well-produced, hand-coloured maps, and transcriptions of related documents. The tone of the writing is measured and detached; it is in the third person, a fitting mode for what is a general rather than personal record. In writing, as in self-display, Mrs Robinson would prove herself adaptable. She got no credit for the work, but some knew her as author; warning Cornwallis of Tarleton's intentions, Lieutenant-General Grant wrote saying that 'he does not mean – or rather the author to whom he lends his name does not mean – to compliment [you]'.[38] Tarleton and Cornwallis had fallen out, Cornwallis having been angered when the young man did not follow the prescribed path for him in France. In consequence, when Cornwallis was finally posted as Commander-in-chief to India, he did not take Tarleton with him, and in turn, Tarleton switched support to Clinton.

The *Campaigns* were in general favourably received, but Tarleton's enemy, Roderick MacKenzie, immediately published a series of 'Strictures' on them, condemning Tarleton with such malevolence that on his friend's behalf Hanger undertook a response. *An Address to the Army* ridiculed the errors in MacKenzie's account and revealed his malice (Hanger also argued that the decisive failure in North America was not military but naval, when the French fleet was allowed to cross the Atlantic unmolested).[39] There were no profits to be made from the *Campaigns*, but Ban's family agreed to pay him an allowance, so he took up again the life of a man-about-town, gambling, playing cricket, going to the races, attending boxing matches. He rejoined Mary in Paris in the winter of 1787, and no doubt found a little woman or two at other times. In the summer of 1788 there was another Westminster election, a very violent affair, with Tarleton and Hanger among those accused by the *Post* of being 'bludgeoners': using heavy sticks against political opponents. It was said that Mrs Robinson lent her vis-à-vis in Fox's support.[40]

Mary had returned to London at the beginning of the year, 'having appealed without success to every remedy on the Continent for the restoration of her limbs' and said by the *Post* to be 'deeply affected and oppressed in spirits'.[41] It was hardly surprising; she had returned to a social scene in which she could no longer fully participate, and after two and a half years of disability must have known that it was permanent (it is to her credit that she was never to blame Tarleton for what had happened). Nevertheless, by April she was reported to be in good looks, living stylishly in Clarges Street in a house near to him. She began to entertain, and both the Prince and the Duke of York 'frequently honoured her residence with their presence'.[42] But in the summer she withdrew herself to Brighton, principally for the sake of Maria, who had been 'threatened with a consumptive disorder' and advised to try sea-bathing. It was a melancholy period for Mary, worried both about her daughter and her own future. That had become complicated by a quarrel with Ban, over what we do not know; he did not come to Brighton but went north to Liverpool to campaign ahead of the next general election.

The quiet time by the sea at least enabled her to devote time to poetry. A new daily had been launched, the *World*, which made a feature of its publication of poetry, and Mrs Robinson became a regular contributor under a variety of pseudonyms. On 31 October a poem with a very personal theme was printed as by 'Laura', but authorship of 'Lines to Him Who Will Understand It' ('Them' in later versions) would have been recognised by Tarleton. Not for the last time she appealed to her lover through verse. She reveals her plans to leave for Italy, to forget her sorrows in its landscapes, and to absorb herself in history, philosophy, and poetry. Yet she also expresses yearning to recapture love, in the knowledge that his image will always present itself to her:

> Driven by my FATE, where'er I go,
> O'er burning plains, o'er hills of snow,
> Or on the bosom of the wave
> The howling tempest doom'd to brave,–
> Where'er my lonely course I bend,
> Thy image shall my steps attend;
> Each object I am doom'd to see
> Shall bid remembrance PICTURE THEE.[43]

Whether Tarleton read and was touched by the lines or not, the relationship survived, and Mary stayed in England.

She had taken lodgings in a cottage hard against the sea wall and, as if to prove Reynolds prophetic, spent hours watching the sea dashing itself on the beach beneath. There, during one wakeful night, she witnessed a disturbing incident. After she had watched a small boat struggle ashore she saw two fishermen bear from it the body of another; unable to revive him they disappeared, abandoning the corpse on the beach. Next day it lay there still, while 'bathers passed and repassed with little concern'. While many came to look, none would take responsibility for the body:

> Mrs Robinson, humanely indignant at the scene which passed, exerted herself, but without success, to procure by subscription a small sum for performing the last duties to a wretched outcast. Unwilling, by an ostentatious display of her name, to offend the higher and more fastidious female powers, she presented to the fishermen her own contribution, and declined further to interfere.

> The affair dropped; and the body of the stranger, being dragged to the cliff, was covered by a heap of stone, without the tribute of a sigh or the ceremony of a prayer.[44]

Probably a third-person rendering of her own writing, it is clear that Mary identified with the unclaimed, unsanctified corpse, victim of an uncaring society. The episode troubled her mind, and in the year of her own death she gave it imaginative expression in 'The Haunted Beach'. This poem fictionalises the experience, making the wretched deceased one who alone of a crew survives shipwreck, only to be murdered as he reaches shore for the gold he carries with him:

> The Spectre band, his messmates brave
> Sunk in the yawning ocean,
> While to the mast he lash'd him fast
> And brav'd the storm's commotion.
> The winter moon, upon the sand
> A silv'ry carpet made,
> And mark'd the Sailor reach the land,
> And mark'd his murd'rer wash his hand
> Where the green billows play'd.[45]

The fisherman-murderer is, by heavenly compulsion, forced to live out his remaining life in wretchedness on the haunted shore. The poem shows the influence of 'The Rime of the Ancient Mariner', and was admired by Coleridge.[46] But unlike the Mariner who finds redemption through confession, Robinson's murderer, like the poet herself, cannot be free from the consequences of a single act:

> But, destin'd mis'ry to sustain,
> He wastes, in Solitude and Pain
> A loathsome life away.

The lonely isolation of sea, sands and jutting cliffs, wrecked ship with phantom crew, images Mary's later life; like the victim and assassin of her poem she was never to escape from the haunted landscape of her own calamity.

10

The English Sappho

This ingenious and celebrated lady has attracted the attention of the public, both by her personal charms, and her mental accomplishments; and who can withstand the united powers of beauty and of wit?
(Review of *Poems*, by Mrs M. Robinson, *Monthly Review*, December 1791)

On 4 May 1791 a small but handsomely bound volume with marbled end papers was published. It was called, simply, *Poems*. The book had been printed on quality paper and 'in his best stile of neatness' by John Bell, book-seller founder of the *World* and later the *Oracle*, daily papers in whose pages many of the poems had first appeared. Publication had been made possible by an impressive list of 600 subscribers, whose names flow over sixteen pages. As Roger Lonsdale has shown, volume publication by subscription was an option adopted by several women poets, one amassing a list of 2,000 subscribers.[1] But in terms of rank and fame none could rival Mrs Robinson's prestigious list. The preliminary page reads:

HIS ROYAL HIGHNESS
George Prince of Wales

❖

HIS ROYAL HIGHNESS
Frederick Duke of York

❖

HIS ROYAL HIGHNESS
William Henry Duke of Clarence

❖

HIS ROYAL HIGHNESS
William Duke of Gloucester

❖

HIS SERENE HIGHNESS
The Duke of Orleans
❖
HIS SERENE HIGHNESS
Prince Frederick Duke of Würtemberg

Among the other names are no fewer than sixteen Dukes and Duchesses, thirty-three Earls and Countesses, and Honourables, Right Honourables, baronets, and lords and ladies in abundance. Many of the 'envelopes' on which Mary wrote her memoirs are dated between March and April 1790, and are annotated with the names of these illustrious personages; they must have contained their subscription promises.

The theatrical world was represented by the managers Sheridan and George Colman, playwrights Richard Cumberland and Arthur Murphy, and actresses Dorothy Jordan, Elizabeth Billington and the singer Madame Mara. Royal Academicians Sir Joshua Reynolds, Philippe de Loutherbourg and Richard Cosway were subscribers, and journalist friends the Reverend Henry Bate (or Bate-Dudley as he had become) and John Taylor (a drama critic who had edited the *Morning Post*). Among politicians were Charles Fox, Richard Fitzpatrick and James Hare (who had written so rudely of Mary in 1782), William Addington, Speaker of the House of Commons, and the newly promoted Colonel Banastre Tarleton, who had achieved his ambition of becoming one of Liverpool's two MPs in 1790. He must be credited with securing the sponsorship of fellow MPs and army personnel (including George Hanger and Gerard Lake, who had once advised the Prince to avoid a 'certain sort of Ladies'); despite their previous hostility to Mrs Robinson, all Ban's family, including his mother, subscribed for copies. Mary's brother John had died the previous year but her mother and her remaining brother George and his wife were subscribers (George, like John Darby, had become a merchant in north Italy). As the *Gentleman's Magazine* noted, the list comprehended 'almost the whole circle of Rank, Fortune, and Fashion of the Country'.[2] All that was lacking, it slyly remarked, was any representative from the '*Bench of Bishops*'.

No doubt Mrs Robinson sought neither the company nor approval of bishops, but the omission encapsulates what was to be her problem during the last decade of her life, when she sought to reinvent herself as a serious writer but could not totally rid herself of her former identity as Perdita. Though so many ladies of the fashionable world agreed to pay their guineas for a copy of *Poems* (payment was on collection from 45 Clarges Street) it is unlikely that they would have left cards inviting the author to one of their card parties, concerts or conversaziones. Moreover the Royal Highnesses so prominently featured were none of them known for probity (the grossly fat Duke of Würtemburg was to marry the Princess Royal in 1797, against public suspicion that he had ill-treated his first wife and possibly even connived at her death). Despite its meditative quality the frontispiece engraving by Thomas Burke, taken from Reynolds's second portrait, also looked back to the time when Mary was accounted the foremost of the Cyprian crew. As the sceptical *Gentleman's Magazine* put it:

> We are inclined to apprehend that, had she been less distinguished by her personal graces and accomplishments, by the impression which her beauty and captivating manners have generally made, her poetical taste might have excited the complacent approbation of her friends, with little attention, and with less reward, from the publick.

Other critics were more generous, if a little bemused by the *Poems*. How was it possible to connect the frivolous woman of 1780s gossip with a writer of pensive odes, elegies and sonnets? Commentators tended to connect the beauty and elegance of the author with the beauty and elegance of her verse, as if the personal graces of the writer transmitted a seductive quality to the poetry. That she acquired the title 'The English Sappho', possibly at her own instigation, may have added to this sense of being wooed.[3]

Yet *Poems* is a volume of high seriousness, and the titles of the odes which open the volume indicate Mrs Robinson's ambition as a poet. The 'Ode to the Muse' is followed by odes to Reflection, Envy, Health, Vanity, Melancholy (pre-Keats), Despair, *two* Odes to the Nightingale (also pre-Keats but like him seeking solace for personal distress in the bird's song), Adversity, Beauty, the Moon, Meditation, Della Crusca, and Valour (the poem dedicated to Tarleton). Odes are of their nature passionate, declamatory and of elevated diction, but a comparison might be made between her poetry and the former life, where Perdita took pride in colourful, highly ornamented chariots, in the extravagance of language in which the sentiments are conveyed. The 'Ode to the Muse' opens the volume:

> O, LET me seize thy pen sublime
> That paints, in melting dulcet rhyme,
> The glowing pow'r, the magic art,
> Th' extatic raptures of the Heart . . .[4]

To a modern ear the language is overblown, but Mrs Robinson had been influenced by an ornate style made fashionable by the poet Robert Merry (also a subscriber).

Merry, yet another man who had abandoned his legal studies and fled to the continent after squandering his money, settled in Florence where he became the centre of a literary coterie including Hester Piozzi, Bertie Greatheed and William Parsons. They were known as the Della Cruscans, after the Academy of Della Crusca there, and when Merry returned to England in 1787 he sent poems to the *World* using Della Crusca as his pen-name. Soon his poetic personality was exerting a compelling effect on female poets. To 'The Adieu and Recall to Love', which begins by banishing Cupid but ends 'O rend my heart with ev'ry pain/But let me, let me love again', one Anna Matilda replied: 'O! SEIZE again thy golden quill/And with its point my bosom thrill'. Thereafter the couple, unknown to each other in real life, conducted an amorous relationship through the *World*'s pages, the poetic courtship made all the more intriguing by the pseudonyms.[5] Then Laura (Mrs Robinson) entered the scene. Her 'Lines to him who will understand it' prompted a sympathetic response from Leonardo ('LAURA! I heard thy warbled woes/At fading Twilight's solemn close'); Leonardo was another of Merry's pseudonyms and Anna Matilda became jealous ('Yes, write to LAURA! Speed thy sighs/Tell her her DELLA CRUSCA dies'). With a *ménage-à-trois* established, the poetical soap opera reached its peak. It came to an end after Merry discovered that his 'enchanting Maid', Anna Matilda, was in reality the dramatist Hannah Cowley, a respectably married matron in her forties. The mutual admiration of Della Crusca and Laura continued however, and Mrs Robinson paid several poetic tributes to Merry in the 1791 *Poems*.

It is easy to mock the quivering sensitivities of Della Cruscanism, but its association of feeling with natural phenomena leads literary historians to discuss it in connection with Romanticism.[6] However, the movement was dealt, if not a death blow, at least a knock-out punch by the acerbic William Gifford in his satire *The Baviad* (1791). Gifford's couplets are laboured, but his prose introduction to *The Baviad* sufficiently ridicules the movement when 'not a day passed without an amatory epistle fraught with thunder and lightning . . . Laura Maria, Carlos, Orlando, Adelaide, and a thousand nameless names caught the infection; and from one end of the kingdom to the other, all was nonsense and Della Crusca'. Laura Maria and Adelaide were pen-names of Mrs Robinson; in his verse satire Gifford is heartless about her: 'See Robinson forget her state, and move/On crutches tow'rds the grave . . .'.[7] Despite his contempt, however, Mrs Robinson thrived as a poet and through gathering together all her pieces under different newspaper identities, and reprinting them under her own name and with such wide support, she acquired literary confidence and discovered new poetic voices. Poetry was to be her great solace in her years of declining health, something to which she could turn at moments of personal crisis, and use to comment on contemporary events. It was also an art form which gave satisfaction in its mechanical aspects; she told John Taylor in 1794 that 'I am never happy but when I am *tagging* rhymes'.[8] Coleridge was to admire her particularly as a metricist, writing to Southey of the 'fascinating Metre' of 'The Haunted Beach', and exclaiming 'ay! that woman has an ear'.[9] In poetry Mary Robinson did *not* move on crutches.

Mrs Robinson had another literary triumph when on 31 January 1792 her first novel, *Vancenza*, sold out before noon on the day of publication. A second edition was ready a week later; third, fourth and fifth editions followed. The novel's success was very gratifying to the author, and must have been a relief too, as this work was not published by subscription. Collecting subscriptions ensured a specific number of sales, providing of course that everyone paid up; there is no way of knowing how many of Mary's 600 subscribers had defaulted, but there must have been more than a handful, for in the *Oracle* of 26 October 1793, just before she published her second volume of poems, she inserted a notice 'respectfully' requesting those who had not yet paid their guineas for the first, to do so. *Vancenza* therefore was produced by John Bell 'for the authoress', where she paid the printing costs plus a small commission on each copy sold, after which the profits were hers. It was the riskiest method (she might alternatively have sold the copyright for a fixed sum, or entered into a profit-sharing arrangement with the printer), but also potentially the most lucrative if she judged price and print run successfully.[10] Publishing on commission was the method used by Jane Austen for several of her novels, with consequent ups and downs: she made a profit of £310 on the first edition of *Mansfield Park* (1814) for example, but lost on the second when copies did not sell.

Characteristically, Mary took a gamble on success; she could have printed a bigger first run, but perhaps the rapid sellout helped stimulate further sales. Unlike her poetry, novel-writing was a commercial venture, even if in the Preface she loftily declared that 'I disdain the title of a Writer of Novels' (worse titles had been bestowed on her before), because 'the species of composition generally known under that denomination, too often conveys a lesson I do not wish to inculcate'. Since many disapproved of novel-reading as frivolous and even corrupting for young (female) minds, she must not be writing for Lydia Languishes. On the other hand she constructed a carefully worded pre-publication advertisement to intrigue a public well-versed in her earlier history. *VANCENZA; or, The DANGERS of CREDULITY*, price 5*s*, was announced with a tantalising epigraph from *Hamlet*: 'Be wary then, best SAFETY lies in FEAR', Laertes' words of warning to Ophelia against listening to the addresses of the Prince. What hints or revelations of the author's past might be found within?

As readers opened *Vancenza*'s pages they would discover that Mary had distanced herself from her own era by setting the novel in fifteenth-century Spain. However, it is a Spain which Isabella and Ferdinand would have had difficulty recognising, its manners and morals being those of late eighteenth-century England, and not a priest of the Inquisition in sight. The physical setting is romance-Gothic territory, an ancient castle placed at the edge of a forest below a 'towering precipice' down which 'rushing torrents scattered their white foam'.[11] In the castle lives fifteen-year-old Elvira, 'The Rose of Vancenza', supremely beautiful and supremely talented (and with Mary's auburn hair), an orphan who has been brought up by her guardian, Count Vancenza, with his widowed sister and her daughter. One day a boar hunt brings to this obscure corner handsome, accomplished Prince Almanza and his friend the Duke del Vero.

Elvira falls in love with the Prince, but he is for the moment preoccupied with manly, chivalrous pursuits. Three weeks later the sound of a guitar in the darkness draws Elvira to her window where she hears a voice calling 'Beautiful Elvira! . . . Accept the heart of your Almanza'. The voice invites her to a meeting in the forest, but she discovers that she has been duped, for it is the Duke del Vero who awaits her; her credulity has exposed her 'to the artifice of an abandoned libertine'. Here the author inserts some moral reflections on the difficulties of preserving female reputation and, in a passage which her audience would have recognised as being less to do with the heroine than an eloquent plea on her own behalf, declares:

> Small is the triumph of chastity that has never been assailed by the cunning of a seducer. The snows of Lapland preserve their whiteness and solidity, as long as they escape the dissolving glances of the burning orb. The female heart has little right to exult in its resolution, 'till it has resisted the fascinations of pleasure, the voice of insidious flattery, and the fatal allurements of pernicious example.[12]

During a visit to Madrid some villainous plotting leads to the fatal stabbing of the Count, and the three women return grieving to the castle. To them then comes Prince Almanza; he now wants to marry Elvira, and seals the engagement with a kiss '*that angels might have envied!*' (readers' eyebrows no doubt rose). Wedding preparations are underway when Elvira discovers a hidden panel behind a portrait of a beautiful woman. Inside a recess is a gold casket, and inside that a death-bed confession signed 'Madeline Vancenza'. She had been 'the credulous victim of an illicit passion', seduced by the present Prince's father, another Prince Almanza. The child of this ill-omened liaison was of course Elvira. Elvira collapses, and when the young Prince comes to claim his bride he is in time only to hear her exclaim 'I cannot wed my BROTHER!' before she sinks into 'the arms of DEATH'.[13]

Readers of *Vancenza* would have enjoyed measuring up the two Princes Almanza with the contemporary Prince and their knowledge of Mary's relationship with him, but she had cleverly opted for dead perfidy and living virtue, so no offence was given. Reactions in the literary journals were mixed. (Reviews in these journals, the *Analytical*

Review, *Critical Review*, *English Review*, *Monthly Review* and others, were anonymous and theoretically impartial.) The *English Review* suggested that it would be a churlish critic who refused to recognise Mrs Robinson's 'genius', adding that 'we are disposed to think that she has more successfully climbed the Parnassian heights than any female votary of the muses which this country has produced', praise which could hardly have been exceeded.[14] The critic of the *Analytical Review*, however, found *Vancenza* moral but surprisingly insipid: 'we expected to have met with more passion and character in the production of a female who has not been an idle spectator of life'.[15] The reviewer complains of a 'milk and water' heroine and condemns the construction of the novel for lacking a 'connecting thread', episodes being introduced only to 'spin it out'. This criticism can be made of other of Mary's novels as she dashes into the writing without sufficient organisation; the time she took over *Vancenza* is suggested by her later heroine Martha Morley, who produces a two-volume novel in only six weeks.

Mary Robinson was to publish six more novels: *The Widow* (1794) and *Angelina* (1796), both written in letter form, *Hubert de Sevrac* (1796), *Walsingham* (1797), *The False Friend* (1799) and *The Natural Daughter* (1799). The 1790s was the decade of the Gothic novel, and *Vancenza*, with its historical setting, isolated castle, mysterious panel and touch of incest (as in Walpole's *The Castle of Otranto* of 1764) is of that genre, though without the ghostly hauntings which are usually a feature. Mary did not attempt a historical setting again, but in other respects *Vancenza* has much in common with the later novels. Plots tend to melodrama, with beautiful young heroines of refined sensibility threatened by the devious designs of rapacious men and scheming women. But Mary was clever in springing surprises on readers as well as heroines; in *Vancenza* the significance of the subtitle seems to have been revealed, but a more horrid truth emerges at the end. *The False Friend* was to trick similarly: the false friend appears to be an unscrupulous clergyman, Treville, but is finally discovered to be Lord Denmore, the heroine's guardian and would-be husband, who is revealed as her father (more spine-chilling incest). The most startling revelation, however, is in *Walsingham*, where Sir Sidney, the hero's cousin and apparent rival in love, turns out to be a woman in love with him herself (she was brought up as a boy to preserve an inheritance). Such unexpectedness makes Mrs Robinson's novels page-turners rather than pot-boilers. They also engage the reader's attention biographically. All contain passages where Mary uses her novel to plead for understanding of her past, and they have central figures who represent herself. In *Angelina* she splits herself between two characters: Sophia Clarendon, who is a poet (the inclusion of poetry was a feature of novels then), and Angelina, a woman of Mary's years, who like her has a 'profusion of dark auburn hair' and eyes of the deepest blue. She has been abandoned by her lover, Lord Acreland (affianced to the unwilling Sophia), but he nevertheless instructs a friend to trace Angelina. In a remote Welsh village the friend discovers a mysterious 'woman in white' living in an old castle tower; she has been observed with a 'small picture, all done round with precious stones, which she will sit and cry over for hours without ceasing'.[16] *Angelina* has its sentimental aspects, but it is a spirited novel, with sharply-drawn characters such as Sophia's father, Sir Edward, both a glutton and chauvinist; he says that 'Women have no business ever to read – or to write either', but his sister proves the quicker-witted. Criticising his 'guzzling' she says:

> 'I am sure it is no wonder that you are such a monstrous porpoise.'
> 'Why yes,' replied Sir Edward, 'all the city will bear witness that I am of some weight.'
> 'So is an elephant, brother,' said Lady Watkins.[17]

At her best Mrs Robinson is a lively satirist, often drawing on her own experiences, especially in the later novels. In *The Natural Daughter*, for example, Martha Morley offers her novel to a publisher who advises her:

> . . . if your fertile pen can make a story out of some recent popular event, such as an highly-fashioned elopement, a deserted, distracted husband, an abandoned wife, an ungrateful runaway daughter, or a son ruined by sharpers; with such a title as 'Noble Daring; or, The Disinterested Lovers;' '*Chacun à son Tour*; or, The Modern Husband;' 'Passion in Leading Strings; or, Love's Captive;' 'Modern Wives and Antique Spouses,' 'Old Dowagers and Schoolboy Lovers,' or anything from real life of equal celebrity and notoriety, your fortune is made.[18]

Unfortunately for Martha, however, it is the publisher who makes a fortune from her novel. Martha then turns to poetry and, having written some odes, seeks a patron, as once Mary had approached the Duchess of Devonshire. When she knocks on Lady Eldercourt's door Martha explains to the housekeeper:

> 'I wish to dedicate some Odes to her ladyship; for I have been informed that she is the patroness of the Muses.'
> 'Of whom?' inquired the housekeeper.
> 'The Muses.'
> 'They are not on our visiting list: I cannot say that I ever heard of them. Are they noble?'
> 'Of the most exalted nobility!' said Mrs Morley smiling. 'They are nine lovely sisters.'
> 'And patronised by my lady? Impossible!' interrupted the housekeeper.[19]

Mary could joke at her own expense too. In Lady Eldercourt's drawing-room Martha is quizzed by one of the guests:

> 'Pray, ma'am, do you write in the newspapers?' said the young lady who introduced the conversation: 'Are you Anna Matilda, or Della Crusca, or Laura Maria? Comical creatures! They have made me shed many a tear, though I never more than half understood them.'[20]

There is nothing so sharp in *Vancenza*. Nevertheless she had reason to congratulate herself in the spring of 1792, and probably did so by inserting this paragraph in the *Oracle*:

> Mrs ROBINSON'S literary productions have been honoured with singular marks of attention. Her Poems have been selected by our best Musical Composers; and WESTALL has employed his exquisite genius in painting a Subject from them, which is now engraving. Several of her Poems have likewise been translated into the French language, and greatly admired in the fashionable world the other side of the water.[21]

(Richard Westall illustrated 'Cupid Sleeping', a poem dedicated to the Duchess of Devonshire.) But if she could celebrate professional success, Mary could not be so complacent about her personal life. And 'the fashionable world' on the other side of the Channel was fast changing for ever.

For liberal-minded Britons, the onset of the French Revolution heralded a golden age of liberty. 'How much the greatest event that ever happened in the world! And how much the best', declared Fox after the fall of the Bastille on 14 July 1789.[22] It was not only the destruction of the old order which that event symbolised, but the inauguration of a new one in the decrees of the National Assembly; when it adopted the Declaration of the Rights of Man, France appeared to have outstripped the achievements of the English 'Glorious Revolution' of 1688. Mary celebrated in a long poem, *Ainsi va le Monde* [Thus goes the world] published in 1791, showing her confidence in the progressive nature of events:

> Who shall the nat'ral Rights of Man deride,
> When Freedom spreads her fost'ring banners wide?
> Who shall contemn the heav'n-taught zeal that throws
> The balm of comfort on a Nation's woes?
> That tears the veil from superstition's eye,
> Bids despots tremble, scourg'd oppression die?[23]

The poem, so spontaneously felt that its 350 lines were written in twelve hours, was also an answer to Edmund Burke's expression of doubt, *Reflections on the Revolution in France*, which warned of the dangers of extremism.[24] For enthusiasts like Fox and Mary he was an old Cassandra, though even in France, the Vicomte de Noailles, veteran of the American war, who had electrified the National Assembly in urging the abolition of all aristocratic privileges, warned of the dangers of anarchy.

Yet there was one category of mankind to whom the Revolution did not extend its ideals of liberty, equality and fraternity: the slaves on their West Indian sugar plantations. In England, however, the abolition of slavery had become a major issue of debate. For Mary Robinson the Rights of Man were as applicable to the African native as to the French peasant, and several poems reveal her outrage for the sufferings of the 'dark sons of pain'.[25] But though they agreed on most political issues, slavery was a subject on which she and Tarleton differed; his family fortunes were built on it and his brothers still engaged in the trade in Liverpool, the foremost port in Europe for slavery. Approximately 100 ships a year set sail from Liverpool, taking goods down to the west coast of Africa to be traded for slaves; appalling cruelty was involved both in the seizure of the Africans and in their transportation in the slave ships, lying shackled in rows in filthy, reeking holds. Consciences were aroused and William Wilberforce led the anti-slavery campaign in the House of Commons, where two great debates were staged in 1791 and 1792. But each time the Member for Liverpool rose to oppose 'a speculation which, if carried into effect, must eventually prove destructive to the interests of the country'.[26] On the first occasion Wilberforce's motion was heavily defeated; a year later public opinion had been strongly mobilised against the trade and the House carried an amendment that it 'ought to be gradually abolished'.[27] Mary reputedly helped Tarleton prepare his parliamentary speeches, though on this subject it would have been from love, not conviction. But in 1792 he would have had to write his own, because by then he had left her for another woman.

The relationship had been a passionate affair, but given his libertine reputation it is perhaps surprising that he had been faithful so long. Ban must have held to Mary partly out of a sense of guilt following her tragic illness, and partly from his consciousness of her emotional dependence on him. Her health was not good; in May 1791, for example, 'scarcely able to hold herself upright', she sought relief in Bath for what was diagnosed as 'gout' in her head.[28] Illness would have exacerbated her quick temper and sharp tongue, making her difficult to live with at times, though she and Tarleton had separate houses and he largely went his own way, attending Parliament and royal levées, visiting Liverpool for his family and Paris to observe the Revolution. In London he spent much of his time in Brooks's club; if Mary did not squabble with him over slavery it is likely that she nagged him about his gambling, a social vice she deplored, particularly if he sometimes drew on her slender resources for stake-money, as was later claimed. Brooks's ran 'The Bett Book' in which, in handwriting often the worse for drink, members challenged each other on topics of the day. Tarleton makes frequent appearances in it: 'Mr Sheridan bets Col[l] Tarleton one hundred Guineas to fifty that Mr Pitt is first Lord of the Treasury on the 28th of May 1792' (Sheridan won with ease); 'Col. FitzPatrick betts Col. Tarleton 10gs that the slave trade is abolished before Episcopacy' (Tarleton won, but not much).

While Robinson's infidelity had been a matter for indignation, Tarleton's was devastating to Mary's pride. To those in the know her bitterness was made public in the *Oracle* of 12 December 1791, in a poem 'To ——' by 'Julia' which records 'one proud indignant tear' as the 'signal of expiring love'. 'Stanzas Written on the 14th February 1792 to My Once Dear Valentine' was softer in tone, full of yearning; if she sent it to him (what point an undelivered Valentine?) he did not respond. Mary was also in further financial trouble, despite the success of *Vancenza*. Once more she decided to leave England, to revisit Spa and then to travel on to Italy and her brother George. Even for this she needed money, so on 23 July she turned in desperation to Sheridan, telling him what had happened and appealing for a loan:

> You will perhaps be surprised to hear that, after an irreproachable connection of more than *ten years*, I am suffered to depart an *Exile* from my Country, and all my hopes, for a few paltry debts. I sail this evening for *Calais*, *alone*, – broken-hearted.
>
> My state of health is too deplorable to bear description, and I am depressed in spirits beyond what my strength can support. I conjure you not to mention this letter to anyone. I am sufficiently humbled by the base ingratitude of the world, without the additional mortification of public exposure. Since Colonel Tarleton has suffered me to be thus driven a wanderer upon the mercy of an unfeeling world, after having endured every insult from his present low associate, I am resolutely determined never to accept of any favour from him. Will you, my dear Sheridan, do me the kindness to lend me *one* hundred pounds? I will pay you, upon my honour.[29]

Sheridan seems to have obliged, perhaps recalling the 100 guineas won from her former lover. She had added a post-script to her letter: 'Pray, don't tell Tarleton – he will triumph in my sorrows'.

Despite this plea, as she crossed from Dover to Calais next evening Mary composed a last message to Tarleton, both a lament and a renewed declaration of love, using the restless sea as metaphor for her turbulent feelings:

BOUNDING BILLOW, cease thy motion;
Bear me not so swiftly o'er!
Cease thy roaring, foamy OCEAN,
I will tempt thy rage no more.

Ah! within my bosom beating,
Varying passions wildly reign!
LOVE, with proud resentment meeting;
Throbs by turns, of joy and pain!

JOY, that far from foes I wander,
Where their ARTS can reach no more;
PAIN, that woman's heart grows fonder,
When the dream of bliss is o'er! . . .[30]

The poem was sent back to the offices of the *Oracle* (unless it was prepared in advance, but it is more romantic to think of Mary sitting on deck watching the white cliffs disappear, feeling the boat lurching through the crests and troughs of the waves, and reflecting that motion in the poem's bouncing trochaic metre). It was published as by Julia on 2 August, and became one of Mrs Robinson's best-known poems, set to music and sung in many a respectable parlour where she herself would scarcely have been welcome.

Mary was not, in fact, journeying to Calais alone, for though she was without her lover, Maria and her widowed mother went too. But it was a bad time for travelling. France was in turmoil, following its declaration of war on Austria, and an ultimatum from the Prussian Duke of Brunswick. The same edition of the *Oracle* which announced her departure (with the reassurance that readers would not thereby be deprived of 'the elegant Communications of our LAURA MARIA') carried a report of dangerous conditions:

> The principal Towns are full of enraged Troops; and the *Peasantry* are without subordination, and almost without reason. Several parties who were going to *Spa* are returned; and many French Families of distinction are preparing to quit France.[31]

It was impossible to journey on, and they waited in Calais among other frustrated travellers, down-on-their-luck English, and fleeing French aristocrats. The situation deteriorated further after 10 August when the Tuileries, where the royal family had been held as semi-prisoners since the abortive flight to Varennes, was attacked and the King's Swiss Guard massacred. The royal family was taken to the grim fortress inappropriately called the Temple; shortly afterwards a republic was declared. Mary would have gone home, but an 'extreme and alarming indisposition' kept her in Calais.[32]

Stress may also have been a cause of illness, for at some time in August, out of the blue, Thomas Robinson arrived. There is little record of communication between husband and wife, but it can be presumed that he sought money from her whenever he thought she had some to give. In 1780, at the height of her affair with the Prince, Mary had told Sophia Baddeley that Thomas would waylay her when she rode out to take the air, 'at which times he generally emptied her purse', and occasional notices in the press thereafter suggested that Mrs Robinson should pay him an allowance.[32] According to the *Memoirs* he had crossed the Channel to claim his daughter, whom he wished to introduce to his brother, Commodore William Robinson, who was offering to sponsor Maria in society. (In an unpublished note in the manuscript *Memoirs* Mary gives William's addresses as Gower Street and Abinger near Dorking, so he must have prospered in the East Indian Service.) Mary could do little herself to advance Maria's interests as she neared her eighteenth birthday; the elder Robinson could provide her with a dowry and make her marriageable. But there was a catch:

> Miss Robinson received from her new relation the promise of protection and favour, upon condition that she renounced for ever *the filial tie*, which united her to *both* parents.[34]

Was this condition, so contemptuous of the younger brother, known to Thomas beforehand? The proposal was indignantly rejected.

According to the *Memoirs* Mary agreed to go back to England for this interview. But there had been another surprise arrival in Calais: Tarleton. Worn down by poetry presumably, he was anxious to make things up with Mary before travelling on to Paris to assess the political situation for himself. Repossessed of Ban's love Mary speedily recovered her health, and this was the true reason for the family's return to England on 2 September, by good fortune a few hours before an *arrêt* banned all British from leaving France. (It may be noted that the only reference to Tarleton's part in Mary's life in the published *Memoirs*, though much may have been suppressed from the manuscript, is in a footnote which acknowledges a relationship of sixteen years, and the Colonel's 'affectionate attentions' to one of whose sufferings 'he had been the involuntary occasion'.[35])

Mary returned home (now 13 St James's Place) while Tarleton went on to Paris; there he witnessed the horrific September Massacres when upwards of 1,200 prisoners were dragged from the gaols and battered and hacked to death on the pretext of being royalists. He never gave a public account of the horrors he witnessed, though he declared in Parliament that they were such as 'would bring the tears of pity from the most iron heart that ever inhabited the breast of man'. One story, however, is recorded.[36] On 3 September he was dining in a party with the Duc d'Orléans when they were drawn to the window by the howlings of a mob. There, born triumphantly aloft, was a head and other body parts on pikes; imperturbably the Duc declared 'C'est la Lamballe; je la connais à ses cheveaux' [I recognise her hair]. The Princesse de Lamballe, faithful companion of Marie Antoinette, had been dragged from imprisonment, savagely killed and mutilated; reports suggest that the head was taken to her hairdresser to make it recognisable for gloating display to the Queen. When Tarleton did not return because of the difficulty of obtaining a passport it was rumoured that he too had been 'Lamballed', but somehow he wangled one and was back by 29 September.

That evening he accompanied Mary to the theatre, an occasion when she was reported to be 'in good health, and never looked better'.[37] It was probably at this time that Mary gave Ban a gold chain ring as emblem of the bond between them; it came with a tender little poem:

Oh! take these little easy chains
  And may they hold you while you live;
For know, each magic link contains
  The richest treasure I can give!

An emblem - earnest of my love!
  Pure as the gold that forms the toy;
The more 'tis try'd, the more 'twill prove
  Beyond the touch of base alloy.

As even as the links, shall be
  The giver's mind, that scorns to range;
And like the heart ordain'd for thee,
  They may be broke! but cannot change!

Then, take the little shining toy,
  And may it never quit thy sight;
And let it be my proudest joy,
  To know my chains, though lasting, light![38]

In the glow of reunion she even composed an adulatory sonnet to the Prince of Wales. The Prince had found himself very unpopular, following his behaviour during the 1788 crisis over his father's health (the King's supposed 'madness'), and because of his over-spending. But he had been mending his ways, supporting the British constitution in his maiden speech in the House of Lords earlier in the year, and attempting to moderate his expenses.[39] A panegyric was printed in the *Oracle* on 18 October saying that the Prince had gone to Brighton to enjoy 'the unspeakable delight of CONSCIOUS RECTITUDE', in which state 'He WILL HAVE the good report of ENLIGHTENED PENS'; this, undoubtedly written by Mary, paved the way for a sonnet by 'Julia' two days later. It is of no poetic merit, remarkable only for its extraordinary commendation of the Prince as formed for 'SAGE PRECEPTS' to prove 'all trivial, empty Pleasures, VAIN!' This was wishful thinking, but as the chaos and bloodshed increased in France, the Prince, tutored in political thinking by Fox, remained the hope of British liberals.

By the end of 1792 it was only a matter of time before war between Britain and France was declared. Tarleton expressed himself opposed to war, arguing in parliament that though 'no exertion of head, heart, and hand shall be wanting to give vigour and effect to any charge committed to my care' the country ought to negotiate peace, for 'no human being can foresee or controul the fortune of war'.[40] But when on 21 January 1793 Louis XVI, Citizen Capet, was guillotined, war became inevitable and there was a French declaration on 1 February. As Tarleton had warned, the outcome was unpredictable, and a state of war would be almost continuous for twenty-two years. But he was never to play more than a marginal role. Unluckily, at a moment when he was high in the favour of the Duke of York who led the initial campaign in Flanders, he was struck down by persistent illness, said to be rheumatic fever.[41] It took most of 1793 for him to recover, and by then events had moved on. Despite her own helpless state Mary devoted herself to his needs, though in August she herself needed nursing after a horrible accident which was a consequence of her physical dependency. She was staying in Cobham in Surrey when a flight of stone steps down which a servant was carrying her crumbled, and he dropped her. She was badly cut about the head and it was a month before she could return to London.[42] For the rest of the year, however, it was not her own troubles but those of the unfortunate former Queen of France which absorbed Mary.[43] She knew that the revolutionary mob saw the head of La Lamballe as only the forerunner of the one they really wanted: that of the hated Antoinette.

Marie Antoinette's fate preoccupied many British women writers, some (like Mary Wollstonecraft) hostile to her past errors of extravagance and show. Mary's attitude was coloured by the brief encounter she had had with the Queen ten years before when, as pseudo-royalty and dressed by Marie Antoinette's own milliner, the ex-mistress of the Prince of Wales had exchanged looks with the Queen of France in, for her, an intensely intimate moment. Since then the campaign of vilification against the Queen would have increased her sense of identification; if Mary had suffered infinitely less, she had likewise been the victim of lewd pamphleteering. Haunted by the Queen's plight she had already tried to help in the only way she could, by employing her pen.

Mrs Robinson's address to the National Assembly, *Impartial Reflections on the Present Situation of the Queen of France* of 1791 tries, unlike Burke's *Reflections*, to be even-handed, praising the achievements of the Revolution while pleading for the persecuted Queen. In Fox-like terms she salutes it as 'the most glorious achievement in the annals of Europe', and the Assembly members for their 'eloquent debates, and temperate proceedings', a temperance she would like to see extended to their treatment of the Queen.[44] 'Has she not borne her sufferings, her humiliations, her anxieties, with the magnanimity of a Heroine?' she asks, and appeals to the 'moderation, virtue, and discretion' of the Assembly to disprove Burke's assertion that the days of chivalry are at an end.[45] The pamphlet was published as by 'A Friend to Humanity'; it would not be the only time when Mary felt she must protect the cause for which she argued from her name. However, no English plea from whatever source would have altered events two years later, when Robespierre and the Jacobins were in control. The 'Widow Capet' was brought to trial on 14 and 15 October 1793, her once golden hair white, her features haggard, for a trial which was a travesty of justice, the guilty verdict predetermined. The ex-Queen was guillotined on 16 October, news reaching England five days later. Next day the newspapers had black borders, and over the days to come Mary must have read both avidly and with horror the details of the trial, which showed how well the Queen had answered her implacable accusers.

The reasoned argument of the *Impartial Reflections* had achieved nothing; now Mary Robinson paid tribute in impassioned verse.[46] *Monody to the Memory of the Late Queen of France* was published in December with an engraved frontispiece of the Queen as widow, a black-shrouded, unadorned figure whose severity of expression and plainness of attire are in marked contrast to the luxuriance of language with which the poet champions her. Burke had famously depicted Marie Antoinette as Dauphiness, 'just above the horizon . . . glittering like the morning star' (Venus), but Mary's chosen image is of the most powerful (and masculine) of the heavenly bodies:

OH! I have seen her, like a SUN, sublime!
Diffusing glory on the wings of TIME![47]

The poem also celebrates the Queen for her 'DOMESTIC VIRTUES' and charity, and more controversially for her mental accomplishments, her 'Immortal GENIUS!' 'Genius', that spark animating the souls of the elite, was Mary Robinson's highest accolade, and it shows how she wished to link herself with the subject of her poem. In handing the French Queen a laurel crown in verse, she crowns herself too. The *Monody* also makes sweeping criticisms of the path the Revolution has taken since its auspicious beginnings, from the peasant forced to leave land and family for the war to the aristocrat condemned solely for his birth. By the time Mary published this poetic protest many had died for the 'crime' of aristocracy, including some she knew. The Duc d'Orléans, who had voted for the death of Louis XVI, followed him to the guillotine in November; on the last day of the year the Duc de Biron (formerly Lauzun) would perish likewise. The Duc and Duchesse du Châtelet, Mary's hosts in Aix, had also paid the price of their aristocratic births. On the day of his execution the Duc tried to dash out his brains against the prison wall; that failing, he smashed a piece of glass and stabbed himself with the shards, but was dragged bruised and bleeding to the scaffold. Little more than a year after the dinner party attended by Tarleton, he was the only guest 'whose head was left on the shoulders of its owner'.[48]

There is a curious rider to Mary's preoccupation with Marie Antoinette. An unpublished biographical account of Mrs Robinson, written immediately after her death by a young friend, Jane Porter, makes reference to her 1781 visit to France:

> At this time . . . her society was sought by the first literary characters, male and female, in that country. Even Antoinette herself used to say, 'Send for the lovely Mrs Robinson. Let me look at her again, and hear her speak, before I go to sleep!'[49]

Either Miss Porter spun this tale or it was spun to her by Mary. In empathising with the imprisoned Queen, did she fantasise about easing her misery by coming in spirit to read to her, and did she make-believe to friends that it was true?

11

Discontent

Oh, I am TIRED of the *WORLD and all its mortifications*.
(Mary Robinson to John Taylor, 5 October 1794)

'Now I will impart to you a secret,' wrote Mary to her friend John Taylor on 5 October 1794; 'I think that before the 10th of December next I shall quit England for ever'.[1] Restless and at the mercy of her rollercoaster emotions she had decided to accept the invitation of her younger brother George Darby, who was in England on business, to return with him to Italy. For years she had nursed the idea of an Italian escape route from the pressures and, as she saw it, the persecutions of her life, and on this occasion came close to taking it, lured by her brother's offer of a villa which had belonged to the novelist Tobias Smollett. George, who had shared the difficult years of childhood and marriage with her, was the last of her Darby relations; her mother had died the previous summer. Mary grieved deeply for her, though she left no commemorative poem as with her father and brother John who had died suddenly on 7 December 1790 at Leghorn.

John Taylor, the recipient of her news, had trained as an eye-surgeon, but his love of the stage and facility for writing led him to abandon the profession for journalism; he wrote plays himself, became theatre critic of the *Morning Post* and for three years from 1787 its editor. To him Mary had dedicated a long and grandiloquent poem, 'Sight' ('Transcendant gift! But for thy light divine,/Oh! What a chaos were the mind of MAN!').[2] A poetic dabbler himself, every year from 1790 he had sent a poem of admiration to his 'dear mistress of the plaintive lyre'. Mary's letter to him on this occasion, however, was plain grumbling, explaining that she wanted to give up writing because she felt unappreciated:

> Yet, my dear Juan, I shall feel a very severe struggle in quitting those paths of fancy I have been childish enough to admire – false prospects. They have led me into the vain expectation that fame would attend my labours, and my country be my pride. How have I been treated? I need only refer you to the critiques of last month, and you will acquit me of unreasonable instability. When I leave England – adieu to the *muse* for ever! – I will never publish another line while I exist, and even those manuscripts now finished I WILL DESTROY.[3]

Taylor's prompt reply not only soothed but encouraged her into two further letters, in which she re-engaged with the unkind world she had wanted to forget, asking 'What news is there in town?'[4]

Mary had continued her prolific publishing career, both in newspaper and volume form, and at the end of 1793 she had not only issued the second volume of her *Poems*, but adopted a new poetical voice, joining William Gifford, Anthony Pasquin (John Williams) and Peter Pindar (her friend John Wolcot) as a verse-satirist. *Modern Manners*, in two cantos, was published under the ambitious pseudonym of Horace Juvenal, and was thought at first to be by a man. Literary critics are the poem's main target, those who 'With pens, deep drench'd in Satire's *thickest* ink,/*Condemn*, before they condescend to *think*', and it becomes clear that she has Gifford in mind when *The Baviad* is named as causing the muse to blush in shame.[5] The couplets are neat enough, but the poem has no developed argument, probably because with the exception of the *Baviad*, there was none to make. Reviews to date had been more favourable than unfavourable; the impartial reader feels that critics generally recognised Mrs Robinson's talent and were not instinctive sneerers.

When she turns to the world of fashion a more sustained picture of the fatuities to be found in London life is presented. Hyde Park, scene of Perdita's chariot triumphs in the 1780s, had witnessed a fitness fad:

> The tender MISS, who scarce could bear to tread
> A narrow dressing-room, with carpets spread,
> Now, with *Herculean* strength, more boldly tries
> To walk four miles – *for gentle exercise*!
> The cheek, that met the morn with blushing grace,

Enflam'd and scarlet, as an housemaid's face:
Those eyes, that twinkled at the taper's ray,
Now meet unhurt the burning glance of day!
Those locks, of late so decently confin'd,
Now fly, the sport of every wanton wind!
While poor MAMA is forced behind to lag,
Puffing and panting *like a hunted stag* . . .[6]

But Mrs Robinson's satire was primarily directed at reviewers, and she thereby 'rouzed a Nest of Hornets'.[7] They might have stung more fiercely than they did, though the *Monthly Review* mocked the pretensions of the pseudonym, while the *Critical Review*, which identified the author belittlingly as one of our 'pretty poetesses', condemned its unpolished, incoherent nature.[8]

Mary's second novel, *The Widow; or, A Picture of Modern Times*, published in February 1794, picks up the social themes of *Modern Manners*. It is very different from *Vancenza*, not only in its modern setting but in being written in letter form. The plot has sentimental aspects, but the centre of interest is a vicious group from fashionable society. In their letters they circle each other, planning seduction, conniving, betraying, as a lesser version of Laclos' *Les Liaisons Dangereuses* (mentioned in the course of the novel); they relieve the *ennui* of country life by cruel teasing of the honest peasantry. Mrs Robinson could hardly expect the *haut ton* to accept meekly a moral lashing from the former Perdita, but most reviewers approved; the *English Review* thought that 'Many of the sentiments do honour to the mind and heart of our authoress', and the *Monthly Review* that 'the features of fashionable folly and depravity are drawn with a skilful hand'.[9] Then in September came a malevolent blast from the *Critical Review*:

> This is one of the most insipid novels which . . . we have had occasion to peruse. The characters are fashionably vicious, without any fashionable brilliancy to compensate the depravity. O! for a warning voice to prevent those, at least, in whom age has not yet destroyed the capabilities of improvement, from dreaming away their hours in turning over publications like these, while the interesting walks of history, and the fair fields of fancy, and the rich

> mines of science, solicit their notice and offer their treasures to their persevering investigation.[10]

This was the review which had distressed her, particularly since she knew who had written it – William Gifford. As relayed indignantly to Taylor, she had been warned that he planned to '"*cut up my* work" *before* he had *read it*'.[11] The journal's motto was 'Nothing extenuate,/Nor set down aught in malice', from *Othello*, but since Mary had attacked him Gifford would have felt himself excused from fairness. However, he did not have to revenge himself on Mrs Robinson's daughter too.

Maria had grown up attractive and accomplished, described in February as one of the 'prettiest women' present at a masquerade attended by the Prince of Wales.[12] He was dressed as 'a British Tar', while she went as a nun, a popular disguise but perhaps connected with her novel, *The Shrine of Bertha*, published soon after, which has a convent setting. Like *The Widow* it is in letter form, using a variety of voices which she manages adroitly. Modern readers may not like the deep attachment of the heroine to the unknown Bertha's grave (the dead woman inevitably turns out to have been her mother), but the general run of criticism was that for a beginner the writing promised well. But it was destroyed by two brutal sentences in the *Critical Review*:

> Novels, as their sole purpose is entertainment, must either be the most amusing or the most insipid of publications. We cannot say that the two volumes before us belong to the former class.[13]

While there is no proof that Gifford wielded the hatchet, the language suggests that he did; *The Shrine of Bertha* made a second edition, but Maria never wrote fiction again. Her novel has one original claim: it must be unique in having a footnote explaining that 'The Authoress is indebted to her Mother' for the poetry.[14] It was also almost certainly to her mother, in her attack on Gifford, that she was indebted for the damning review.

It is unlikely that Gifford bothered to read much of *The Widow*, but in disdainfully flipping through its pages he would, as a dyed-in-the-wool Tory, have noticed much to displease him anyway. Mary believed that the French Revolution had been sparked by the gulf between rich and poor, but in embracing the cause of the poor she was treading on dangerous political ground. Initial enthusiasm for Revolutionary ideals had spawned reform societies dedicated to the extension of civil and voting rights, but events in France showed how quickly extremists could take over and mobilise the mob. When war broke out Pitt's government introduced repressive measures, suspending habeas corpus and arresting suspected subversives; their trials were in preparation as Mary wrote gloomily to Taylor, and the poisonous political atmosphere in England may have added to Italy's attractions.

But it was perceived lack of appreciation for her writing which was the root cause of her discontent. As she expressed it in verse in the third of her letters to Taylor:

> Heav'n knows, I never would repine,
> Though fortunes fiercest frowns were mine,–
> If Fate would grant that o'er my tomb
> One *little Laurel wreath*, might bloom,
> And mem'ry, sometimes wander near,
> To bid it live, – and drop a tear![15]

Had she possessed a crystal ball to see that 200 years after her death her laurels are flourishing, it might have consoled but would not have substituted for the recognition of her contemporaries. After five more stanzas the poem ends in a desire to '*die, – and feel no More*!' But she comments self-mockingly, 'My *Muse*, always makes me melancholy, and I fear, her somniferous qualities communicate to those, who read her productions'. Taylor would have recognised from the very sending of this poem that she would not, could not, renounce the muse; as if writing of a lover she adds, 'I swear every day to quit her for Ever; and am, every day, as constantly forsworn'.

In John Taylor, Mary discovered an apparently staunch friend; it is therefore a disappointment to find in his two-volume *Records of My Life*, written thirty years after her death, almost nothing about her, despite their being packed with tales of seemingly everyone else he knew. Early in the first volume, while recalling the poet S.J. Pratt, Taylor writes that he 'met him frequently at the house of the celebrated Mrs Robinson, whom I shall mention in the course of these records'.[16] But the only other reference comes when he tells how the actor

William Smith (Leontes to Mary's Perdita), came out of retirement in 1798 to recreate his original role of Charles Surface in *The School for Scandal* (at sixty-eight!) in a benefit for Tom King; on this occasion Taylor 'joined with my friend the celebrated Mrs Robinson in taking a box sufficient for herself, her daughter, one of her female friends, and myself'.[17] 'Celebrated' is a distant, impersonal word: friendship is somehow betrayed. But Taylor was not all that he seemed; unknown to Mary (and unconfessed in his memoirs) he was, at least till 1793, a secret government agent, in receipt of three guineas a week to disseminate its propaganda through his journalism.[18]

Mary's depressed state focused on her writing but she was again harassed for money, another reason to leave for Italy. She no longer spent wildly, but she maintained an elegant house in London, entertained, dressed herself and her daughter fashionably, kept a carriage and engaged a box at the theatre, had medical bills to pay. Income did not match expenditure, though she did not see this as her fault:

> Let common sense judge how I can subsist upon £500 a year when my carriage (a necessary expense) alone costs me £200. My mental labours have failed through the dishonest conduct of my publishers. My works have sold handsomely but the profits have been theirs.[19]

In *The Widow* she had, with considerable hyperbole, lauded the Prince as one 'whose mind . . . deserves that adoration, which it is beyond the reach of earthly power to exalt!'[20] Privately she was resentful:

> Have I not reason to be disgusted when I see him, to whom I ought to look for better fortune, lavishing favours on unworthy objects . . . while I, who sacrificed reputation, an advantageous profession, friends, patronage, the brilliant hours of youth, and the conscious delight of correct conduct, am condemned to the scanty pittance bestowed on every indifferent page who holds up his ermined train of ceremony![21]

Perhaps Mary should not be taken literally here, but Pages of Honour holding up the Prince's train earned £47 10*s* per quarter, well below her 'scanty pittance'.[22]

In the unlikely event that the Prince ever gave thought to how poor Mrs Robinson was managing, he could have done nothing for her since he had colossal debts himself; he had borrowed so much to finance the building of Carlton House, his London residence, that even the money lenders would oblige him no more. He needed an escape route too: his was marriage and the allowances Parliament would grant him. He set aside Maria Fitzherbert, whom he had secretly and illegally married in December 1785, and announced his intention to wed his cousin, Caroline of Brunswick. He had not given much thought to his choice of bride and it was to prove a disastrous union, but public reaction was favourable. Mary told Taylor that she had heard that the Princess was 'handsome, and amiable', adding sententiously, if accurately, 'I don't think the most exalted situations promise the fairest prospects'.[23]

About her other grouse, her publishers, she seems to have been wrong, though possibly there were grounds for complaint against the first of them, John Bell, whose records no longer exist. For *The Widow* and her two following novels she turned to Hookham & Carpenter, while the last three were published by the firm of Longman; her records with both these firms have been studied by Jan Fergus and Janice Farrar Thaddeus.[24] All publications with Hookham & Carpenter were 'for the author', which required the tricky judgement of print run. Bearing in mind the success of *Vancenza*, for *The Widow* Mary doubled the normal edition to 1,500 copies. A third of them sold quickly; thereafter sales stalled, and little profit was made. Moreover there were publicity costs of front-page advertisements in the newspapers, to which must be added the 'puffs' of advertising disguised as news items. For her next novel, *Angelina* (1796), Mary sensibly limited the print run to 750 copies; when these sold out rapidly a second edition was called for, but again sales collapsed dramatically and reduced her profits.

From Longman Mary received straight copyright payments of £150 for the four-volume novels *Walsingham* and *The False Friend*, and £60 for the two-volume *The Natural Daughter*, with 1,000 copies printed of each. In this, her last novel, fairly or unfairly, she gives vent to her irritation with the publishing trade. When Mrs Morley presents Mr Index, the publisher, with her manuscript novel he offers her just £10 for what later proves to be a best-seller, telling her that the warehouses are full of such novels, fit only to be sold as waste-paper for 'lining trunks, or enveloping the merchandize of pastry-cooks and cheese-mongers'.[25] Ten pounds, however, was a usual sum for an untried author, and 10 guineas was what Ann Radcliffe received for her first novel; she was later paid £500 for *The Mysteries of Udolpho* (1794), while for the novel which makes fun of *Udolpho* and the Gothic genre, *Northanger Abbey*, Jane Austen received £10 from a publisher (who then hung on to the manuscript, which was not printed till after the author's death). Pages from unsold copies of Mrs Robinson's novels may have wrapped cheeses, but it seems that Mary's publishers did not treat her unjustly.

Authorship had its hazards, yet it was a way for women to earn an independent living and, as Judith Phillips Stanton has shown, in every decade of the eighteenth century more of them tried authorship.[26] Yet a feeling persisted that it was indecorous for women to make money; a review of her second volume of poems reproved Mrs Robinson for writing for 'calls more pressing than the impulse of genius or the desire for fame', making the work a mere 'article of merchandise'.[27] She would have bridled at that; in *Walsingham* she would again, in a chapter connected by the loosest of threads to the narrative, castigate those anonymous 'journeymen of Parnassus' who from envy, political bias or sheer caprice destroy a writer's hopes of earning an 'honourable subsistence'.[28] Amazingly, reviewers of *Walsingham* made little protest, perhaps because they felt sorry for her. Her condition *was* pitiable: chairbound, daily humiliated in every physical need, often in pain and of necessity resorting to mind-clouding drugs. It is unsurprising that she suffered from bouts of depression and needed to express the wretchedness in grumbling.

Another long-held ambition was to write for the stage. In 1792 it had been announced that Mrs Robinson had composed an 'opera' (a play with songs), but when a year later, and despite much press prompting, Drury Lane had still not brought it out she withdrew it.[29] Next she wrote a comic afterpiece, but it too was long in the managers' hands. The delay was partly caused through changes at Drury Lane since Mary's acting days, notably that Sheridan, preoccupied with politics, had passed the day-to-day management of the theatre to John Philip Kemble, brother of Sarah Siddons, while retaining the right to vet all new plays, unread piles of which gathered dust in his study. Moreover the old theatre had been demolished in 1791 for a replacement to accommodate a larger audience, but the new Drury Lane (designed by Henry Holland) did not open until March 1794. Even then the outside was unfinished, and was in fact still incomplete when the theatre burnt down fifteen years later.[30] But the inside, which could hold an audience of 3,611, was impressive, 'of a most stupendous height, chastely and richly ornamented in the Gothic and Chinese styles'.[31] Ladies were assured that the boxes, 123 of them, were of an 'airy spaciousness', lined with blue silk to 'heighten the effect of female attire'. The stage was enormous and most suited to spectacle; an afterpiece, *Alexander the Great; or, The Conquest of Persia*, designed to 'shew the extent and powers of the new Stage', ended with a procession involving 200 soldiers, a chariot drawn by three white horses, and another by two elephants.[32] Mary's little farce *Nobody* was hardly fitted to such a location.

Nobody takes up the theme of 'the frivolous manners and gay dissipation of high life', focusing on the so-called faro ladies, whose use of their houses as gambling salons had become a general scandal, and of personal concern to Mary because Tarleton was a regular visitor to their tables.[33] Faro (or pharaoh, because one of the cards bore an image of a pharaoh) was a form of gambling whereby players bet against the bank on the sequence of cards turning up. Since the banker controlled play, running a faro bank could be lucrative. Opposition to the gambling culture was already reflected in plays such as Thomas Holcroft's comedy *The Road to Ruin* (1792); society found it particularly disturbing that aristocratic women should not only gamble (risking their husband's fortunes) but run the gambling salons (pocketing male inheritances). Two aristocratic ladies, fat Lady Buckinghamshire and the painted scarecrow Lady Archer, were widely reviled, and in 1796 Lord Chief Justice Kenyon threatened to 'exhibit them in the PILLORY'.[34] But it was one thing for a Lord Chief Justice to threaten, another for the former Perdita to condemn the titled gamesters.

Nevertheless, *Nobody* was put into rehearsal on 18 November. Because she had been one of them, 'once favour'd here' as she reminded the audience in her Prologue, some of Drury Lane's best players agreed to appear, apart from Elizabeth Farren who refused the main role of Lady Languid, claiming that it ridiculed a friend.[35] A substitute was found, and Drury Lane's leading comic actress Dorothy Jordan, known as Dora, agreed to play Nelly Primrose, a country bumpkin, the kind of part in which she specialised. James Boaden, who knew both women, remembered 'the delight she [Mary] expressed at Mrs Jordan's heading the list'.[36] Between Mary and Dora there was warmth of feeling, even fellow-feeling, since Dora was the mistress of William, Duke of Clarence (bearing him ten children before she too was cast off); in *The False Friend* Mary would pay tribute to Mrs Jordan's 'resistless and magical influence' on the stage.[37] Mary was also allowed new costumes for her play, writing directions about Lady Languid's Act II dress which show she had not lost her eye for exhibition: 'a white Chemise with *No Waist* – a Turban with *One Feather of enormous length* – Short Sleeves much above the Elbows – A *very large Medallion* at her Bosom'.[38]

The first night was Saturday, 29 November, when *Nobody* followed the mainpiece, Congreve's tragedy *The Mourning Bride* with Mrs Siddons. As ever the audience hoped to end the evening with a good laugh, or the majority of them did, for the faro ladies had organised a spoiling party. They had already sent Mrs Jordan an intimidatory letter declaring that '*Nobody* should be damned!', while Mary herself received a 'scurrilous, indecent, and *ill-disguised* scrawl, signifying to her that the farce was already condemned'.[39] Titled ladies would not themselves yell abuse, but they sent their servants to the gallery and had paid others to disrupt the performance. Shouting soon began and the ladies 'hissed through their fans'. Yet although 'the MANY had a struggle against the ILL NATURE which a FEW were forward in displaying', the majority prevailed and the play was given a hearing.[40]

The title, *Nobody*, is unconnected with the story, but is explained in the Prologue as ironic disclaimer: 'When Satire shews the portraits fancy drew,/Sure Nobody will say, they're meant for you' (the afterpiece was never printed, but a theatre copy is held in the Huntington Library in California). The play opens with Mrs Goodly attempting to teach Nelly what Lady Languid will expect:

Mrs Goodly:	You must put your best face on.
Nelly:	Why this be my best – I ha' got no other, won't it do?
Mrs Goodly:	Alack-a-day, I fear 'twill soon be spoilt in London.

Nelly:	Why lord bless ye, you do know nothing about it – No matter what be done to un – I do wash un wi soap & suds every Morning, and a looks as good as new.
Mrs Goodly:	Very likely; but your face won't last forever.
Nelly:	Efecks it has lasted a good bit, for father always did say 'twas Grandmothers *own* face, and she ha been dead these 50 years.[41]

If the dialogue does not sparkle, a good actress could nevertheless get some laughs. Nelly spells trouble for Lady Languid, smearing rouge all over her face and, when told to fetch a pair of boots, bringing in a man's boots with spurs; Lady Languid's fashionable friends visiting her in her boudoir suspect the worst. These are the not-too-subtly named Ladies Faro, Squander, and Rouleau (a gambling token for 100 guineas), Miss Cassino, Lord Courtland and a coxcomb, Sharply, who is looking to marry money. In the second act Lady Languid is lectured by Sir Henry Rightly, a banker, on the virtues of giving money to the poor rather than losing it at the faro tables: 'Explore some wretched habitation . . . Relieve their Wants – & then tell me if ever you felt *such rapture* in the Paths of dissipation'.[42] She strikes a bargain: if he will run a faro bank that evening at Lady Squander's, she will try his idea of fun next morning. The play ends at the party, where Lady Languid loses her 'last 9,000 guineas' to the bank, the ladies treat her disdainfully because of the boots, and Sharply withdraws from the marriage stakes. But Sir Henry restores her money and gives the repentant lady his heart as well. The summary shows the play's weakness: there is not enough incident (and too much of Sir Henry's moralising). As a critic wrote next day, it is not funny enough for an afterpiece, 'where to laugh, and laugh heartily, is always expected'.[43]

Reviews nevertheless suggest that the first act, when Mrs Jordan held the stage, went quite well; she sang a song which was 'rapturously encored' (*Morning Chronicle*), but booing and jeering broke out again, and rose to a crescendo just before the Epilogue. James Boaden describes what happened next:

> Our dear Mrs Jordan . . . was not made for a storm; and grew pitiably nervous if the house shewed marks of displeasure and

> contest, which they liberally or illiberally did in abundance on this present occasion. One might have supposed Mrs Robinson prescient of her fate, by her epilogue – for Mrs Jordan hurried on to address the audience in the words following, 'half dead and scarce recovered from my fright.' Recovered! She was so far from being recovered, that she only repeated twenty lines out of the epilogue, that had no connexion with each other; and the authoress was indignant with manager, actress, proprietor, and even the public, for not embalming *Nobody*.[44]

The last remark is surprisingly acid from a man who, like Taylor, wrote adulatory verses to Mrs Robinson in her life (another newspaper man, Boaden was editor of the *Oracle* which encouraged the publication of Mary's poetry, and a theatre devotee who wrote plays himself). He explained *Nobody*'s failure as stemming from a superior cast showing the audience that they recognised the 'trivial business' they were engaged in. But forty years after the event he had forgotten that the first night fiasco resulted from the furore in the audience; the prompter noted the 'Opposition of Hisses and Applauses', so Mary had some supporters. Moreover Mrs Jordan herself scribbled an indignant note afterwards to the Duke of Clarence saying that 'The play has been DAMND most unfairly', and explaining that she had been 'most unwell and c[d] not speak the epilogue'.[45]

Nobody was tried again on the following Monday (omitting the Epilogue) when it passed off quietly. There is an undated letter of Mrs Jordan's to the Duke headed '*Monday, 11 o'clock at night*' saying 'I am this moment returned from the theatre – the Farce went off so much better that it is to be repeated tomorrow', which may refer to it.[46] But if so the actress was misinformed about the repeat, as it was scheduled, foolishly one would think, for another Saturday. This repeated not only the play but the disorder, the Prompter noting that 'Considerable disapprobation was expressed through the whole of the Second Act, and towards the conclusion a disposition to riot began to manifest itself, which confusion continued for a considerable time after the Curtain dropt'.[47] No management could allow such a situation, nor would Mary have wished to embarrass her friends, so *Nobody* was withdrawn. It was fortunate for her pride that there were those on whom the blame for failure could be thrown.

One dramatic form remained to try, so she produced a blood-spattered blank-verse tragedy, *The Sicilian Lover*. Sheridan had little enthusiasm for unsolicited new tragedies, however, and not finding theatrical backing Mary had it printed. But the general public wanted to read a new verse tragedy as little as Sheridan, and only thirty-two copies sold. Fortunately Mary's next work, *Hubert de Sevrac*, published at the end of 1796, did well, trailing in the wake of *The Mysteries of Udolpho*. Hubert has similar exotic elements, with a sinister mouldering castle in a dark Italian forest, feuds, murders, false accusations, abductions, disembodied voices and other strange goings-on, in a world peopled by innocent victims, wicked nobles and noble peasants. Though it had a contemporary rather than a historical setting (and included pointed commentary on social injustice) Mary had got the formula right. However, because of the failures of *The Sicilian Lover* and *Angelina*, when she concluded business with Hookham & Carpenter she had cleared only £10.[48]

Fifty-nine copies of *The Sicilian Lover* were expensively bound and sent out as gifts; one is likely to have gone to Sarah Siddons in the hope that she would want to play the suffering heroine, Honoria. Mrs Siddons was sympathetic to Mary, but wary for her reputation's sake of any connection; when she received a volume of Mrs Robinson's poems she returned thanks through John Taylor, which made it clear that she would not risk acquaintance:

> If she is half as amiable as her writings, I shall long for the *possibility* of being acquainted with her. I say *possibility*, because one's whole life is one continual sacrifice of inclinations, which to indulge, however laudable or innocent, would draw down the malice and reproach of those prudent people who never do ill . . . The charming and beautiful Mrs Robinson: I pity her from the bottom of my soul.[49]

The English Sappho continued to be haunted by the shade of the sapphic Perdita.

The year 1796 was Mary Robinson's literary *annus mirabilis*. Not only did she publish two novels (*Angelina* and *Hubert*) and her verse tragedy, but also her most ambitious poetic work, the sonnet sequence *Sappho and Phaon*; this links her even more closely with the Greek poetess from whom she took her nickname. Such an output is astonishing, though the sonnet sequence was being referred to at least a year before publication, and was no hasty assemblage for profit. Her care with this work is shown in its presentation, advertised as 'on fine Wove Paper, hot-pressed, and embellished with a beautiful engraving [of the head of Sappho] . . . from an antique at Rome'; 'hot-pressed', for a work which has a strong erotic charge, is curiously appropriate.[50] The price was half a guinea.

Sappho and Phaon is learned in its classical references, innovative in its use of the sonnet (the 'legitimate' sonnet of Petrarch and Milton, with division into octave and sestet, rather than Shakespearean with concluding couplet), and bold in a Preface claiming poetry as the means towards a more enlightened world.[51] The forty-four sonnets are mainly in the voice of Sappho herself, based on a narrative myth found in Ovid which tells how the poetess follows her faithless lover Phaon from Lesbos to Sicily; failing to win him back, she throws herself from a cliff. A striking feature of the work is the poet's control over the form even as she uses it to express 'the destructive controul of ungovernable passions'. Readers today will respect the technical mastery and recognise the passion; some may, like Mary's contemporaries, feel uncomfortable with the opulent language and unabashed emotion, though Jerome J. McGann argues that such poetry should be read on its own terms as a poetry of sensibility that is 'specifically gendered female'.[52] Sonnet XXIII will stand as an example:

> To Aetna's scorching sand my Phaon flies!
> False Youth! Can other charms attractive prove?
> Say, can Sicilian loves thy passions move,
> Play round thy heart, and fix thy fickle eyes,
> While in despair the Lesbian Sappho dies?
> Has Spring for thee a crown of poppies wove,
> Or dost thou languish in th'Idalian grove,
> Whose altar kindles, fann'd by Lover's sighs?
> Ah! think, that while on Aetna's shores you stray,
> A fire, more fierce than Aetna's, fills my breast;
> Nor deck Sicilian nymphs with garlands gay,
> While Sappho's brows with cypress wreaths are drest;

Let one kind word my weary woes repay,
Or, in eternal slumbers bid them rest.[53]

In her Preface Mrs Robinson pays tribute to those of her 'illustrious countrywomen', including another pioneering sonneteer Charlotte Smith, who 'persevere in the paths of literature' despite lack of patronage in a country 'most neglectful of literary merit'. In this rebuke we recognise the familiar theme of disregarded genius. Equally, the voice of Sappho, that 'illustrious woman' whose 'soul was replete with harmony', is Robinson's own poetic one, while Sappho's emotional sensibility is underpinned by Mary's – 'Ah! why is rapture so allied to pain?'[54]

Though it would be grotesque to match the golden-haired Phaon with the greying Tarleton, Sappho's despair will have owed something to the failing relationship. Its on-off nature is already illustrated in the autumn of 1794, when Mary wrote her letters to John Taylor. The pair had retreated from the London summer to Salt Hill near Eton; at some time there was a quarrel followed by a reconciliation, signalled by a paragraph in the *Oracle* in September that 'A certain LITERARY FEMALE has good-humouredly received a gallant COLONEL into those habits of friendly attendance, so reciprocally gratifying, and which *misconception* alone could have broken off'.[55] Then comes her unhappy letter to Taylor in which he is not mentioned. It becomes clear in the third letter that he has been in London; no doubt Mary had worried that he would not return. But he had, bringing news of his promotion to Major General, and in her third letter his greetings are included with hers and Maria's. Now Mary cheerfully recounts all the places where they had earlier been 'rambling' – [Thomas] Gray's tomb and the churchyard at Stoke Poges, the woods of Cliveden, Windsor, 'and many more *strange* things'.[56] There had been poetic badinage too; in late August Tarleton sent some verses to Taylor, to which Mary attached dismissive quatrains scoffing that 'the lyre of *Apollo* is tuned by an ass'. Ban riposted:

The limbs may languish, but the mind can't faint,
Genius like freedom bows not to restraint;
Down with all tyrants strikes upon my ear!
Alas! I've got a female Robespierre.[57]

Since no correspondence survives, these verses represent the only recorded exchange between the pair. Ban shows his admiration for the way Mary surmounted disabilities, but even used jestingly his 'female Robespierre', responding to her 'ass', suggests the fracture lines in their union, that she asserted intellectual superiority and that he resented it. The Reign of Terror had come to an end less than a month before with the guillotining of its chief architect, Robespierre: it was not a name to joke comfortably with.

Two years later they returned to the area, taking at least one pleasure trip on the Thames past the wooded steeps of Cliveden reach, a day spoiled for Mary when she was refused permission to land and take refreshment from Cliveden's natural spring. In indignation she penned a note to Lady Orkney, owner of the estate, from the Sun Inn in Maidenhead:

> Mrs Robinson presents her Compliments to Lady Orkney, and begs leave to explain a mistake, which alone could have provoked the rudeness she experienced this Evening.
>
> Mrs Robinson, with General Tarleton, and a small party, having been on the water the whole day, and being extremely oppressed by the heat of the Sun, took the liberty to stop for a few minutes near the spring, in order that her Servant might procure, for her, a glass of water.
>
> Mrs Robinson was not conscious of any impropriety in so doing, having observed many parties land, during the evening; and having, the Summer before last, been favoured with Lord Kirkwalls permission to do the same.
>
> Mrs Robinson, as she is the last person, who would be guilty of any impropriety, is also the first to feel an unprovoked incivility.[58]

Though it is not clear quite what happened, it is difficult to believe that Lady Orkney had put Mrs Robinson's name on a blacklist. The incident reveals her touchiness, while also showing that she and Tarleton could enjoy themselves together.

But Tarleton could travel more widely, and was entertained more freely; when he was away, Mary grew jealous of potential rivals. She was still a beautiful woman, but she could also be a difficult one, with mood swings, a temper easily provoked, and an unwillingness to give way in an argument. She disliked Tarleton's gambling, his support of the slave trade, and his enjoyment of vicious sports like boxing; being, as James Boaden noted, 'tolerably free in her remarks', she would not have hesitated to say so.[59] No doubt Tarleton gave as good as he got, objecting in turn to her growing feminism; Treville in *The False Friend*, supposedly based on him, annoys the heroine Gertrude St Lawrence as Tarleton must have goaded Mary, by declaring that 'I make no doubt that you will shortly become a *he-she* philosopher . . . you will hope to equalise the authority of the sexes, and to prove that woman was formed to think, and to become the rational companion of man; though we all know that she was merely created for our amusement'.[60]

In his mid-forties Tarleton had reached an age when such men look for young women to bolster their self-image as still dashingly irresistible, though he could have done that without an absolute rupture. He must have been irritated, not just by Mary's feminism, but also by her assumption of the moral high ground (her heroines when misunderstood always fall back on their enjoyment of 'conscious moral rectitude'). But money probably precipitated the final break. Ban's mother died in May 1797, leaving him only £1,500 (in her will Jane Tarleton listed the debts which she had paid for him, regarding them as part of his inheritance); he had his half-pay but no other (reliable) source of income, felt himself to be a poor man, and was not prepared to pass his inheritance over to Mary to solve her problems.[61] On 10 May 1797 the *Oracle* reported that General Tarleton had lost his mother, and 'if we mistake not this is not the *only loss* he has recently sustained, in that which comes nearest to the heart'.

No doubt Mary thought that he would come back to her, as he had done before. Was he not tied to her, not just by the passion they had shared but by years of friendship, the obligations of her illness, her loving attention in his, her financial assistance, help with his writing, by all their shared memories? A little flurry of entries in the *Oracle* in October show her using its pages to try to prick his conscience, first with the rebuke indirect:

> The work which Mrs ROBINSON is finishing [*Walsingham*] will probably be her *last*. Her health declines rapidly. The sting of *ingratitude* wounds deeply in a sensible heart.

Three days later there follows the attack direct:

> Mrs ROBINSON denies that General GREY CROP is to make his appearance in her NOVEL. She only pourtrays [*sic*] the *follies*, not the VICES of individuals.

(Cropped hair was fashionable for men, and supposed to show support for the Revolutionary ideals.) And lastly the plea pathetic:

> Mrs ROBINSON has constantly experienced the most unremitting attentions from her truly estimable daughter. But all the virtues of filial affection cannot stop the progress of declining health.[62]

Tarleton's contrasting inattention is implied. Mary also tried poetry again. 'The Sorrows of Memory', published as by Laura Maria in the *Morning Post* on 26 January 1798, in the midst of plentiful congratulatory press notice of *Walsingham* and just after she had begun her memoirs, is directed at one who has 'broke my heart'. Each verse ends with the phrase 'lov'd thee dearly', the second stanza with a variation, and reminding him of what he owes to her:

> How many summers pass'd away,
> How many winters sad and dreary,
> And still I taught thee to be gay
> Whene'er of life thy soul was weary;
> When ling'ring sickness wrung thy breast,
> And bow'd thee to the earth, or nearly,
> I strove to lull thy mind to rest –
> For then I lov'd thee, Oh! How dearly![63]

The poem ends with the threat that she will haunt him after death. But poetry no longer had power over his heart.

The worst was yet to come. On 14 December, along with several other papers, the *Morning Post* announced:

> General TARLETON is on Monday next to be married to Miss BERTIE, a young lady very nearly related to Lord CHOLMONDELEY. Report gives her 20,000L to her fortune.

Mary knew very well who Susan Priscilla Bertie was: the illegitimate daughter of Captain Robert Bertie, one of Tarleton's hell-raising friends in youth. She was born not long after he became Duke of Ancaster, and just before his death in July 1779; her mother was a Rebecca Krudener. However, the Duke had in his will bequeathed his daughter both his name and money for her upbringing, which was undertaken by Lord Cholmondeley, her uncle by marriage. The morally free-ranging Lord Cholmondeley, former friend and perhaps lover of Perdita, had brought her up along with Grace Dalrymple Elliot's daughter Georgiana (possibly his, possibly the offspring of the Prince of Wales). Susan had been impeccably educated and, as the *Post* revealed, was a copy-book model of the politely schooled young lady, speaking several languages, artistic, musical, 'mistress of Astronomy, Geography, etc.'[64] That she was indeed such a paragon is borne out in the memoirs of Frances Lady Shelley, who describes her as 'the most *spirituelle* and clever person I ever met with' and 'very handsome and attractive'.[65] By an irony that Mary would not have appreciated Lady Shelley also calls her 'the illegitimate daughter of the celebrated Mrs Robinson'. Though £20,000 may have been an over-estimate she brought a good sum to the marriage, which took place on 17 December.

Thus Tarleton acquired a pretty young wife, with money to boot. Moreover his prospects had advanced through the good offices of the Duke of York, who had secured for him an active military post as commander of the land forces in Portugal. Napoleon, who came to power in the aftermath of the Revolution, had set his sights on the conquest of Spain and Portugal, and the Portuguese had called for British assistance. In early February, therefore, the newly married couple went to Portsmouth to await embarkation. Through 1798 Mary had been writing *The False Friend*, with its black portrayal of Tarleton as the cynical womaniser Treville, and that too was launched in February. On the day prior to its publication, the Tarletons, waiting for favourable winds, would not have been comforted to read in the *Morning Post* that Treville, his lady companion and other enemies of the heroine, all perish at sea while on a voyage to Lisbon.[66]

12

Friends and Foes

O! not to me, stern DEATH, art thou a foe;
Thou art the welcome messenger, which brings
A passport – to a BLEST AND LONG REPOSE!
(Last lines of 'To Spring, Written after a Winter of Ill Health in the Year 1800')

Unlike Gertrude in *The False Friend*, Mary did not die of a broken heart. Nor did Tarleton's ship founder in the Bay of Biscay. However, it must have given her satisfaction to learn that things did not go well in Portugal and that by the summer the cavalry commander had become incapacitated with gout.[1] Luckily Bonaparte looked away from the Iberian peninsula to Egypt and Tarleton was recalled; someone seemed to have taken Mary's part when they sailed back in a ship called the *Walsingham*.

In *The False Friend* Mary poured resentment of her faithless lover into the Reverend Treville, whose most infamous moment comes when he attempts to seduce Gertrude over the coffin of his former mistress. But Treville represents more than Tarleton. In 1798 Mary was writing not just *The False Friend* but her *Memoirs* and, consciously or unconsciously, Treville is surely a composite of all those libertines who aimed at or succeeded in charming her into their beds, from Lord Lyttelton onwards. That Treville is made a minister of religion emphasises the hypocrisy of the English social code which indulged the male fornicator but allowed a woman not a single lapse at his hands. 'Man first degrades, and then deserts her' is a trenchant line from Mary's *Letter to the Women of England*, which takes up the issue.[2] This pamphlet, together with *The False Friend* and her final novel *The Natural Daughter*, were all published in 1799; all were influenced by the example of Mary Wollstonecraft, whose *Vindication of the Rights of Woman* had been published in 1794. In *The False Friend*, written in the year following Wollstonecraft's death from puerperal fever, Gertrude/Mary declares, 'I preach, and I shall never fail to feel those precepts which have been inculcated by one who now sleeps in the grave', footnoted as 'The late Mrs Wollstonecraft', while the *Letter* predicts that it will need a '*legion of Wollstonecrafts* to undermine the poisons of prejudice and malevolence'.[3]

Mrs Robinson and 'Mrs' Wollstonecraft probably met through William Godwin, of whom Mary saw a great deal following their introduction in 1796. Godwin, who like Mary was (if she did not admit it) in his fortieth year, was a very different kind of man from the self-indulgent lords of her earlier life. Trained as a dissenting minister he had lost his faith and turned instead to high-minded philosophy, combining a distrust of the institutions which control society with a belief in the individual's capacity for reason and justice. In Utopian innocence he envisaged a world where, with property held in common, the institutions of government, monarchy, the church, the law, and even marriage would wither away. These ideas he elaborated in the book which made his name, his *Enquiry into Political Justice* of 1793. The following year brought the Treason Trials, when Godwin went to the support of friends such as the playwright Thomas Holcroft; while not accused himself he was regarded with suspicion by the authorities.

It was in the spring of 1796 that, as he remembered, Godwin was introduced by the poet Robert Merry to 'a most accomplished and delightful woman, the celebrated Mrs Robinson'.[4] By her own account she was nervous of meeting him, afraid he would prove 'fastidious, stern, austere, and abstracted from worldly enjoyments'; instead she found him possessed of 'a thousand amiable qualities'.[5] They met first on 9 February, when in Godwin's brief, precise way he notes in his Journal that he had tea at Mrs Robinson's, where he also found Tarleton and Francis Twiss, brother-in-law of Sarah Siddons.[6] Next day he supped at her house, and thereafter Mrs Robinson's became a frequent port of call for tea, supper, or just a visit (when sometimes she was 'na' – not at home). Occasionally she paid a return visit to his lodgings in north-east London. He was soon reading *Angelina*, recording his daily page progress though never any opinion, and he went on to *The Sicilian Lover* and later *The Shrine of Bertha*. Godwin gave his mornings to study and writing, but the rest of the day was devoted to social visits, many of them to his entourage of literary lady friends. They formed a formidable group: Elizabeth Inchbald, dramatist and novelist, Amelia Alderson (later Opie), prolific novelist and poet, the feminist and novelist Mary Hays, Anna Barbauld, the poet Mary had admired in youth, poet and novelist Charlotte Smith, and Mary Wollstonecraft herself. These women buzzed round the bachelor with a fervour not totally dissimilar from lecherous lords round the young Mary Robinson.

On 1 June Godwin recorded: 'Theatre: sup at Mrs Robinson's w. Wolstencraft [*sic*] & Twiss'.[7] Mary Wollstonecraft had already encountered Mrs Robinson at least on a literary level, publishing a very favourable account of *Angelina* in the *Analytical Review*. Angelina herself she described as 'an assemblage of almost every excellence which can adorn the female mind', while 'The sentiments contained in these volumes . . . breathe a spirit of independence, and a dignified superiority to whatever is unessential to the true respectability and genuine excellence of human beings'.[8] She must therefore have been well-disposed to meeting the author. Though records are sparse, there were friendly encounters; Wollstonecraft asked Godwin in a letter to lend her Mrs Robinson's poems; she invited her and Maria to tea, and arranged to bring the novelist Mary Hays to tea at St James's Place. On this occasion Mrs Robinson offered her carriage so that 'little *Fannikin*', two-year-old Fanny Imlay, could accompany her mother; Mary Imlay, as she called herself then, confirmed the arrangements by letter, also sending 'kind rememberance [*sic*] to your Mary'.[9] Twenty-two-year-old Maria perhaps enjoyed amusing the little girl, maybe wondering if she would ever have a child of her own.

Unfortunately, as Mary Wollstonecraft grew intimate with Godwin she also became jealous of his other lady friends. One of the many notes they exchanged suggests that they had argued over his going to a play with Mrs Robinson when she could not; she urges him after all to attend because 'I am not such a child as I thought myself'.[10] In another note she wrote to Godwin that she was 'vext' with herself for staying to supper with 'Mrs R.' the previous evening, and had only done so to gratify him.[11] Perhaps it was not Mrs Robinson whom she wanted to avoid but Elizabeth Inchbald who, according to Godwin's journal, was also present and whom she decidedly did not like. Nevertheless, hostility emerges in a review of *Hubert de Sevrac*; after the eulogy for *Angelina* it is startling to read something so dismissive:

> Mrs Robinson writes so rapidly, that she scarcely gives herself time to digest her story into a plot, or to allow those incidents gradually to grow out of it, which are the fruit of matured invention. She certainly possesses considerable abilities; but she seems to have fallen into an errour, common to people of lively fancy, and to think herself so happily gifted by nature, that her first thoughts will answer her purpose . . .[12]

There is simple irritation with the novel's careless construction, but also a sharpness which does not suggest the work of a friend; Mrs Robinson would not have enjoyed reading that 'she could write better, were she once convinced, that the writing of a good book is no easy task'. The review is signed simply 'M', so she may never have realised who the author was, but she was certainly aware that in 1797 her society was sought less and less by Godwin and the woman who, despite all his objections to marriage, became his wife on 29 March. Godwin came seeking Mrs Robinson again after his wife's death; when in 1800 he accused Mary of 'inconstancy in Friendship' (her quotation from his letter), she defended herself saying:

> You have frequently withdrawn yourself from my society during many successive months. Two years elapsed after your marriage, and I never saw you! – This circumstance I did not fail to feel, – though I felt it – in silence.[13]

(Godwin's journal shows that she exaggerates the gap in their intercourse.) But she did not let personal resentment distort her admiration for Mary Wollstonecraft; of course it is easier to forgive the dead than the living.

Aware that her own past history would be used to resist her arguments as Wollstonecraft's was, *A Letter to the Women of England on the Injustice of Mental Subordination* was published under the respectable-sounding pseudonym of Anne Frances Randall (Mary reclaimed authorship for the second edition). Its primary aim was to contest male-constructed stereotypes of women's inferiority:

> There are but three classes of women desirable associates in the eyes of men: handsome women; licentious women; and good sort of

> women. – The first for his vanity; the second for his amusement; and the last for the arrangement of his domestic drudgery. A thinking woman does not entertain him; a learned woman does not flatter his self-love, by confessing inferiority; and a woman of real genius, eclipses him by her brilliancy.[14]

She argues her 'incontrovertible' case with examples past and present, incorporating a list of contemporary thinking women which includes herself and her daughter. She also urges more liberal intellectual and physical expectations of women. Why are they forbidden to attend debates in Parliament? Women hunt, so why is it considered 'not feminine' for them to swim, to play ball-games and run races? ('I can only conclude that a wife has full permission to break her neck; though she is forbid to think or speak like a rational creature.'[15]) The argument is sustained and vigorous, though it did not strike many male critics as unanswerable; they did not know Anne Frances Randall, but she could be damned through her championship of Mary Wollstonecraft.

The *Letter* makes an important contribution to the 1790s debate about the position and education of women which Mary Wollstonecraft initiated and which others, such as Mary Hays, joined. Hays' *Appeal to the Men of Great Britain on Behalf of the Women* (1798), possibly stirred Mary Robinson to her own appeal.[16] But it also reflects her personal frustrations. She had helped write Tarleton's speeches: why could she not hear them delivered? More fundamentally, she had been abused for her relationship with the Prince and excluded from the negotiations which ended it; Tarleton had abandoned her for a wealthy, healthy young wife, and she had no redress – in her *Letter* she exposed herself to some mockery by suggesting that women should have the right to defend their honour in a duel. But if she could not draw a pistol Mary did have a weapon, her pen, and she made use of it in *The False Friend* and *The Natural Daughter*.

The full title is *The Natural Daughter with portraits of the Leadenhead Family*, and it was with the self-made, social-climbing, vulgar Leadenheads that Mary revenged herself, not just on Ban but on the whole Tarleton tribe. Like them the Leadenheads acquired their money through the slave trade, and they live in Plummet Castle, just as the Tarletons had bought Bolesworth Castle in Lancashire for their 'seat'.[17] Young Humphrey Leadenhead's career resembles Ban's, and his absurdly fashion-conscious sister is called Bridget, as was Tarleton's (Elizabeth Robinson may have contributed to Miss Leadenhead, since Mary had never met Ban's sister). In case anyone failed to recognise the caricatures, inserts in the *Post* made it clear. '*The Leadenhead family* in Mrs ROBINSON'S last Novel, are too strikingly like to be mistaken' was placed above a notice that the Mrs Robinson who had died in a coach accident was sister of the 'wife of Thomas Tarleton Esq. of Liverpool'. Four days later news of the arrival from Portugal of General Tarleton and his lady was slyly placed almost adjacent to a notice that *The Natural Daughter* 'is likely to have an extensive circulation in the county of Lancaster'.[18] At this time Mary was closely associated with the *Post*, so could have arranged such things. More amusing than this spitefulness was her parody of Susan Priscilla's wedding encomium for Humphrey Leadenhead's bride Lady Penelope Pryer, who is not only 'mistress of all living and dead languages', but understands 'the most profound mysteries of astrology and theology, mythology, philology, etymology, and phisiology [*sic*]', is 'well versed in philosophy, psalmography, biography, topography, orthography, and phytography', and much more.[19]

The novel's title may have been aimed at Susan Tarleton, but the story has nothing to do with hers, though there is an apparently illegitimate child at its centre. Set in 1792 at the height of the French Revolution, the plot concerns two sisters of contrasting temperaments.[20] Martha, undemonstrative but compassionate, becomes a social outcast when she adopts a baby in her husband's absence and is believed to be its mother herself. Julia, whose excessive display of sensibility suggests a tender nature, is in reality hard-hearted: she is the one who actually bears a child out of wedlock (and poisons it!). She comes to a bad end, committing suicide at the downfall of her lover, the real-life tyrant Robespierre. A good deal of disbelief has to be suspended, but there are lively satirical scenes, and the revelation of the child's true parentage is startling. But by general agreement the 'portraits of the Leadenheads' are the novel's weakest aspect: Mrs Robinson's squib failed to ignite.

Politically nothing improved in the last years of the eighteenth century. The land war with France was going badly, and by 1797 Britain no longer had military allies in Europe, other nations having been defeated or made their peace. Fears of invasion were rife. There was French-backed rebellion in India in 1797 and Ireland in 1798. The navy mutinied at shipboard conditions in 1797, but thereafter victories at sea and the discovery of a hero in Nelson gave people something to celebrate. War does not come cheap and new taxes were introduced, including a tax on hair-powder which effectively ended its use; the cost of living steadily rose, prompting bread riots and protests. A meeting in Bristol in 1795 to congratulate the King on his escape from a mob which had stoned his coach, shouting 'Bread! Peace! No Pitt!', had been electrified when the young Samuel Taylor Coleridge reminded those present that if the war was costly for the rich 'a PENNY taken from the pocket of a poor man might deprive him of a dinner'.[21] Mary Robinson would have applauded.

Mary hated Pitt for his policies and, as she saw it, corruption and nepotism. In a ditty to a well-known song-tune, published in the *Morning Post*, she mocked him as the 'VIRGIN-BOY', made fun of his long face and tip-tilted nose, and accused him and his 'Treasury boys' of pocket-picking:

O! RARE ***** **** [Billy Pitt]! he's the wonder of nature!
For taxing and talking, no man can be greater!
He perks up his nose, and he lengthens his chin,
And, as Dian though chaste, he's the Demon of Sin!
Derry down, down, down derry down.

Oh! B—y loves War, for he pockets the shiners;
And mocks the plain sense of the patriot diviners;
While he pays all his cronies, with other folks' pelf,
And, by bankrupting millions, enriches himself!
Derry down, &c. &c . . .[22]

There was personal anger behind the attack: inflation was steadily making Mary's financial situation more precarious. She had economised by moving from smart St James's Place to somewhat cheaper accommodation but still in the westend (Clifford Street adjoining Cork Street, a 'temporary habitation' in Piccadilly, Curzon Street and Chapel Street); in 1799 she announced her intention to live permanently in a cottage at Englefield Green near Windsor, though she never actually gave up a London base.[23] Her position was made worse when Pitt introduced a 10 per cent Income Tax at the beginning of 1799.

The effect of taxation is well illustrated by the mast-head of the *Morning Post*, which daily reminded its readers: 'Price in 1783–3*d.* Taxed by Mr PITT, 3*d.* Price 6*d*'. The *Post* was one of the few papers not controlled by the government (that is, subsidised by the Treasury). Through the efforts of the brothers Daniel and Peter Stuart it had risen from a period of decline, and in 1798 passed into the sole proprietorship of Daniel Stuart who, by his moderate political stance and skilled use of good writers, made it the best-selling newspaper of the day. It was not popular with conservatives, and when Gifford launched his *Anti-Jacobin Review* in 1798 an accompanying Gillray caricature targeted everything that reactionaries saw as threatening the state, including a deformed news-boy crying the *Morning Post*, and creatures holding up a cornucopia from which fall, among other publications, Godwin's *Memoirs* of Mary Wollstonecraft, her [*Maria, or the*] *Wrongs of Women*, and Mrs Robinson's *Walsingham*. Godwin rides an ass while reading *Political Justice*, and both Coleridge and his friend Robert Southey have asses' ears. Stuart had engaged Southey as Poetry Editor of the *Post* and had weaned Mrs Robinson from the *Oracle*; when Southey gave up the 'Laureateship' of the paper in February 1800 it went to her. If she received similar payment she earned herself thereby a guinea a week.

At the end of 1799 Coleridge became for a few months a principal journalist on the *Post*. This was when he came to know Mrs Robinson. Godwin's journal notes occasions when he met Coleridge at her home, and he was no doubt entertained there at times when Godwin was not present.[24] Though her former life was one of which the poet could not approve, he admired her. 'She is a woman of undoubted Genius,' he told Southey; 'I never knew a human Being with so *full* a mind – bad, good, & indifferent, I grant you, but full, & overflowing.'[25] He sent Southey copies of 'The Haunted Beach', and a ballad poem, 'Jasper' (an atmospheric poem of a man distraught at the loss of his 'Mary'), for an anthology he was editing. Of one of its lines – 'Pale moon! Thou spectre of the sky!' – Coleridge told Southey that it 'would of itself redeem a worse poem'.

Apart from poetry, they were linked by ill health and the use of opiates to control pain. Mary showed him 'The Maniac', a poem she is said to have written under the influence of nearly 'eighty drops of laudanum' while staying in Bath in the summer of 1791.[26] There she became obsessed with the image of an old man known as 'mad Jemmy' after seeing a crowd pelt him with mud and stones. According to the *Memoirs*, she woke one night, called Maria and 'desired her to take a pen and write what she would dictate'. The poem, speculating on the cause of the madness, was dictated with her eyes closed and in the voice of a sleep-talker; in the morning she remembered nothing about it. Whether she had the twenty stanzas in her head beforehand or worked on them afterwards, the story of the composition so impressed Coleridge that he gave her a manuscript copy of his own opium-inspired 'Kubla Khan', then unpublished and unknown. She responded with 'To the Poet Coleridge', recognising the power of his vision and incorporating echoes of it into her own poem:

Now by the source which lab'ring heaves
  The mystic fountain, bubbling, panting,
While Gossamer its net-work weaves,
  Adown the blue lawn slanting!
I'll mark thy *sunny dome*, and view
Thy *Caves of Ice*, thy fields of dew!
Thy ever-blooming mead, whose flow'r
Waves to the cold breath of the moonlight hour! . . .[27]

There were further poetic exchanges; when in her last illness Mary published a blank-verse ode celebrating the birth of Coleridge's son Derwent, he sent her a poem which he later thought 'excessively silly', but which shows his feeling for her. In 'A Stranger Minstrel' the poet, lying on the flanks of Skiddaw in the Lake District, confesses his yearning for her:

A Lady of sweet song is she,
Her soft blue eye is made for thee!
O ancient Skiddaw! By this tear,
I would, I would, that she were here![28]

He had invited her to join him and his family at Greta Hall near Keswick, but her health had made it impossible. The spectacular scenery might have proved a tonic; whether the relationship could have survived a domestic encounter is uncertain.

'A Stranger Minstrel' was not published in the *Post*, though it would not have been out of place. As editor, Mary herself published an ode in praise of Mrs Jordan (Mrs Jordan was reciprocally setting some of her verses to music), and three days later some 'Lines on Seeing the Duchess of Devonshire in Her New and Splendid Carriage', both poems printed under the pseudonym of 'Oberon'.[29] Judith Pascoe has identified eight pseudonyms – 'Laura Maria', 'Oberon', 'Sappho', 'Julia', 'Lesbia', 'Portia', 'Bridget', and 'Tabitha Bramble' – which, together with her own name, enabled her to bring diversity of form and mood to the poetry columns.[30] 'Tabitha Bramble' was a name adopted from the crotchety spinster created by Smollett, and was used for satirical verses or narratives with an abrasive edge. Even if readers did not recognise all the identities, they could hardly fail to be aware of Mrs Robinson; as Pascoe notes, over a few days a *Post* reader 'might come across a front-page advertisement for a subscription to a new Robinson volume, a poem, a puff, a promotion for a soon-to-be-published poem, and a medical prognosis'.[31]

The editorship allowed Mary to exercise patronage on behalf of those she admired, such as Samuel Jackson Pratt and the handsome young Porter sisters, dark Jane and fair Anna Maria. Pratt was a prolific writer, forgotten today, but with the memorable pen-name Courtney Melmoth. The two women were to make their marks as novelists, Jane anticipating Sir Walter Scott in her use of real historical figures (*Thaddeus of Warsaw* of 1803 is her best-known work). Mary cultivated Jane's friendship, though she shocked her 'sweet young friend' when she confessed that she had found her own sex 'almost universally . . . unkind and hostile' towards her.[32] The girls had a brother Robert, an artist, whose painting *Storming of Seringapatam*, an immense canvas displayed in a three-quarter circle, was a sensation of 1800. He illustrated one of Mary's sonnets and produced her portrait for a short biography.

There were poets, like Wordsworth, who disdained publishing in the prints. It was true that what was read by thousands one day would light the fire the next, but the poem could be kept for volume publication. In 1800 Mary was collecting subscriptions for her complete works, this time asking for half a guinea in advance, and planning a volume which she called *Lyrical Tales*. Though she did not know him personally, through Coleridge she had fallen under the influence of Wordsworth, whose *Lyrical Ballads* of 1798 she admired. Her own volume was to consist, she told her printer, of 'Tales, serious and gay, on a variety of subjects in the manner of Wordsworth's Lyrical ballads'.[33] (Hearing of this, Wordsworth considered changing his own title before the famous 1799 reprint.) Included in the *Lyrical Tales* are 'The Haunted Beach' and other supernatural stories, comic tales in which someone (usually an interfering old woman) gets their come-uppance, tales of loneliness and loss, and others of rich oppressors and poor oppressed. Several of Mrs Robinson's tales can be paralleled with Wordsworth's 'ballads', but they are not simply pastiche. 'The Poor Singing Dame', for example, is not unlike Wordsworth's 'Goody Blake and Harry Gill', his often mocked story of a man whose teeth 'chatter, chatter' for ever more after old Goody curses him for stopping her gathering sticks from his hedge. Mary's is the more compelling tale, largely because its landscape is that of romance and fairy-tale rather than the 'real' countryside, which suits its supernatural elements better. Moreover, the poem does not just point a moral, but is invested with personal feeling. 'Poor singing MARY' lives cheerfully in her 'hovel' in the valley below a great castle, where she is persecuted by its surly Lord who resents her simple happiness. When she will not cease her singing he sends her to prison where she dies. But she is revenged:

The Lord of the Castle, from that fatal moment
 When poor Singing MARY was laid in her grave,
Each night was surrounded by Screech-owls appalling,
 Which o'er the black turrets their pinions would wave!
On the ramparts that frown'd on the river, swift flowing,
 They hover'd, still hooting a terrible song,
When his windows would rattle, the Winter blast blowing,
 They would shriek like a ghost, the dark alleys among![34]

Day and night the avenging birds pursue him and he is haunted to his death. As the editor of Mary's *Selected Poems* points out, this poem can be read as a 'revenge fantasy' for the impoverished poet/singer's treatment by royalty.[35]

An advantage of publishing her poems in the newspaper was the opportunity to respond to events and seasons. On 4 January when skaters thronged to Hyde Park, the *Post* printed 'The Wintry Day'. This presents Mary's favourite theme, the gulf between rich and poor, in a series of contrasting scenes:

Is it in mansions rich and gay
On downy beds, or couches warm,
That Nature owns the Wintry Day,
And shrinks to hear the howling storm?
Ah! no!

'Tis on the bleak and barren heath,
Where mis'ry feels the shaft of death,
As to the dark and freezing grave,
Her children (not a friend to save)
Unheeded go![36]

Mary told Jane Porter that the artist Maria Cosway was producing illustrations for the poem, one for each of the twelve stanzas; for these two verses one shows a woman reclining at ease beside a blazing fire, while on the lonely heath a woman with two dying children looks in desperation to heaven.[37] The series is striking, but not entirely at one with the poem, since the scenes of affluence look pleasantly comfortable and lack a Hogarthian edge. Mary told Miss Porter that she was 'wholly unacquainted' with Maria Cosway, though since her husband Richard, miniaturist to the Prince of Wales, had painted her in the 1780s, this is unlikely to be strictly true.[38] There may have been no recent acquaintance, though a biographer of the Cosways says that Mary 'implored' Maria to undertake the illustrations, but cites no documentary proof.[39] Mary would not have wanted Jane to think they knew each other, for Maria had a dubious reputation and had been rumoured to be another of the Prince's mistresses. But if she *was* lying then her denial would acquire later irony.

Unhappily, Mary's own wintry day was upon her, as her twin enemies, sickness and debt, gained ground. Notices of her ill-health had increased; often she is described as suffering from a 'nervous fever', which suggests that depression was a problem, exacerbated by industry with the pen and anxiety about money. But it was not her own financial situation which led to harassment in the summer of 1799; she was lying seriously ill when two men, a clergyman and his attorney, burst into the sick-room and 'with as little decency as humanity' demanded that she appear in a suit against her brother George.[40] One of them sneered, 'Who . . . could believe that she had once been called the *beautiful* Mrs Robinson?' In early November she was 'in better health than she has been for many years', but she was 'very ill' again by Christmas, and in April the *Post* reported that she was showing 'alarming symptoms of consumption', for which Bristol water had been recommended (the natural springs of the Hotwells had a reputation in such cases, which only the numerous deaths of the sick eventually destroyed).[41]

None of the waters drunk and spas visited over the years had cured her crippling 'rheumatism'. It was this problem that Coleridge tried to help, when on 21 May he wrote to Godwin, enquiring after her and making a suggestion:

> Have you seen Mrs Robinson lately? How is she? – Remember me in the kindest & most respectful phrases to her. – I wish, I knew the particulars of her complaint. For [Humphry] Davy has discovered a perfectly new Acid, by which he has restored the use of limbs to persons who had lost them for many years . . . in cases of supposed Rheumatism. At all events, Davy says, it *can* do no harm, in Mrs Robinson's case – & if she will try it, he will make her up a little parcel & write her a letter of *instructions* &c.[42]

When Godwin went to deliver the message he found Mary in a different sort of trouble: she had been arrested for debt and placed in a sponging-house called Allingham's. He wrote in concern, and received a philosophic reply:

> I assure you that my feelings are not wounded, niether [*sic*] is my Spirit depressed by the 'cloud' you mention. And tho' I shall not dart through it like a Sunbeam I shall warmly feel the attentions with which you and my most valued friends, have honoured me.[43]

She explained that the arrest was for 'necessaries' not luxuries, so she could, as a married woman not legally separated from her husband, pass the debt on to him:

> But then I should involve that husband, and act, as I should *feel*, dishonestly towards my creditors. I therefore submit patiently. I have had various proposals, from many Friends, to settle the business – but I am too proud to borrow, while the arrears *now due* on my annuity from The Prince of Wales, would *doubly* pay the sum for which I am arrested. – I have written to the Prince, and his answer is that 'there is no money at Carlton House! – that he is very sorry for my situation, but, that His *own* is equally distressing!!' you will smile, at such paltry excuses, *as I do*! But I am determined to persist in my demand, half a years annuity being nearly *due*, which is Two hundred and fifty pounds, and I am in custody for sixty-three pounds – *only*!

Godwin went to see her at Allingham's on 1 and 2 June, but by 4 June when he saw her again, she had returned home. A receipt in the Royal Archives, signed Mary Robinson, acknowledges on 2 June 'the Sum of One Hundred and Twenty five Pounds – for One Quarter's Annuity due on the 5th April last'.[44] So the Prince, despite his disordered finances, had been persuaded to act, and Mary was released from her humiliating situation. The likelihood is that it was Lord Moira, a close friend of both, who intervened, since a month later 'Sappho' addressed a poem to her 'gen'rous Friend': 'O! MOIRA! Where can grateful GENIUS see/A loftier THEME, a nobler friend – than THEE!'[45] Francis Rawdon Hastings, Earl of Moira, a distinguished soldier, was also an active parliamentarian who in 1793 had tried to bring in a Bill to reform the laws relating to debtors and such petty seizures; he had also been involved in negotiations over the Prince's finances.

Does the choice of pseudonym, used for love poems, have any significance? Despite all the illness, evidence suggests that in the post-Tarleton years Mary was not without her admirers. Moira could have been the 'noble *cecisbeo*' who accompanied her to the opera on 13 April, and there had also been gossipy hints about an 'Ermined Patron' in February 1798. This titled lord had an estate 'S—', where it was imagined that 'venerable oaks' were inscribed to 'our English

Sappho'.[46] In the autobiographical *Natural Daughter* there is an incident, surely based on a real event, when a 'wealthy libertine' tempts the heroine with a proposal of two thousand pounds to settle her debts and an allowance of £300 a year; he argues that it will be of no account because she has 'already "sacrificed her reputation"'.[47] There was also an unidentified nobleman to whom Mary appealed in vain to return a loan so that she could try the Bristol waters, saying she would be 'sorry to *die* at enmity with any person'.[48]

Another 'enemy' was a mysterious woman to whom Mary refers in a letter to Godwin, reminding him that, at a time when she had accounted the woman her friend, Godwin had described her as 'odious', whereas now he was defending her. Godwin and Mary had had a falling-out just before he left on a trip to Dublin; on his return he wrote her a reproachful letter. Something she had said or done had caused him to feel that Mary was 'capricious' in friendship and insincere in her flattery of his intellect (these two highly intelligent beings had easily bruised egos). She denied the offence, counter-charging that she had never been certain that he was a friend, since 'in mixed societies . . . you *appeared* to feel pleasure, in humbling *my* vanity:– for I am *vain* – I am not without ambition, growing out of a rooted, and I once hoped, a distinguished adoration of Superior talents'.[49] She denied insincerity, for 'I cannot, I never could dissemble'. It was a long self-justifying letter, in which she wrote of sensing that her days were 'nearly numbered', provoking a further accusation from Godwin of 'cherishing a discontented Spirit'. She replied:

> Alas! Had even your Philosophy been so tried; Had you been, in the spring and bloom of Youth frost-nipped by sickness and consigned to a premature old age; Hurled from the most flattering prospects of Delight and Fortune to contemplate a long and dreary perspective, which only the Grave could terminate, would not your spirit, like my own, be weary of its Journey? You say that I have 'Youth and beauty'. Ah! Philosopher, how surely do I feel that both are vanished! You tell me that I have 'Literary Fame'. How comes it then that I am abused, neglected – unhonoured – unrewarded.[50]

But Mary did not want to continue the quarrel and she urged him to accept an olive branch and visit her at Englefield Green. This he did on 1 September, staying overnight and taking with him his friend, the translator James Marshall, for whom Mary felt unqualified affection; it would be the last time either man saw her alive.

Mary had then only just said good-bye to visitors who had stayed several weeks. Eliza Fenwick, author of a novel called *Secresy* [*sic*], was a friend of Mary Hays, one who had helped nurse Mary Wollstonecraft in her last illness. She had a difficult life, with a n'er-do-well husband, no money, and two small children; Mary wrote a tender poem, 'To an Infant Sleeping', for her baby boy. The cottage was something of a refuge for Mrs Fenwick and she seems to have had a happy time; she told Mary Hays that she and Maria had been kept busy as there had been no female servants, but they had managed to go out riding for four or five hours a day and she wrote from a garden seat beneath two tall trees, and 'surrounded by a plantation of shrubs'.[51] It is to Mrs Fenwick that we owe the fullest description of the small *cottage ornée* which Mary jokingly called a 'hovel', but of which she must really have been proud. She begins with the neighbourhood:

> Englefield Green is singularly beautiful. Tis a broad plain on the summit of a high hill, the houses are irregularly scattered & the breaks & openings display an astonishing prospect of richly wooded & cultivated country with the Thames pouring through it.

The cottage stood 'aloof' from grander ones of the neighbourhood, backed by the trees of Windsor Great Park and looking towards St Ann's Hill, where Fox had retreated with Elizabeth Armistead, his wife since 1795. In her *Letter to the Women of England* Mary had called for university education for women; by fortunate chance the view from where Englefield Cottage once stood on the summit of Egham Hill now includes the turrets of Royal Holloway College, the women's university established in 1886.[52]

Mrs Fenwick also describes the interior, which revealed the taste to be expected from Mary Robinson, with just a hint of over-spending:

> [T]he papers of the rooms in a particular degree are beautifully appropriated to the building & situation. The furniture is perhaps more ornamental than I should chuse for myself, but still it is elegant & quiet – nothing gaudy nor ill placed.

And she ends with a tribute to a 'woman whose powers of pleasing, ever varied & graceful, are united to quick feeling & generosity of temper'.

Mary was at her best as a hostess. She liked to have guests, and was planning to receive Eliza Parsons, a novelist, and urging both Pratt and the Porter sisters to come too, tempting them with the Egham races and the military camp which had been set up at nearby Winkfield, whose 'confusion, din, and riot' she celebrated in a lively poem, 'The Camp'. An extraordinary invitation went to Elizabeth Gunning, another novelist. She was a friend of the Porter girls but unknown to Mary, yet when her mother died she wrote not only a letter of sympathy but offered her a sanctuary where she might find 'a change of scenery . . . Books, music, conversation and affectionate attentions'.[53] The impulse to entertain Miss Gunning no doubt stemmed from real sympathy, but also belonged to a day-dream of Mary's which she explained a few days later to Jane Porter:

> Oh! Heavens! If a Select Society could be formed, – a little Colony of Mental powers, – a world of Talents, drawn into a small but brilliant circle, – what a splendid sunshine would it display; and how deeply in gloom it would throw the uninteresting vapid scenery of Human life![54]

She knew it could only ever be a 'Visionary Idea', but perhaps the vision sustained her through the days to come.

The literary labours of that summer would have taxed anyone's strength. The demands of the poetry column had to be met (twelve poems in August, including 'The Camp', the descriptive piece 'London's Summer Morning', and 'The Savage of Aveyron', inspired by news of a wild boy discovered in France). *Lyrical Tales* had to be got in the press, the promised subscription volumes put together; she was writing commissioned prose articles, and a new novel had been begun; if these were not enough she spent ten days in August in the 'torment' of translating Joseph Hager's *Picture of Palermo* from the German, while at the same time nursing an alarmingly swollen ankle. ('Thank Heaven,' she told Miss Porter, '[this] has disappeared for I should not admire a mutilated leg.'[55]) It is a pity that she did not get more pleasure from a book which seductively carries its readers to the orange and lemon groves of Sicily. Perhaps she got some amusement from a report of a furore when her friend John Wolcot had attacked William Gifford with his cane, calling him a 'malicious monkey'.[56]

Then, on 2 September, came the accident which together with the medical treatments it occasioned undoubtedly shortened Mary's life, though she described it light-heartedly to James Marshall:

> Not a word, my dear Friend, to enquire about my poor head! which not only escaped distruction [*sic*]; but has been these ten days almost frantic with torture! On the day of your departure my coachman, probably mistaking me for a truss of Hay, in lifting me out of the slanting room where I slept, forgot the low roof, or rather penthouse, and threw me with considerable violence so high in his arms, that the top of my head absolutely cracked the ceiling. Had the adversary my *brain* encountered, been nearer of its own quality, (*of wood* or *of lead*,) I had never lived to write this letter.[57]

By the end of September her condition had declined sharply, and there could be little doubt about the outcome. On 10 October, in shaky handwriting, she wrote to Godwin, thanking him for his concern, and continuing,

> I am still so feeble, and so depressed in spirit, that I scarcely dare call myself out of danger. The exertion of speaking almost destroys me; to see me, you would not, by any personal feature, know me.[58]

To this atheist she subscribed herself 'God bless you'. Five days later she managed a letter to Jane Porter, her 'sweet Friend', but it conveyed the same message:

> I have scarcely strength to thank you for your kind enquiries. My illness has indeed been so perilous, that I believe little hopes were entertained of my recovery. When my daughter received your letter I was in a state too terrible to describe! – one blister on my shoulders, another on my head; – which, with perpetual bleedings, with the lancet as well as with Leeches, have so reduced me that I am a mere spectre.[59]

This letter, likewise ending 'God bless you, and Bless all that are dear to you', has a postscript in deteriorating writing 'I have but too much reason to believe, that my sojourn on this Earth, will shortly terminate'.

Still the poetic muse hung about her pillows. Lines 'Written on seeing a Rose still blooming at a Cottage Door on Egham Hill', dated 25 October 1800, ask poignantly:

> Why dost thou linger still, sweet flow'r?
> Why yet remain, thy leaves to flaunt?
> This is for thee no fost'ring hour –
> The cold wind blows,
> And many a chilling, ruthless show'r
> Will now assail thee, beauteous rose![60]

The poem was published in the *Post* on 4 November, and others appeared right up to her death; according to the *Memoirs*, 'her unfeeling employers accused her of negligence' when the stream of poetry failed.[61] *Lyrical Tales* was published in November and perhaps it gave Mary some satisfaction to hold the volume which she had told Miss Porter was her 'favourite offspring'. The volume has a vigour belying the physical frailty of their creator.[62] She had been asked to undertake a further translation, Klopstock's *Messiah*, but had had to refuse. She was anxious about unfinished business, however, laying on Maria a solemn injunction to publish both the *Memoirs* and her complete poems. Maria had a friend, Elizabeth Weale, who helped with the distressing tasks of nursing, and it was to her that Mary felt able to talk about her impending death. In an 'unruffled manner' she gave directions for her funeral. She wished to be buried in Old Windsor churchyard for 'a *particular reason*': perhaps because she and Tarleton had been happy in Old Windsor, or maybe because of its nearness to the Castle.

In the last fortnight she endured agony, but may have been able to smile at a letter received from John Wolcot, Peter Pindar:

> I have just heard that you have been exceedingly unwell: for God's sake do not be foolish enough to die yet, as you possess stamina for an hundred years, and a poetical mind that cannot soon be

> replaced. Leave Englefield-green then for London, and let us enjoy our usual laugh and whim. I am much older than you, and yet, I think the Devil at a great distance . . .[63]

On Christmas Eve she asked how near was Christmas day:

> Being answered, 'Within a few days' – '*Yet*,' said she, 'I shall never see it.' The remainder of this melancholy day passed in undescribable tortures. Towards midnight, the sufferer exclaimed, – 'Oh God, oh just and merciful God, help me to support this agony.'[64]

Her last words, the following evening, were to her daughter: '*My darling Mary*!' She died on 26 December at a quarter past noon. The doctors insisted on a post-mortem, and it was found that while the immediate cause of death was 'a *dropsy in the chest*', the intense suffering of her end had probably been caused by six large gallstones.

On the first day of the New Year, the first of the new century, Mary Robinson was interred according to her wishes in Old Windsor churchyard. It was not usual for women to be at funerals, and Mrs Robinson was attended to her grave by just two men, William Godwin and John Wolcot, with one mourning coach and her own. Another of her wishes was carried out when locks of her hair were sent to 'two *particular persons*', assumed to be Banastre Tarleton and the Prince of Wales. What Tarleton did with his can only be guessed, but after the Prince's death a bundle of locks of hair 'of all colours and lengths' was found among his effects; no doubt at least one of them was auburn.[65]

Epilogue

[P]ressing to her heart her daughter, who knelt by her bed-side . . . 'Poor heart!' *murmured she, in a deep and stifled tone*, 'what will become of thee!'

(*The Memoirs of the Late Mrs Robinson*)

Mary Robinson was dead: the talented actress, spectacular Cyprian, accomplished and industrious author, committed feminist and radical, charming and witty hostess, spendthrift, devoted daughter and mother, compassionate, sensitive and sometimes spikily difficult woman. A genius? Perhaps only in her extraordinary versatility, but not undeserving of the 'One little laurel wreath' she craved.

In his diary William Godwin recorded the death in his accustomed manner, 'M Robinson dies', under 26 December 1800.[1] John Wolcot wrote a simple but moving pastoral elegy:

Farewell to the nymph of my heart,
Farewell to the cottage and vine,
From thy scenes with a tear I depart,
Where pleasure so often was mine.

Remembrance shall dwell on thy smile,
Shall dwell on thy lute and thy song,
Which often my hours to beguile
Have echo'd the valleys among . . .[2]

Coleridge also wrote a four-line tributary verse ('O'er her pil'd grave the gale of evening sighs;/And flowers will grow upon its grassy Slope. . .'). It was included in his letter to his friend Thomas Poole:

> Poor dear Mrs Robinson! You have heard of her Death. She wrote me a most affecting, heart-rending Letter a few weeks before she

died to express what she called her death bed affection and esteem for me.[3]

He may have heard the news from Daniel Stuart, whose *Morning Post* gave the event prominence. A long obituary celebrated Mrs Robinson's 'truly liberated and munificent mind' and 'the elevated independence of her spirit', and continued with the confident declaration:

> All honoured her; all were her friends: and, we believe, it might be inscribed on her tomb, without danger of contradiction, that she never made herself an enemy.[4]

Jane Porter could have told Stuart otherwise. She received news of Mrs Robinson's death in a disturbing scene which reveals not only a malignancy of spirit, but even the ambivalence of friendship towards a 'fallen woman'.

At the beginning of January Miss Porter was staying at Champion Lodge, home of a Mr and Mrs Crespigny. Mary de Crespigny, a fifty-year-old matron and minor author, had like Mrs Robinson 'taken up' the young woman. She had recently encouraged Jane to keep a journal, which she opened with a portrait of her 'good-natured . . . religious & charitable' hostess. Then on 3 January, while they were at table, someone abruptly announced the death of Mrs Robinson:

> Obliged as I was to conceal the shock, which this intelligence gave to me, I bore up very composedly, till after the company had dined. Then finding, that in spite of Mrs Crespigny's penetration, (for to her severe enquiries, I had denied my knowledge of Mrs Robinson,) I must be overcome, I pleaded a nervous head-ache, and made that an excuse for the tears which poured down my cheeks. Oh! How did it cut my heart, that I was thus forced to hide a regret which I thought laudable! I one moment despised myself, for being ashamed to avow feelings, which I could not condemn; and the next, I excused myself, from the conviction that it was only a prudence due to my sister and myself, not to publish a conduct, which however guiltless, would draw on us the disrespect of many of our friends, and most likely the scandal of the world.[5]

Mrs Crespigny warned that if she admitted knowing Mrs Robinson, 'all the world would cut me – that she must drop me – that I should be shunned by all decent people'.[6] To assuage the guilt she felt at denying knowledge of one whom she both admired and pitied, she immediately wrote a tribute, intending it for a monthly magazine. She portrayed Mary as a 'lovely Magdalen', emphasising her faith and trust in a just God, but in the end withheld the piece on the advice of her sister, who feared her being suspected as its author.[7]

Mrs Crespigny appears a bullying prude, but she was worse; she hid from Miss Porter that *she* was almost certainly acquainted with Mrs Robinson and may well have been the 'odious' friend turned enemy referred to in the letter to Godwin. On several occasions when he met Mary, his journal shows that a 'Crespigny' was also present, and once 'Miss R J [?] Crespigny' (not a daughter, as there was a son only).[8] He also records reading Mrs Crespigny's novel *The Pavilion*. As with Coleridge, there would have been occasions when one or more Crespignys were entertained by Mrs Robinson when Godwin was not present. Perhaps the wife felt that her husband was seeing too much of Mrs Robinson; perhaps Mrs Robinson turned down a poem of hers for the *Morning Post*. The 'terrifying interview' had its effect on Jane Porter, convincing her that she had engaged in an 'imprudent friendship'. Maria Robinson called in April and spoke 'in a manner that made me love her, and more tenderly regard the memory of her dear injured parent', but Miss Porter made no effort to maintain the acquaintance.[9] The sins of the mother were to be visited upon the daughter.

Maria Elizabeth was twenty-six in 1800, the same age as Mary when she suffered her crippling illness, and it might be said that her mother's death exercised a similarly crippling effect on her life. To be the daughter of 'the late Mrs Robinson' was to reduce her status both socially and financially. No one had a bad word to say about Maria, indeed when Richard Polwhele published his satire *The Unsex'd Females* in 1798, a footnote to a couplet condemning Mrs Robinson (for admiration expressed in *Walsingham* for Rousseau) exempted her 'beautiful' daughter, 'whose personal charms are only equalled by the elegance of her mind'.[10] She was the girl who drew all eyes at a masquerade and who introduced the '*gypsy hat*' and '*Grecian head-dress*' to fashionable society.[11] When Mary contemplated leaving

England for Italy it was reported that her daughter would be married from her brother's house with an appropriate 'fortune' to a 'Mr. H.', but if so nothing came of it, and George Darby did not help his niece after his sister's death.[12] Perhaps Mary and George quarrelled after she failed to take up his offer of a home.

Mary's daughter faced 1801 saddled with debt, and with an annual income of £200, according to the bond of twenty years earlier. A quarterly payment for her mother had fallen due the day before her death, and the Prince magnanimously agreed that this would be paid to Miss Robinson 'as a present'.[13] But by June she had only received £50 of her mother's £125, and none of her own annuity. It is pleasing to discover in the Royal Archives a letter signed Ban: Tarleton on her behalf; he was on his way to Dublin to take over the military organisation of southern Ireland, but he wrote to Colonel John McMahon, the Prince's Treasurer, begging him to attend to the situation both to oblige him and 'thereby do an infinitely better thing – assist one, who I am sorry to say from a variety of unpleasant events is become almost friendless'.[14] His intervention seems to have had little effect – probably because Carlton House coffers were empty – and in late November, 'compelled by dire necessity', Maria pleaded to have three-quarters of a year's annuity paid.[15] To her anger and embarrassment she then learned that Thomas Robinson was claiming the £125, exerting his rights as a husband over his wife's estate in the absence of a will.[16] She replied to Robert Gray, the administrative official at Somerset House, describing her father's actions as the '*most harmful* and indelicate proceeding he could have been guilty of'; she gave Gray permission to show him her letter.[17] It was pointed out that her father was legally responsible for her mother's debts, but the ones Maria was concerned with were the local ones, 'Butchers Bakers &c &c', who were pressing for payment. She was always to dread the knock of the local tradesman, and the Royal Archives reveal that a pattern of the rest of her life was writing letters begging for money owing, or advances to meet their bills.

If abandoned by some of her mother's former friends, others, like Tarleton, tried to help, and she wrote of that 'most truly excellent man, – Lord Moira, – who has been the only *true friend* I ever found'.[18] But she kept up, at least for a while, epistolary acquaintance with Godwin, Coleridge, and Pratt; Pratt received a cheerful letter thanking him for all his 'good offices' to her, and for his recommendation of one Robert as a servant:

> He must understand waiting at Table. – the care of the Horse & chaise – In short, he must be a *Footman/Groom*, – I allow one Suit of Working cloths [*sic*], and one afternoon Suit, a best, and a working Hat per An.^{m} a Great Coat every three years – sixteen pounds p^{r} Ann^{m}. He must find his own boots in case they are wanted which is not very often as I do not take him out with me on Horse back, but to make very *formal visits*! – You know how quietly we live . . .[19]

'Footman/Groom' is a joke: she cannot afford both.

In this letter Maria also refers to her 'excellent Bessy', Elizabeth Weale, who was to be her lifelong companion at Englefield Cottage. Because of the troubles over her mother's property Maria drew up her will in 1801, leaving everything to Elizabeth.[20] She is described as the daughter of Thomas and Ann Weale, late of Evesham in the county of Worcester, but though the records of St Lawrence's Church in Evesham reveal a string of children, including three daughters, Mary (1770), Sarah (1775) and Martha (1781), there is no Elizabeth.[21] Sarah Weale was a witness to the will; perhaps Elizabeth was a second name for Mary, the closest in age to Maria. The will leaves to Elizabeth 'all and singular my household goods furniture plate linen china jewels diamonds Rings Monies and Securities for Money'. Jewels, diamonds, and rings! Mrs Robinson must have hung on to the Prince's gifts and refused to realise their cash value for her debts. Maria seems to have done likewise.

Following her mother's death Maria set about the publication of the *Memoirs*, with the assistance of the 'Friend', censoring, recasting and completing the manuscript autobiography, before who knows how many pages were destroyed. The *Memoirs* were published in four volumes, rather deluding the public, who found that the last two were made up of poetry, prose articles, and the opening chapters of the unfinished novel, *Jasper*. They aroused interest, but were only reviewed at length in the *Monthly Review*, which noted their resemblance to a novel, the problem of 'truth' in autobiography, the absence of Thomas Robinson's side of the story, and the blame that must attach to the author for putting herself in dangerous situations: 'Mrs R. played the part of a *pretty*, but not a *prudent* wife'.[22] The *Memoirs* may have shocked those who knew only the older Mrs Robinson; Coleridge did not read them, but the tenor of a letter to Maria shows him aware that they covered the early years of indiscretions. He wrote pompously that 'it was my Hope, my heart-felt wish, my Prayer, my Faith, that the latter age of your Mother would be illustrious & redemptory – that to the Genius & generous Virtues of her youth she would add Judgement, & Thought – whatever was correct & dignified as a Poetess, & all that was matronly as Woman'.[23] The problem, as Maria was only too aware, was that the *Memoirs* revived memories of the Perdita, rather than the poet. In 1814 Pierce Egan, producing a gleeful volume of imaginary letters between Florizel and Perdita, noted an 'afflicting drawback' to her story:

> That the ELEGANT, ENLIGHTENED, INTERESTING,
> BEAUTIFUL PERDITA
> was unchaste![24]

Though one may deplore Maria's censorship of the *Memoirs*, her instinct was right. She also saw to the publication of the complete poetical works in 1806, but her mother's literary reputation was eroded during the nineteenth century as she, and all contemporary women poets, were eclipsed by the dominance of male Romantic writers. What remained of Mary Robinson, until the late twentieth century and her rediscovery by literary academics, was the story of the abandoned royal mistress. This was kept alive by the *Memoirs*, reprinted many times in the nineteenth century and with no suspicions of any tampering.[25]

Maria also produced a poetic anthology of her own, *The Wild Wreath* (1804). This contains a few of her own poems, previously unpublished ones by her mother, and poems by other authors, including Pratt, Merry, Southey, Coleridge, M.G. Lewis, and one 'SUSAN'. This was Susan Priscilla Tarleton, who may not have been mistress of all the *-ologies* and *-ographies*, but showed her accomplishments not only in some competent verse, but in five attractive vignettes, though Mary would surely not have relished having a poem of hers illustrated by Mrs B. Tarleton. It must have been because of Tarleton's friendship with the Duke of York that

Maria got permission to dedicate the volume to the Duchess, which she described as 'the most honourable and flattering event of my life'. A second anthology was put together in 1805, this time to be dedicated to the Countess of Loudoun and Moira (Lord Moira had married in 1804); it was offered to publishers, but they declined it.[26]

Another duty was fulfilled when the Old Windsor grave was completed. One side was inscribed with a tributary sonnet by Pratt to the 'fairest of the fair', the other reproduced an epitaph written for a character in *Walsingham*:

> No wealth had she, nor power to sway;
> Yet rich in worth, and learning's store:
> She wept her summer hours away,
> She heard the wintry storm no more.
>
> Yet o'er this low and silent spot,
> Full many a bud of Spring shall wave,
> While she, by all, save ONE forgot,
> SHALL SNATCH A WREATH BEYOND THE GRAVE.[27]

Half a century later a couple writing a book about the Thames visited the churchyard where they talked with an 'old labourer'; he recalled, perhaps with some exaggeration, the 'loads of lords and gentlemen . . . but not so many ladies' who at first flocked to see the tomb of the 'Fair Shepherdess'. He also remembered how he would open the gate to her daughter,

> . . . and she'd bow and smile like a real lady: but always . . . always she came either at early morning or in the gloom before night. She'd hang over the railing, even in winter, like a wreath of snow: it always seemed as though she loved, yet was ashamed of her.[28]

Maria was certainly self-conscious about her situation, asking that her annuity be paid discreetly, so that she could pay her taxes but avoid any 'awkward explanation' as to the source of her income.[29]

After her quarrel with her father there is evidence of a later reconciliation. As discovered by local historian Janet Kennish, Land Tax records show a Thomas Robinson as the occupier from 1809 of property owned by the Lascelles estate in Datchet, on the other side of the Thames from Old Windsor. In 1813 he was living in Southley House, a substantial property (now demolished), though he had gone by 1815.[30] The parish register for Datchet shows the burial there of a Thomas Robinson, who died on 30 July 1814 aged sixty-four, an appropriate age for Mary's husband. These facts fit with black-edged letters in the Royal Archives in late 1814, in one of which Maria writes of 'recent family affliction'.[31] She had no family left but her father, so the Datchet Thomas Robinson must be him, lying just a mile from his wife (there is no gravestone, nor was there a will, and his £100 annuity from his father died with him). He went to the grave silent on the events of his life; in contrast to his wife, whose pen was ever poised to counter misrepresentation, Robinson published no rebuttal of her black portrayal of him in the *Memoirs*. There may have been no defence to make, but perhaps, in his way, by not revealing all that he might have done, he did after all show matrimonial loyalty.[32]

After 1814 Maria's letters to Robert Gray asking, and apologising for asking, for advances on her income, making promises not to do it again and apologising for breaking those promises, show that she was losing spirit. She was distressed when he accused her of 'imprudence' and 'bad management', describing herself as 'an unoffending Being who has *deserved a better fate* than she has met with in her journey through life'.[33] But Gray showed his humanity by advancing her money from his own purse, and though they never met, except as she said 'through the medium of the *general Post Office*', she called him 'the best Friend I have met with, in my many vicissitudes'.[34]

Between the summers of 1815 and 1816 Maria may have had a visitor in Mary Godwin, when she was living with Shelley close by at Bishopsgate on the edge of Windsor Forest. It seems probable that she would have sought out the daughter of the friend of her father and mother, and that she did so is suggested by her 1826 science-fiction novel *The Last Man*, in which the narrator's sister, living in a cottage at Bishopsgate, is called Perdita. After 1816 Maria's health declined; in 1817 she wrote of a 'lingering illness of near fourteen months'.[35] She died in January 1818. Her quarterly allowance had been sent two days earlier, and to defray expenses was allowed to Miss Weale, who expressed gratitude that she could attend to 'my beloved late friends concerns'.[36] Maria was buried with her mother, the inscription reading

'Maria Elizabeth Robinson, daughter of Mary Robinson of literary fame, who died at Englefield Cottage on January 14th 1818, in the 43rd year of her age'.[37] Thus in death she was defined by her mother's life; time has obliterated even this record of her existence.

Elizabeth Weale thereupon inherited all remaining jewels, diamonds, rings and other property, including literary effects. She disappears from Englefield Green, but may well be the Elizabeth Weale who ran a business of some kind at 70 Berniers Street in London, and whose own will was proved on 25 May 1833, leaving the shop, goodwill and stock to a niece and her husband.[38] If this was Maria's Bessy, she must have sold her inheritance to buy the business. Who but Miss Weale could have put up for sale the manuscript of Mary's memoirs? Sotheby's records of the period were lost in a fire, but a biography of Gainsborough refers to the sale in the late 1820s, when the pages fetched a mere £3 8*s* at auction, a sign of how Mrs Robinson's star had fallen.[39]

Of Mary's lovers, Charles James Fox died first, in 1806, his beloved Liz at his side. The Prince of Wales was deeply affected, contributing £500 towards the funeral in Westminster Abbey and wearing black for months afterwards. Ten years later, when he heard that Sheridan was dying in penury and squalor, the Prince sent a representative with £200 for immediate relief. Sheridan too was buried in Westminster Abbey.

General Sir Banastre Tarleton, Baronet, Knight Grand Cross of the Most Noble Order of the Bath, lived on, a respected member of the establishment, until 16 January 1833; his wife died in 1864. They had had no children. George Capel, Earl of Essex, formerly Lord Malden, also died childless in 1839, a year after making a second marriage to an opera singer.

George Prince of Wales, Prince Regent from 1811, George IV from 1820, ended his days on 26 June 1830. The dashing Prince Florizel had become a grossly fat old man (his underpants in Brighton Museum are of a size to marvel at), with an almost equally fat last mistress in Lady Conyngham, though he was buried with a miniature of Mrs Fitzherbert round his neck. His letters to Perdita had long been consumed by flame, but large packets of love letters to others were found, 'descriptive of the most furious passion', which went the same way.[40]

What happened to the jewelled miniature which enshrined the pledge to be '*Unalterable to my Perdita through life*'? Portraits of the 1790s show Mary wearing it; it was a treasure she would never yield up. The miniature must surely have accompanied her to the grave in Old Windsor and be there still, two miles from where George IV lies in St George's Chapel. Of all his many mistresses, in death at least, Perdita, the first, lies closer to Florizel than any other.

Appendix

MARY ROBINSON'S DRAMATIC ROLES
(Compiled in order of first performances from *The London Stage 1660–1800: Part 5 1776–1800*, edited by Charles Beecher Hogan, Carbondale, Southern Illinois University Press, 1978). All plays mainpieces unless stated. *New play.

Juliet in *Romeo and Juliet* (altered by Garrick): 10, 12, 21, 27 December 1776; 23 May 1777 (benefit for a group of actors); 27 December 1779.

Statira in *Alexander the Great; or, The Rival Queens* (Nathaniel Lee, 1677, but with alterations): 17 February 1777; 10 May 1780.

Amanda in **A Trip to Scarborough* (Sheridan's reworking of Vanbrugh's *The Relapse*): 24, 25, 27 February, 1, 4, 6, 8, 18, March; 2, 8 April 1777; 21 December 1778; 13 January, 18, 30 November 1779; 10 January, 24 February, 19 April 1780.

Fanny in *The Clandestine Marriage* (Colman and Garrick, 1766): Benefit performance 10 April 1778.

Ophelia in *Hamlet* (altered by Garrick): 30 September, 4 October, 29 December 1777; 17 March, 19 September, 16 October 1778; 6 February, 18 September 1779.

Lady Anne in *Richard III* (altered by Colley Cibber): 7, 11 October 1777; 8, 26 May, 26 October, 23 November 1779; 12 May 1780.

Araminta in *The Old Bachelor* (Congreve 1693, with alterations by Sheridan): 9 October 1777; 18 May 1778.

The Lady in *Comus* (Milton's masque adapted as an afterpiece by George Colman): 15, 16, 17, 19, 22, 23, 29, 31 December 1777; 7 January (following *The School for Scandal* 'By command of Their Majesties'), 23, 26, 31 January, 5, 17, 24 February, 9 March 1778, 13 April 1779.

Emily in *The Runaway* (Hannah Cowley, 1776): 10 January, 28 April (benefit for Mrs Wrighten), 22 May, 14 November 1778; 7 January, 26 February, 14 April, 16 May 1780.

Araminta in *The Confederacy* (Vanbrugh, 1705): 9 April 1778.

Fanny in *Joseph Andrews* (an adaptation as an afterpiece, author unknown, of Fielding's novel): 20 April 1778.

Octavia in *All for Love* (Dryden's neo-classical version of *Antony and Cleopatra* 1678): 23 April 1778 (benefit for Mr Palmer).

Lady Macbeth in *Macbeth*: Benefit performance 30 April 1778, with the addition of her own musical afterpiece, *The Lucky Escape*.

Lady Plume in **The Camp* (afterpiece devised by Sheridan, with music by Thomas Linley): 15, 16, 17, 19, 20, 21,23, 24, 26, 27, 28, 29, 30, 31 October; 2, 3, 4, 5, 6, 7, 9, 10, 11, 12, 13, 14, 16, 17, 18, 21, 23 November 1778; MR replaced for subsequent performances until 11 February, when she took role of **Lady Sash**, 13, 15, 25 February; 12 April; 3 May 1779.

Palmira in *Mahomet* (translation from Voltaire by James Miller and John Hoadly, 1744): 11, 13, 17 November 1778; 18 January 1779.

Miss Richly in *The Discovery* (Frances Sheridan, 1763): 3, 5, 27 February, 18 March, 9 April, 9 November 1779.

Alinda in **The Law of Lombardy* (Robert Jephson, 1779): 8, 9, 12, 13, 15, 16, 20, 22, 23 February 1779.

Cordelia in *King Lear* (Tate/Garrick version): Benefit performance 14 April, 4 May 1779.

Jacintha in *The Suspicious Husband* (Benjamin Hoadly, 1747): 10 May 1779; 1, 6 April 1780.

Fidelia in *The Plain Dealer* (William Wycherley, 1677, bowdlerised version by Isaac Bickerstaffe): 15 May, 9, 28 October 1779; 8 February 1780.

Viola in *Twelfth Night*: 23 October, 21, 31 December 1779, 29 April, 20 May 1780.

Nancy in *The Camp* (Sheridan, 1779): 6, 13, 16 November; 17, 27 December 1779 (17 December as part of a royal command performance following *The Way of the World*).

Perdita in *The Winter's Tale* (Garrick's shortened version, 1756): 20, 26, 29 November, 1, 3 December ('By command of Their Majesties'), 11 December 1779, 1, 11, 22 January, 10 February, 30 March, 12 April, 18, 24 May 1780.

Rosalind in *As You Like It*: 28 January, benefit performance 7 April, 2 May 1780

Prologue to *The Double Dealer* (Elizabeth Richardson, 1779), 29 January 1780.

Oriana in *The Inconstant; or,* The *Way to Win Him* (George Farquhar, 1702): 3, 25 April 1780.
Imogen in *Cymbeline* (altered by Garrick): 18 April 1780.
The Widow Brady in *The Irish Widow* (afterpiece by Garrick, 1772): 4, 16, 19 May 1780.
Eliza Camply in **The Miniature Picture* (afterpiece by Elizabeth, Baroness Craven, 1779): 24, 27, 31 May 1780.

Notes

The following abbreviations have been used:

Angelina	*Angelina; A novel*, Hookham & Carpenter, 1796
Bass	Robert D. Bass, *The Green Dragoon: The Lives of Banastre Tarleton and Mary Robinson*, Alvin Redman, 1957
Biographical Dictionary	Philip P. Highfill Jr, Kalmin A. Burnim, Edward A. Langhams, *A Biographical Dictionary of Actors, Actresses, Musicians, Dancers, Managers & Other Stage Personnel in London, 1660–1800*, 16 vols, Carbondale, Southern Illinois University Press, 1991
Coleridge Letters	Samuel Taylor Coleridge, *Collected Letters of Samuel Coleridge*, ed. Earl Stanley Gibbs, 2 vols, Oxford, Clarendon Press, 1956
Correspondence	A. Aspinall, ed., *The Correspondence of George, Prince of Wales 1770–1812, Vol. 1 1770–1789*, Cassell, 1963
False Friend	*The False Friend: A Domestic Story*, T.N. Longman & O. Rees, 1799
Garrick	Harry William Pedicord and Frederick Louis Bergmann (eds), *The Plays of David Garrick*, 5 vols, Carbondale, Southern Illinois University Press, 1981
Georgiana	Georgiana Cavendish, *Georgiana: Extracts from the Correspondence of Georgiana, Duchess of Devonshire*, ed. The Earl of Bessborough, John Murray, 1955
George IV	Christopher Hibbert, *George IV*, Harmondsworth, Middlesex, Penguin, 1976
Hawkins	Laetitia-Matilda Hawkins, *Anecdotes, Biographical Sketches and Memoirs*, F.C. and J. Rivington, 2 vols, 1822
Hubert	*Hubert de Sevrac, A Romance, of the Eighteenth Century*, Hookham & Carpenter, 1796
Letter/Natural Daughter	*Letter to the Women of England and The Natural Daughter*, ed. Sharon M. Setzer, Ontario, Canada, Broadview Press, 2003

Levy	M.J. Levy, *George IV and his Mistresses*, Peter Owen Publishers, 1996
London Stage 4	*The London Stage 1660–1800, Part 4: 1747–1776*, ed. with a Critical Introduction by George Winchester Stone Jr, Carbondale, Illinois, Southern Illinois University Press, 1968
London Stage 5	*The London Stage 1660–1800 Part 5: 1776–1800*, ed. with a Critical Introduction by Charles Beecher Hogan, Carbondale, Illinois, Southern Illinois University Press, 1968
Memoirs	*Perdita: The Memoirs of Mary Robinson (1758–1800)*, ed. M.J. Levy, Peter Owen Publishers, 1994
PRO	Public Record Office
RA	Royal Archives
Selected Poems	*Mary Robinson: Selected Poems*, ed. Judith Pascoe, Ontario, Canada, Broadview Press, 2000
Vancenza	*Vancenza; or, The Dangers of Credulity*, J. Bell, 1792
Walpole	W.S. Lewis *et al.*, *The Yale Edition of Horace Walpole's Correspondence*, Oxford and New Haven, Oxford University Press and Yale University Press, 1937–83
Walsingham	*Walsingham; or, The Pupil of Nature*, ed. Julie Shaffer, Ontario, Canada, Broadview Press, 2003
The Widow	*The Widow; or, A Picture of Modern Times*, Hookham & Carpenter, 1794

CHAPTER ONE: BRISTOL BELLE

1. *Oracle*, 25 January 1798.
2. *Morning Post*, 2 December 1797.
3. See David V. Erdman, 'Lost Poem Found: The co-operative pursuit & recapture of an escaped Coleridge "sonnet" of 72 lines', in *New York Library Bulletin* 65, 1961, pp. 249–68.
4. *Memoirs*, p. 46.
5. *Ibid.*, p. 62. See Eleanor Ty, *Empowering the Feminine: The Narratives of Mary Robinson, Jane West, and Amelia Opie, 1796–1812*, Toronto, University of Toronto Press, 1998, pp. 23–35 for discussion of MR's self-presentation in the *Memoirs*.
6. 'Stanzas to a Friend, Who Desired to have my Portrait', ll. 43–8, first published in *Poems* (1793). *Selected Poems*, pp. 139–42.
7. Horace Walpole to George Montagu, 22 October 1766, Walpole 10, p. 232.

8. Facts of Nicholas Darby's life are mainly drawn from William H. Whiteley's account in the *Canadian Dictionary of National Biography*.
9. *Memoirs*, p. 18.
10. A George Pettit was a mercer in Bridgwater in 1708, and a Jonathon Vinicott (James's brother?), whose wife was called Ann, was a tinman, later wine merchant (Somerset Archive and Record Service, DD/DP 93/5). There was also a 'Vinicott's workhouse' in Bridgwater in 1721. In this year too 'John Vinicott the elder' leased the Star Inn, Bridgwater (DD/X/SEA 1). Thanks to P.J. Hocking for this information.
11. Bristol Record Office, P/St.Aug/R/1(e)1 for John; P/St.Aug/R/(e)2 for Elizabeth's baptism; P/St.Aug/R1(e)6 for Mary Darby's and Elizabeth's burials.
12. William was baptised at St Michael Without, Bristol Record Office, P/St.Aug/R/1(c).
13. See John Rogan (ed.), *Bristol Cathedral: History and Architecture*, Stroud, Tempus, 2000, p. 42 for the picture, p. 60 for Minster House's history.
14. *Memoirs*, p. 18.
15. *Walsingham*, p. 41.
16. 'Mistaken or Misled? Mary Robinson's Birth Date', in *Women's Writing* 9, No. 1, 2002, pp. 139–42. Thanks to Alix Nathan for replying so quickly to my query.
17. The manuscript is held in a private collection.
18. Bristol Record Office, P/St Aug/R/1(e). The copy is P/St Aug/R/1(f).
19. *Memoirs*, pp. 20–1.
20. See 'Thomas Chatterton' in Richard Holmes, *Sidetracks: Explorations of a Romantic Biographer*, HarperCollins (Flamingo Paperback), 2001, pp. 5–50. Holmes argues convincingly that Chatterton's death was accident not suicide.
21. See 'Women teachers and the expansion of girls' schooling in England, c.1760–1820', in Hannah Barker and Elaine Chalus (eds), *Gender in Eighteenth-Century England: Roles, Representations and Responsibilities*, Harlow, Addison Wesley Longman, 1997, pp. 101–25.
22. *Felix Farley's Bristol Journal*, 16 February 1765.
23. *Walsingham*, p. 117.
24. Quoted in Anne Stott, *Hannah More: The First Victorian*, Oxford, Oxford University Press, 2003, pp. 9–10.
25. Walpole to Hannah More, 17 August 1788, Walpole 31, p. 277.
26. Katherine C. Balderston (ed.), *Thraliana: the Diary of Mrs. Hester Lynch Thrale (later Mrs. Piozzi) 1776–1809*, Oxford, The Clarendon Press, 1942, vol. II, p. 82.

27. The deleted passage is found on p. 18 of the manuscript.
28. *Memoirs*, p. 22.
29. *Ibid.*, p. 25.
30. *Ibid.*
31. He was buried 17 October 1766 (Bristol Record Office, microfiche P/St.Aug/R/1E(6), frame 32).
32. PRO PC1/3185 (from which document also comes the sum invested and number of men engaged).
33. *Felix Farley's Bristol Journal*, 20, 27 February, 5 March 1768.
34. 'London's Summer Morning', ll. 1–14, first published 23 August 1800 in the *Morning Post*. See *Selected Poems*, pp. 352–3.
35. *Memoirs*, p. 29.
36. See Julie Shaffer's introduction to *Walsingham*, p. 27, and pp. 19–34 for relevant educational issues.
37. *Letter/Natural Daughter*, p. 214.
38. *Memoirs*, p. 32.
39. *Ibid.*, p. 30.
40. *Ibid.*, p. 34.
41. *Ibid.*, p. 35.
42. Quoted in Ian McIntyre, *Garrick*, Harmondsworth, Allen Lane, 1999, p. 484.
43. R.B. Sheridan to Thomas Linley, undated but 1775, in Cecil Price (ed.), *The Letters of Richard Brinsley Sheridan*, vol. III, Oxford, The Clarendon Press, 1966, p. 297.
44. *Memoirs*, p. 37.
45. Journal entry for 19 February 1773, in Lars E. Troide (ed.), *The Early Journals and Letters of Fanny Burney Volume I, 1768–1773*, Oxford, The Clarendon Press, 1988, p. 242.
46. *Memoirs*, p. 36.
47. *Town and Country Magazine*, January 1781, p. 10.

CHAPTER TWO: THE DISASTROUS MARRIAGE

1. *Memoirs*, p. 48.
2. Theophilus Jones, *History of Brecknockshire*, Edwin Davies, 1898, p. 339.
3. *Letters from Perdita to a Certain Israelite and His Answers to them*, J. Fielding, 1781, p. 7.
4. *Memoirs*, p. 42.
5. *Ibid.*, p. 43.
6. *Ibid.*, p. 48.

7. Lucyle Werkmeister, A *Newspaper History of England 1792–1793*, Lincoln, University of Nebraska Press, 1967, p. 33.
8. *Letters from Perdita*, p. 35.
9. *Ibid.*, p. 26.
10. The view can still be enjoyed, though the house, a nineteenth-century replacement, is offices for hospital administration.
11. *Memoirs*, p. 49.
12. *Ibid.*, p. 51.
13. *Ibid.*, p. 54.
14. *Ibid.*, p. 56.
15. *Humphrey Clinker*, Oxford, Oxford University Press World's Classics Edition, 1949, p. 109.
16. *Ibid.*, p. 105.
17. *Memoirs*, p. 53.
18. *Ibid.*, p. 54.
19. *Letters from Perdita*, p. 11.
20. *Town and Country Magazine*, October 1773, p. 514.
21. See I.M. Davis, *The Harlot and the Statesman*, Bourne End, Bucks, The Kensal Press, 1986, p. 22.
22. Thomas Frost, *The Life of Thomas Lord Lyttelton*, Tinsley Brothers, 1876, p. 125.
23. *Life of Lord Lyttelton*, p. v.
24. *Memoirs*, p. 56.
25. *Ibid.*, p. 57, and *see also* pp. 67 and 79.
26. *Ibid.*, p. 58.
27. *Ibid.*, p. 59.
28. *Ibid.*, p. 68.
29. *Ibid.*, p. 71.
30. 'Ode to Virtue', in *Poems by Mrs Robinson*, C. Parker, 1775, p. 45, ll. 1–2.
31. *Life of Lord Lyttelton*, p. 246.
32. *Selected Poems*, ll. 1–4, p. 72.
33. PRO PRIS 10/21. It is curious that among his creditors is listed one Mary Darby, to whom he owed £10.
34. *Memoirs*, p. 64.
35. PROB 11/1096.
36. J.W. von Archenholtz, A *Picture of England*, Edward Jeffery, 1789, II, p. 53.
37. Quoted in John Ashton, *The Fleet, Its River, Prison, and Marriages*, T. Fisher Unwin, 1888, p. 299.
38. *Selected Poems*, p. 69, ll. 9–12.

39. *Monthly Review*, September 1775, p. 262.
40. *Memoirs*, p. 80.
41. See Amanda Foreman, *Georgiana: Duchess of Devonshire*, HarperCollins, 1998, pp. 22–43.
42. *Memoirs*, p. 84.
43. *Ibid.*
44. PRO PRIS 10/21.

CHAPTER THREE: GARRICK'S GIRL

1. *Memoirs*, p. 85.
2. *Letter/Natural Daughter*, p. 160.
3. *London Stage* 4, pp. xli–ii.
4. *Biographical Dictionary*, 13, p. 32.
5. *London Stage* 5, p. 11.
6. Quoted in Jean Benedetti, *David Garrick and the Birth of Modern Theatre*, Methuen, 2001, p. 195.
7. *Letter/Natural Daughter*, p. 179.
8. As described by Sheridan in *The Critic*. For details of stage history, see the introduction to *London Stage* 5.
9. Garrick 3, *Romeo and Juliet*, Act V, Sc. iv, ll. 93–109.
10. *Memoirs*, pp. 87–8.
11. Quoted *London Stage* 5, p. 43.
12. *Memoirs*, p. 89.
13. *Morning Advertiser*, 25 February 1777.
14. *Memoirs*, p. 89.
15. *Gazetteer & New Daily Advertiser*, 26 February 1777.
16. The tickets sold for a benefit were printed pieces of paper, but normal 'tickets' were reusable metal disks. None guaranteed a particular seat.
17. See Linda Kelly, *Richard Brinsley Sheridan: A Life*, Pimlico, 1997, p. 78. Miss Hopkins became a stalwart of Drury Lane; she married William Brereton, and after his death John Philip Kemble.
18. Date identified by M.J. Levy in *Memoirs*, p. xi.
19. *Ibid.*, pp. 90–1.
20. *Ibid.*, pp. 88–9.
21. *Ibid.*, p. 100.
22. *Morning Post*, 26 August 1779. Squib's sneering reply appeared on 30 August.
23. Kelly, p. 81.
24. *Biographical Dictionary*, 13, p. 35.
25. *Morning Post*, 1 October 1777.

26. *Morning Chronicle*, 8 October 1777.
27. See *Morning Post* and *Morning Chronicle*, 22 May 1778.
28. Foreman, *Georgiana*, pp. 63–4.
29. *Morning Chronicle*, 9 February 1779.
30. Mary wrongly dates the events to 1776; it was in 1778 that Miss Farren played at the Haymarket.
31. Quoted in *Biographical Dictionary* 5, p. 164. Fox's affair with Miss Farren was chronicled in newspapers from late autumn 1780 to early 1781.
32. *Morning Post*, 27 April 1778.
33. *Ibid.*, 1 May 1778.
34. Her manuscript of the songs, beautifully bound, was presented to the British Library by Coventry Patmore (Additional MS 25984).
35. Ll. 17–20. First printed in the *Oracle*, 26 September 1789.
36. *Memoirs*, pp. 93 and 99.
37. Wrongly dated as 1778 in the *Memoirs*.
38. *Ibid.*, pp. 95–8.
39. *Ibid.*, p. 100.
40. See Saul, David, *Prince of Pleasure: The Prince of Wales and the Making of the Regency*, Little, Brown and Company, 1998, pp. 130–3. In 1787 Sir John married Laetitia Darby, former doxy of a condemned highwayman, whose language awed even the Prince of Wales.
41. *Gazetteer*, 9 November 1779.
42. *The Town and Country Magazine*, May 1780, p. 235.

CHAPTER FOUR: ENTER THE PRINCE

1. See Olwen Hedley, *Queen Charlotte*, John Murray, 1977, pp. 72–7.
2. The building was demolished in 1802; the site is marked by a sundial on a lawn in Kew Gardens.
3. *Correspondence*, p. 5.
4. Mrs Vernon Delves Broughton (ed.), *Court and Private Life in the Time of Queen Charlotte: being the Journals of Mrs Papendiek, Assistant Keeper of the Wardrobe and Reader to her Majesty*, 2 vols, Richard Bentley & Son, 1887, I, p. 132.
5. Robert Huish, *Memoirs of George IV*, 2 vols, Thomas Kelly, 1831, I, p. 49.
6. *Journals of Mrs Papendiek*, I, p. 91.
7. Quoted in *The Farington Diary* in Frederick Whiley Hilles (ed.), *Letters of Sir Joshua Reynolds*, Cambridge, The University Press, 1929.

8. Elizabeth and Florence Anson (eds), *Mary Hamilton at Court and at Home from Letters and Diaries 1756 to 1816*, John Murray, 1925, p. 72.
9. *Ibid.*, p. 73.
10. *Ibid.*, p. 75. The mottos translate 'Always loved', and 'Engraved for ever in my heart'.
11. *Ibid.*, pp. 83–4.
12. *Ibid.*, p. 88.
13. *Morning Chronicle*, 20 September 1779.
14. *Morning Post*, 20 September 1779.
15. *Morning Chronicle*. The Garrick version was abandoned this season.
16. *London Stage V*, pp. 274, 277.
17. Cecil Price (ed.), *The Letters of Richard Brinsley Sheridan*, vol. I, Oxford, The Clarendon Press, 1966, p. 103.
18. *Gazetteer & New Daily Advertiser*, 22 November 1779.
19. *Morning Post*, 22 November 1779.
20. *Ibid.*, 6 December 1779. The story appears with slight variations in other sources.
21. See Harry William Pedicord, *"By Their Majesties' Command": The House of Hanover at the London Theatres, 1714–1800*, The Society for Theatre Research, 1991, p. 32.
22. *Memoirs*, p. 101.
23. *Ibid.*, p. 102.
24. *Ibid.*, p. 103.
25. *Morning Post*, 12 February 1780. The quotation adapts Perdita's own words when Polixenes has demanded an end to his son's romance: 'Being now awake, I'll queen it no inch further/But milk my ewes and weep.'
26. Mary Hamilton's *Diaries*, p. 90.
27. In 1785 Mary Hamilton married John Dickenson of Taxall. She maintained lifelong support for the Prince of Wales.
28. *Memoirs*, p. 105; Mary Hamilton's *Diaries*, pp. 72, 75, 76–7.
29. *Memoirs*, p. 105.
30. Garrick 3, *Florizel and Perdita*, Act II, Scene I, ll. 40–2.
31. *The Memoirs of Perdita* (anon.), G. Lister, 1784, p. 95.
32. For the Prince's pursuit of Mrs Fitzherbert see *George IV*, pp. 71–85.
33. *Memoirs*, p. 114.
34. *A Picture of England* II, p. 181.
35. *Morning Post*, 5 April 1780.
36. *Walsingham*, p. 285.
37. *Morning Post*, 3 May 1780.

38. *Town and Country Magazine*, p. 235. The reference to MR refusing Sir John Lade's offer occurs in this article.
39. For the significance of portrait miniatures see Marcia Pointon, '"Surrounded with Brilliants": Miniature Portraits in Eighteenth-Century England', in *Art Bulletin*, March 2001, pp. 48–71.
40. Georgiana, p. 292.
41. *Memoirs*, p. 114.

CHAPTER FIVE: FLORIZEL AND PERDITA

1. *Memoirs*, p. 107.
2. MER to William Godwin, undated letter, Abinger Deposit Dep.b.214/3, Bodleian Library. She was seeking to print in the *Memoirs* letters from her mother which would 'do her credit'.
3. *Memoirs*, p. 108.
4. *Morning Herald*, 21 November 1780. This may well be the only reference to the Prince's 'temperance'!
5. See *George IV*, pp. 73–4, for an account of the Prince's attempted 'suicide' as a way to secure Mrs Fitzherbert.
6. *Memoirs*, p. 111.
7. Robert Huish, *Memoirs of George IV*, Thomas Kelly, 1831, p. 75.
8. *Memoirs*, p. 111.
9. Composite of quotations principally from Marguerite Steen, *The Lost One: A Biography of Mary (Perdita) Robinson*, Methuen, 1937, pp. 130–1, with contributions from Philip Lindsay, *A Piece for Candlelight*, Hutchinson, 1953, and Stanley V. Makower, *Perdita: A Romance in Biography*, Hutchinson & Co., 1908.
10. A.A. Barkas, *Richmond Notes*, vol. 1, pp. 137–8, and Levy, p. 24.
11. Elizabeth Steele, *The Memoirs of Mrs. Baddeley*, Literary Press, 1787, Vol. 6, p. 174.
12. *Ibid.*, pp. 178–9.
13. *Morning Post*, 9 March 1780.
14. First produced 28 April 1779, never published.
15. It hangs in the Garrick Club.
16. *Morning Chronicle*, 29 January 1780.
17. Horace Walpole to the Reverend William Mason, 28 May 1780, Walpole, 29, p. 434. He later printed one of her plays at Strawberry Hill, and 'forgave her the scandal for her prettiness'.
18. *London Courant*, 29 May 1780.
19. *Morning Chronicle*, 27 May 1780.
20. *London Stage*, p. 347.
21. *Biographical Dictionary* 13, pp. 35, 36.

22. *Memoirs*, p. 118.
23. *Biographical Dictionary* 14, pp. 386–8.
24. *Public Characters of 1800–1801*, Dublin, J. Moore, 1801, p. 267.
25. *Town and Country Magazine*, January 1781, p. 11.
26. *Morning Post*, 26 March 1781, and *Morning Chronicle*, 1 December 1794.
27. See J. Paul de Castro, *The Gordon Riots*, Oxford University Press, 1926, pp. 4–5. The government wanted to be able to recruit Catholics for the American war.
28. *Ibid.*, pp. 98–9.
29. *Ibid.*, pp. 141–3.
30. *Morning Chronicle*, 6 June 1780.
31. *Memoirs*, p. 117.
32. *Correspondence*, p. 35.
33. Bass, p. 135, but unsourced.
34. *George IV*, p. 63.
35. Sold at Sothebys in 1984 for £2,640, present whereabouts unknown.
36. *Memoirs of Perdita, interspersed with anecdotes of the Hon. Charles F – x* [etc], G. Lister, 1784, p. 105.
37. Hawkins, II, p. 24.
38. *Ibid.*, p. 31.
39. *Memoirs*, p. 113.
40. For full histories of the press see Lucyle Werkmeister, *The London Daily Press 1772–1792*, Lincoln, University of Nebraska Press, 1963, and A. Aspinall, *Politics and the Press c. 1780–1850*, Brighton, The Harvester Press, 1973, reprinted from 1949.
41. Werkmeister, p. 7.
42. See *Town and Country Magazine*, October 1773, pp. 459–61.
43. *Morning Post*, 18 July 1780.
44. *Ibid.*, 20 July 1780.
45. *Morning Post*, 3 August 1780.
46. *Morning Post*, 27 September 1780.
47. *Ibid.*, 28 September 1780.
48. *Ibid.*, 29 September 1780.
49. *Ibid.*, 2 and 9 October 1780.
50. *Ibid.*, 16 November 1780.
51. Dorothy George, *Catalogue of Political and Personal Satires preserved in the Department of Prints and Drawings in the British Museum*, vol. V, British Museum Publications Ltd, 1978, No. 5767, p. 469.
52. *Memoirs of Perdita*, p. 25.
53. *Morning Post*, 7 October 1780.

54. *Town and Country Magazine*, April 1781, p. 203.
55. *Morning Post*, 27 October 1780.
56. *George IV*, p. 37, no source given.
57. *Memoirs*, p. 105.

CHAPTER SIX: YE OLD INFERNAL CAUSE ROBINSON

1. *Memoirs*, p. 115.
2. *Town and Country Magazine*, June 1776, p. 347.
3. Georgiana, p. 291.
4. *Memoirs*, p. 119.
5. *Town and Country Magazine*, January 1781, pp. 9–11.
6. *Correspondence*, p. 41, n.1.
7. Lt Col Lake to George, Prince of Wales, 23 January 1781, *ibid.*, p. 45.
8. *Morning Herald*, 10 April 1781.
9. *Public Advertiser*, 16 January 1781. Levy, pp. 29–30.
10. *Morning Herald*, 5 January 1781.
11. RA GEO/38052.
12. *Morning Herald*, 31 March 1781.
13. George, Prince of Wales to Prince Frederick, 24 March 1781, *Correspondence*, p. 55.
14. *Ibid.*, 10 April 1781, p. 56.
15. *Journal of the Reign of King George the Third*, II, Richard Bentley, 1859, p. 458.
16. King and Mrs Robinson do not seem to have met in later life despite moving in similar circles.
17. *Morning Post*, 29 March 1780.
18. *Morning Herald*, 4 April 1781.
19. *William Felton*, A *Treatise on Carriages*, J. Debrett, etc., 1794, pp. 79–84. A 'plain' chariot cost £114 15*s* 9*d*, and a 'Neat Town Chariot', £191 12*s* 6*d*, pp. 69, 71.
20. Prior to 1786. Centre for Kentish Studies, Streatfeild Manuscripts, U908 T414/1.
21. Emily is pictured as Thaïs, the Athenian courtesan who incited Alexander the Great to fire the palace of Persepolis.
22. The Prince of Wales to Prince Frederick, 17 July 1781, *Correspondence*, p. 67.
23. Lt Col Hotham to Lord Malden, 31 July 1781, Hertford CC Records M274.
24. *Morning Herald*, 31 March 1781.
25. Lt Col Hotham to Lord Malden, 8 August 1781, Hertford CC Records M282.

26. Lord Southampton to Lord Malden, 15 August 1781, *ibid.*, M289.
27. Mary Robinson to George, Prince of Wales, undated, *ibid.*, M280.
28. Lt Col Hotham to Lord Malden, 28 August 1781, *ibid.*, M294.
29. Mary Robinson to Lord Malden, 29 August 1791, *ibid.*, M295.
30. King George III to Lord North, 10 August 1781, *The Correspondence of King George III, 1760–1783*, ed. The Hon. Sir John Fortescue, Macmillan, 1928, p. 269.
31. *The Diaries of Sylvester Douglas (Lord Glenbervie)*, ed. Francis Bickley, Constable & Co., 1928, I, p. 6. Also quoted in Levy, p. 38.
32. *Morning Herald*, 14 August 1781.
33. *Ibid.*, 1 January 1781.
34. 'Anecdotes of Eminent Persons', *The Monthly Magazine and American Review for the year 1800*, Vol. I, pp. 39–40, p. 39.
35. *Morning Herald*, 13 September 1781 for the trees; 3 September for the miniature.
36. *Memoirs*, p. 122. All quotations concerning Mary's Paris visit come from pp. 121–3.
37. Quoted in Kimberly Chrisman Campbell, 'The Face of Fashion: Milliners in Eighteenth-Century Visual Culture', in *British Journal for Eighteenth-Century Studies 25*, no. 2, Autumn 2002, p. 162.
38. *Memoirs*, pp. 122–3, *Morning Herald*, 8 March 1782, and *Morning Post*, 13 April 1782.
39. For details of etiquette at Versailles, see Antonia Fraser, *Marie Antoinette*, Weidenfeld & Nicolson, 2002, pp. 67–72 and *passim*.
40. *Memoirs*, p. 123, and *Monthly Magazine* I, 1800 p. 40.
41. *Memoirs of the Duc de Lauzun*, translated by C.K. Scott Moncrieff, George Routledge & Sons, 1928, p. 211.
42. *Monthly Magazine* II, 1800, p. 390.
43. *Duc de Lauzun*, p. 211. The original is quoted in John Ingamells, *Mrs Robinson and her Portraits*, the Trustees of the Wallace Collection, 1978, p. 30.
44. *Duc de Lauzun*, pp. 207–8.
45. Quoted in Robert A. Selig, *The Duc de Lauzun and his Legion*, www.americanrevolution.org/lauzun.html (26/09/03).

CHAPTER SEVEN: AT THE PORTRAIT PAINTER'S

1. Quoted in Martin Postle, *Thomas Gainsborough*, Tate Publishing, 2002, p. 17.
2. See Martin Postle, '"Painted Women": Reynolds and the Cult of the Courtesan', in Robyn Asleson (ed.), *Notorious Muse: The Actress in*

British Art and Culture 1776–1812, New Haven and London, Yale University Press, 2003, pp. 23–55.

3. Although listed as no. 107 in the list of Academy exhibits in 1781, no trace of it can be found.
4. *Mrs Robinson and her Portraits*, p. 30.
5. See William Vaughan, *Gainsborough*, Thames & Hudson Ltd, 2002, pp. 87 and 104.
6. Quoted in Richard Wendorf, *Sir Joshua Reynolds: The Painter in Society*, National Portrait Gallery, 1996, p. 135.
7. M.J. Levy, 'Gainsborough's *Mrs Robinson*: A portrait and its context', *Apollo* 136, 1992, pp. 152–4, p. 154.
8. *Gainsborough*, p. 154.
9. Claude Phillips, 'Gainsborough's "Perdita" in the Wallace Collection', in *The Art Journal*, May 1904, pp. 145–6, p. 146.
10. Anne K. Mellor, 'Making an Exhibition of Her Self: Mary "Perdita" Robinson and Nineteenth-Century Scripts of Female Sexuality', in *Nineteenth-Century Contexts 22*, 2000, pp. 271–304, p. 278. She also believes that the dog represents Perdita's 'bestial sexuality'.
11. David Mannings, *Sir Joshua Reynolds: A Complete Catalogue of his Paintings*, New Haven & London, Yale University Press, 2000, p. 393.
12. David Mannings, 'At the Portrait Painter's', *History Today*, Vol. 27, 1977, pp. 279–87, p. 284.
13. Quoted in Wendorf, p. 115.
14. *Mrs Robinson and her Portraits*, pp. 31–2.
15. *Morning Advertiser*, 19 April 1781.
16. Ernest Fletcher (ed.), *Conversations of James Northcote RA with James Ward on Art and Artists*, Methuen, 1901, p. 59.
17. Mellor, p. 283.
18. John Thomas Smith: *A Book for a Rainy Day*, Richard Bentley, 1845, p. 71.
19. Hawkins II, p. 31.
20. First published in the *Oracle*, 9 July 1789. See *Selected Poems*, p. 289, ll. 17–20.
21. Letter dated 18 December 1790 and quoted in *Memoirs of the Late Mrs Robinson*, R. Philips, 1801, vol. 4, p. 191.
22. 'Gainsborough's *Mrs Robinson*', pp. 153–4. The unattributed image can also be seen in Marcia Pointon, '"Surrounded with Brilliants": Miniature Portraits in Eighteenth-Century England', in *The Art Bulletin*, March 2001, pp. 48–71, p. 64.
23. A list of over eighty portraits can be found in *Biographical Dictionary* 13, pp. 39–47.

24. One is held by the National Portrait Gallery; another owned by the Folger Shakespeare Library is used as frontispiece to *Letters/Natural Daughter*.
25. British Library, Add. MS. 39781 f.27.
26. *Mrs Robinson and her Portraits*, pp. 5–6.
27. *Selected Poems*, p. 139, ll. 5–6.

CHAPTER EIGHT: RELUCTANT CYPRIAN

1. See I.M. Davis, *The Harlot and the Statesman*, Bourne End, Buckinghamshire, The Kensal Press, 1986, a biography of Elizabeth Armistead, for a general account of the behaviour and expectations of courtesans.
2. *Morning Post*, 29 August 1782.
3. *Morning Herald*, 21 June 1781.
4. *Ibid.*, 9 January 1782.
5. *Ibid.*, 8 March 1782.
6. See *The Art of Dress*, p. 71, though the introduction of the chemise is wrongly credited to the Duchess of Devonshire in 1784. Quotation from *Morning Chronicle*, 28 November 1782.
7. *Morning Herald*, 21 and 31 March 1783.
8. *Ibid.*, 20 January 1783. The coach is described on 4 December 1782.
9. *Ibid.*, 31 May 1783.
10. *The Vis-à-Vis of Berkeley Square*, June 1783.
11. *Morning Herald*, 16 June 1783.
12. *False Friend* I, p. 59.
13. MR to William Godwin, 24 August 1800, Abinger Deposit, Dep.b.215/2, Bodleian Library. Letter quoted in full in *Selected Poems*, pp. 367–70.
14. See the website: http://home.golden.net/~marg/bansite/banecdotes/86perditas.html (1/10/03)
15. For more details of Tarleton's parentage and early life see Bass, pp. 11–16.
16. *Town & Country Magazine*, July 1782, p. 345.
17. For more about Tarleton's military record see Bass's biography, or the many websites devoted to him.
18. G. Scott Withrow, in an essay 'Banastre Tarleton', http://www.nps.gov/cowp/tarleton.htm (1/10/03)
19. See Bass, pp. 51–3.
20. *Williamson's Liverpool Advertiser*, 21 February 1782.
21. *Public Advertiser*, 4 May 1782.

22. See John Ingamells and John Edgcumbe (eds), *The Letters of Sir Joshua Reynolds*, New Haven and London, Yale University Press, 2000, p. 133 and note. Also John Tarleton to Clayton Tarleton, 13 March 1791, Liverpool Library, Tarleton Family Papers, HO920 TAR, 28 (1).
23. John Bonehill, 'Reynolds' *Portrait of Lieutenant-Colonel Banastre Tarleton* and the Fashion for War', *British Journal for Eighteenth-Century Studies 24*, 2001, pp. 123–44, p. 132. The author controversially sees the portrait as 'a knowing piece of ridicule' of the soldier.
24. Horace Walpole to William Mason, 23 February 1781, Walpole, vol. 29, p. 189.
25. *The Memoirs of Perdita*, p. 28.
26. *Ibid.*, p. 160.
27. *Morning Herald*, 4 and 8 June 1782, and see 23 July 1782.
28. Centre for Kentish Studies, Streatfeild Manuscripts U908/T14. This document concerns the sale of furniture from the house in lieu of unpaid rent in 1785.
29. Banastre Tarleton to Thomas Tarleton, 29 July 1782, Liverpool Library, Tarleton Family Papers, HO920 TAR, 13 (11).
30. *Journal of the Reign of King George the Third*, II, Richard Bentley, 1859, p. 598–9.
31. Henry S. Eeles and Earl Spencer, *Brooks's 1764–1964*, Country Life Limited, 1964, pp. 48–52.
32. Horace Walpole to Lord Harcourt, 5 July 1782, Walpole, vol. 35, p. 520.
33. *Morning Herald*, 9 January 1782.
34. James Hare to Richard Fitzpatrick, 31 July 1782, British Library, Add MS.47582, f.131/b.
35. *Morning Herald*, 16 and 17 August 1782.
36. Horace Walpole to Lord Harcourt, 7 September 1782, Walpole, vol. 35, p. 523.
37. *Morning Herald*, 3 September 1782. The destruction of Jezebel by Jehu is found in Kings II, Chapter 9.
38. *Morning Chronicle*, 3 and 13 August 1782.
39. Lawrence E. Babit, A *Devil of a Whipping: The Battle of Cowpens*, Chapel Hill & London, The University of North Carolina Press, 1998, p. xiii.
40. 20 August 1782. On 'The satirist as hireling', see Diana Donald, *The Age of Caricature: Satirical Prints in the Reign of George III*, New Haven and London, Yale University Press, 1996, pp. 23–7.

41. Mary Robinson, *Poems*, J. Bell, 1791, p. 60.
42. *Morning Herald*, 31 December 1783.
43. See Roy Porter, *Quacks, Fakers and Charlatans in English Medicine*, Stroud, Tempus Publishing Ltd, 2000, pp. 140–54; and Tim Fulford, 'The Electrifying Mrs Robinson' in *Women's Writing* 9, no. 1, 2002, pp. 23–35.
44. Quoted from Dr Graham's pamphlet in *Rambler's Magazine*, January 1783, p. 60.
45. Thought to have been Emma Hart before she became Lady Hamilton.
46. Anon., *The Celestial Beds; or, A Review of the Votaries of The Temple of Health, Adelphi, and, the Temple of Hymen, Pall-Mall*, G. Kearsley, 1781, p. 26.
47. *Morning Herald*, 31 July 1782, 27 August 1783.
48. *Ibid.*, 9 March 1782. The author was Dr Charles Burney, whose intention was to puff his daughter Fanny's just-published novel *Cecilia*.
49. *Morning Post*, 5 March 1783.
50. Quoted fully in Bass, pp. 208–25. The originals are in Liverpool Library, Tarleton Family Papers, H0920 TAR 13 (14–24).
51. Mrs Jane Tarleton to Banastre Tarleton, 23 June 1783, *ibid.*, HO920 TAR 14 (8).
52. Banastre Tarleton to Mrs Jane Tarleton, 25 July 1783, *ibid.*, H0920 TAR 13 (25).
53. *Eccentric Biography; or Memoirs of Remarkable Female Characters, Ancient and Modern*, T. Hurst, 1803, p. 289. The Duc de Biron was then the Duc de Lauzun.
54. *Memoirs*, p. 131.

CHAPTER NINE: ILL HEALTH AND BAD DEBTS

1. Hawkins II, p. 33.
2. *Memoirs*, pp. 123–4.
3. *Eccentric Biography; or, Memoirs of Remarkable Female Characters, Ancient and Modern*, T. Hurst, 1803, p. 290.
4. *Ibid.*
5. *Rambler's Magazine*, November 1783, p. 440.
6. Lord Pembroke to Lord George Herbert, 13 August 1783, Lord Herbert (ed.), *Pembroke Papers (1780–1794): Letters and Diaries of Henry, Tenth Earl of Pembroke and his Circle*, Jonathan Cape, 1950, p. 227. 'Sciondalona' has defied all of many books and authorities consulted to explain.
7. For these ideas I am indebted to Dr Lynn Mucklow, Dr Kerry Thomas and Miss Kathleen Whelan.

8. *Morning Post*, 10 September 1783.
9. *Morning Herald*, 28 November 1783.
10. *Ibid.*, 28 January 1784. See also 10, 11, 22 January.
11. *Pembroke Papers*, p. 231.
12. Banastre Tarleton to Thomas Tarleton, 23 September 1783, Liverpool Library, Tarleton Family Papers, H0920 TAR 13 (26). Tarleton's correspondence from France is fully quoted in Bass, pp. 227–32.
13. *Morning Herald*, 19, 22 January 1784. Quotation 28 July 1784.
14. Foreman, *Georgiana*, 1998, pp. 136–59.
15. Charles Ross (ed.), *Correspondence of Charles, First Marquis Cornwallis*, John Murray, 1859, 3 vols, I, p. 166.
16. *Morning Post*, 13 July 1784.
17. George, Prince of Wales to MR, undated, private collection.
18. *George IV*, p. 235.
19. Ingamells, p. 21, and William T. Whitley, *Thomas Gainsborough*, Smith, Elder, 1915, p. 183. See also *Morning Post*, 7 and 14 January 1785.
20. An assignment by David Sands of Great Russell Street, Bloomsbury, upholsterer, to William Lyon of Gray's Inn, County of Middlesex, 27 July 1786, Centre for Kentish Studies, Streatfeild Manuscripts, U908 T414/1.
21. *Morning Post*, 16 August 1784. See also 17 August.
22. *Racing Calendar*, 1 September 1784.
23. John Tarleton to Mrs Jane Tarleton, 10 October 1784, Liverpool Library, Tarleton Family Papers, H0920 TAR 5(15).
24. MR to George, Prince of Wales, 17 January 1785, Westminster City Archives, Broadley Haymarket, vol. 3, p. 187.
25. Dieter P.J. Wynands, *Kleine Geschichte Aachens*, Aachen 1986, pp. 53–4.
26. John Ash, *Experiments and Observations to investigate by chemical analysis, the medicinal properties of the mineral waters of Spa and Aix-la-Chapelle in Germany, and the waters and boue near St. Amand, in French Flanders*, J. Robson and W. Clarke, 1788, p. 306.
27. *Memoirs*, p. 125.
28. *Ibid.*, p. 127.
29. *Ibid.*, poem quoted pp. 127–30.
30. *Morning Post*, 14 July 1786.
31. *Ibid.*, 5 August 1786. Both passages are printed in full in Bass, pp. 252–4.
32. *Ibid.*, 29 June 1786.
33. Private collection.
34. Ash, p. 340.

35. *Ibid.*, p. 347.
36. *The Shrine of Bertha*, W. Lane, 1794, II, p. 128.
37. Bass, p. 247.
38. Lt Gen Grant to Earl Cornwallis, 10 January 1787, *Correspondence of Lord Cornwallis*, I, p. 261.
39. George Hanger, *An Address to the Army in reply to strictures by Roderick M'Kenzie*, James Ridgway, 1789. See also Bass, pp. 255–60.
40. *Morning Post*, 1, 2, 11 August 1788.
41. *Morning Herald*, 24 January 1788; *Morning Post*, 31 January 1788.
42. *Memoirs*, p. 131.
43. First published 31 October 1788 in the *World*. See *Memoirs*, pp. 132–5, and *Selected Poems*, pp. 87–90 for complete poem.
44. *Memoirs*, p. 136.
45. First published 26 February 26 February 1800 in the *Morning Post*. See *Selected Poems*, pp. 217–20.
46. S.T. Coleridge to Robert Southey, 28 February 1800, *Collected Letters* I, p. 575.

CHAPTER TEN: THE ENGLISH SAPPHO

1. Jane Cave in 1873. See Roger Lonsdale (ed.), *Eighteenth Century Women Poets: An Oxford Anthology*, Oxford, Oxford University Press, 1990, p. 373.
2. *Gentleman's Magazine* 61, p. 560.
3. See Judith Pascoe, *Romantic Theatricality: Gender, Poetry, and Spectatorship*, Ithaca and London, Cornell University Press, 1977, p. 69, n. 2; Pascoe cites a paragraph in the *Oracle* of 29 July 1789. Sappho was the Greek poetess of love from Lesbos in the seventh century BC.
4. First published 13 November 1788 in the *World*. See *Selected Poems*, ll. 1–4, p. 76.
5. The poems can be read in order in *The British Album*, 2 vols, J. Bell, 1790.
6. See Jerome McGann, *The Poetics of Sensibility: A Revolution in Literary Style*, Oxford, The Clarendon Press, 1996, particularly Chapter 9 'The Literal World of the English Della Cruscans', pp. 74–93, and '"That fluttering, tinselled crew": Women Poets and Della Cruscanism', in *Romantic Theatricality*, pp. 68–94.
7. *The Baviad and Maeviad*, J. Wright, new edition 1797, ll. 27–28.
8. MR to John Taylor, 13 October 1794, *Collection of Autograph Letters and Historical Documents formed between 1865 and 1886 by Alfred Morrison*, printed for private circulation 1891, vol. V, p. 287.

9. S.T. Coleridge to Robert Southey, 28 February 1800, *Collected Letters*, I, pp. 575–6.
10. For an account of Mary's dealings with publishers, see Jan Fergus and Janice Farrar Thaddeus in 'Women, Publishers, and Money, 1790–1820', in *Studies in Eighteenth-Century Culture 17* (1988), pp. 191–208.
11. *Vancenza* I, pp. 1–2.
12. *Ibid.* I, p. 71.
13. *Ibid.* II, pp. 90, 104, 126, 129.
14. *The English Review*, vol. XX, 1792, p. 111.
15. *The Analytical Review*, vol. XIII, 1792, p. 420.
16. *Angelina* I, p. 204.
17. *Ibid.*, p. 148.
18. *Letter/Natural Daughter*, p. 209.
19. *Ibid.*, p. 229.
20. *Ibid.*, p. 235.
21. *Oracle*, 22 March 1792.
22. Letter to Richard Fitzpatrick, 30 July 1789, in Lord John Russell, *The Life and Times of C.J. Fox*, Richard Bentley 1853, II, p. 361.
23. *Selected Poems*, ll. 293–8, pp. 112–13.
24. *Memoirs*, p. 107.
25. See 'The Negro Girl' and 'The African' in *Selected Poems*, pp. 234–9 and 313–14.
26. *Parliamentary History* 29, p. 1090.
27. Tarleton's vote was one of 85 against 250; the Lords threw the bill out, but it was in any case abandoned when war broke out with France.
28. *Oracle*, 30 May 1791.
29. Quoted in Percy Fitzgerald, *The Lives of the Sheridans*, Richard Bentley & Sons, i, pp. 148–9. The 'low associate' has not been identified.
30. *Stanzas written between Dover and Calais, in July 1792*, ll. 1–12, *Memoirs*, pp. 140–1, and *Selected Poems*, p. 132.
31. *Oracle*, 25 July 1792.
32. *Ibid.*, 28 August and 3 September 1792, though MR had returned on 2 September.
33. *The Memoirs of Mrs. Sophia Baddeley*, vol. 6, p. 177.
34. *Memoirs*, p. 142.
35. *Ibid.*, p. 131.
36. Liverpool Library, Tarleton Family Papers 37, *Hasty Sketch of Colonel Tarleton's speech, on Mr Fox's Motion on Saturday, December 15th 1792*, and undated, unsigned note.
37. *Oracle*, 1 October 1792.

38. *Stanzas, Presented with a Gold Chain Ring*, published in *Poems* of 1793. After Tarleton's defection the title was changed to *Stanzas Presented with a Gold Chain Ring to a Once Dear Friend.*
39. See *George IV*, pp. 154–5.
40. Liverpool Library, Tarleton Family Papers 37, *Hasty Sketch*, and undated, unsigned note.
41. *Oracle*, 26 January 1793.
42. *Ibid.*, 17, 21, 23 August and 14 September 1793.
43. See 'Embodying Marie Antoinette: The Theatricalized Female Subject' in *Romantic Theatricality*, pp. 95–129, and '"The aristocracy of genius": Mary Robinson and Marie Antoinette' in Adriana Craciun, *Fatal Women of Romanticism*, Cambridge University Press, 2003, pp. 76–109.
44. *Impartial Reflections on the Present Situation of the Queen of France*, John Bell, 1791, pp. 8 and 19.
45. *Ibid.*, pp. 17 and 27.
46. She also wrote 'Marie Antoinette's Lamentation, in her Prison of the Temple', see *Selected Poems*, pp. 135–7.
47. *Monody to the Memory of the Late Queen of France*, T. Spilsbury & Son, 1793, p. 10.
48. Liverpool Library, Tarleton Family Papers 37, *Hasty Sketch*, and undated, unsigned note.
49. 'Character of the Late Mrs. Robinson', Misc. Ms. 2296, The Carl H. Pforzheimer Collection of Shelley and His Circle, The New York Public Library, Astor, Lenox and Tilden Foundations.

CHAPTER ELEVEN: DISCONTENT

1. MR to John Taylor, 5 October 1794, *Collection of Autograph Letters*, V, pp. 286–7 (2). Quoted in full in *Selected Poems*, pp. 365–7, and in Bass, pp. 343–5.
2. *Sight, The Cavern of Woe, and Solitude*, T. Spilsbury & Son, 1793. 'Sight' is also printed in *Selected Poems*, pp. 116–22.
3. MR to John Taylor, 5 October 1794, *Collection of Autograph Letters*, V, pp. 286–7 (2). For a denial of the rumour of her departure for Italy see the *Oracle*, 26 September 1794.
4. MR to John Taylor, 13 October 1794, *Collection of Autograph Letters* V, p. 287 (3).
5. *Modern Manners*, I, ll. 3–4; criticism of *The Baviad*, l. 8.
6. *Ibid.*, I, ll. 305–16.
7. *Oracle*, 9 November 1793.

8. *Monthly Review*, 12, 1793, p. 348, *Critical Review* 8, 1793, p. 216.
9. *English Review* 24, 1794, pp. 59–60; *Monthly Review* 14, 1794, pp. 38–40.
10. *Critical Review* 12, 1794, p. 102.
11. MR to John Taylor, 5 October 1794, *Collection of Autograph Letters*, V, pp. 286–7 (2).
12. *Oracle*, 26 February 1794.
13. *Analytical Review* 18, 1794, p. 506; *English Review* 23, 1794, p. 310; *Monthly Review* 15, September 1794, p. 108; *Critical Review* 11, 1784, p. 468.
14. *The Shrine of Bertha*, W. Lane, 1794, I, p. 70. It was 'Printed for the author'.
15. MR to John Taylor, 14 October 1794, W.b.112, Folger Shakespeare Library, Washington DC.
16. *Records of My Life*, Edward Bull, 1832, I, p. 39.
17. *Ibid.*, II, p. 61.
18. See A. Aspinall, *Politics and the Press c.1780–1850*, Brighton, The Harvester Press, 1973 (originally published 1949), p. 164.
19. MR to John Taylor, 5 October 1794, *Collection of Autograph Letters*, V, pp. 286–7 (2).
20. *The Widow* II, p. 182.
21. MR to John Taylor, 13 October 1794, *Collection of Autograph Letters* V, p. 287 (3).
22. I am grateful to Miss Pamela Clark, Registrar of The Royal Archives, for this information.
23. MR to John Taylor, 14 October 1794, W.b.112, Folger Shakespeare Library, Washington DC. The Royal Marriages Act (1772) prohibited marriage without the King's consent; Mrs Fitzherbert was, moreover, a Roman Catholic.
24. Fergus and Thaddeus, 'Women, Publishers, and Money, 1790–1820', pp. 191–208, from which all the further information not otherwise annotated about Mrs Robinson's publishing history is taken.
25. *Letter/Natural Daughter*, pp. 208–9.
26. Judith Phillips Stanton, 'Statistical Profile of Women Writing in English from 1660 to 1800', in Frederick M. Keener and Susan E. Lorsch (eds), *Eighteenth-Century Women and the Arts*, Westport, Connecticut, Greenwood Press Inc., 1988.
27. *Critical Review* 10, 1794, p. 382.
28. *Walsingham*, p. 216.
29. *Oracle*, 2 and 12 July 1792, 23 and 30 March 1793, and 29 December 1795.

30. See *London Stage* 5, III, pp. 1474–5 and 1570.
31. *Oracle*, 13 March 1794.
32. *London Stage* 5, III, p. 1727.
33. *Morning Chronicle*, 1 December 1794. For an account of the scandal, see Gillian Russell, ' "Faro's Daughters": Female Gamesters, Politics, and the Discourse of Finance in 1790s Britain', in *Eighteenth-Century Studies* 33, no. 4, 2000, pp. 481–504.
34. *Ibid.*, p. 490.
35. Miss Farren became the Countess of Derby in 1797 after a platonic partnership of many years with the Earl, which amused the press. She left the stage immediately and bore three children.
36. James Boaden, *The Life of Mrs Jordan*, 2 vols, Edward Bull, 1831, I, p. 271.
37. *False Friend* II, p. 247.
38. Larpent Ms 1046, The Huntington Library, Act II, Scene 2, p. 32.
39. *Memoirs*, p. 143, where the date is wrongly given as 1793.
40. *Morning Post*, 1 December 1794.
41. Larpent Ms 1046, The Huntington Library, Act II, Scene 2, p. 32, Act I, Scene 1, p. 3.
42. *Ibid.*, Act II, Scene 2, p. 34.
43. *Morning Post*, 1 December 1794. See also *Morning Chronicle* and *The Times* for 1 December.
44. Boaden, I, pp. 271–2.
45. A. Aspinall (ed.), *Mrs Jordan and her Family: being the Unpublished Correspondence of Mrs Jordan and the Duke of Clarence, later William IV*, Arthur Barker Ltd, 1951, p. 28.
46. *Ibid.*, p. 21. Aspinall dates it as '[? before 1794]' without explaining why he thinks it likely to pre-date 1794.
47. British Library: *Drury Lane Playbills*, vol. 4, Prompter's note for 6 December 1794.
48. 'Women, Publishers, and Money, 1790–1820', p. 196.
49. Sarah Siddons to John Taylor, undated, J. Fitzgerald Molloy (ed.), *Memoirs of Mary Robinson, 'Perdita'*, Gibbings & Company, 1895, p. xiv.
50. *Oracle*, 22 October 1796; the earlier reference is in the *Oracle*, 14 September 1795.
51. The whole sequence, plus Preface, is in *Selected Poems*, pp. 144–80.
52. See 'Mary Robinson and the Myth of Sappho' in *The Poetics of Sensibility: A Revolution in Literary Style*, Oxford, Clarendon Press, 1996, pp. 94–116, p. 98.
53. *Selected Poems*, pp. 168–9, where the editor glosses 'Idalian' as 'Idalium: a town in Cyprus where Aphrodite was worshipped'.

54. Sonnet XVIII, l. 14. *Selected Poems*, p. 166.
55. *Oracle*, 10 September 1794.
56. MR to John Taylor, 14 October 1794, W.b.112, Folger Shakespeare Library, Washington DC.
57. 'Verses addressed to Mr John Taylor', 20 August 1794, *Collection of Autograph Letters*, p. 286, 1. Tarleton's initial verses are not included.
58. In the collection of John Gardner, by whose kind permission it is printed.
59. James Boaden, *The Life of Mrs Jordan*, 2 vols, Edward Bull, 1831, I, p. 271.
60. *False Friend* II, p. 77.
61. Bass, p. 366.
62. *Oracle*, 17, 20, 24 October, 1798.
63. *Poetical Works* II, pp. 258–60; Bass, pp. 374–6.
64. *Morning Post*, 17 December 1798.
65. *The Diary of Frances, Lady Shelley 1787–1817*, 2 vols, ed. Richard Edgcumbe, John Murray, 1913, I, p. 42.
66. *Morning Post*, 18 February 1799.

CHAPTER TWELVE: FRIENDS AND FOES

1. *Morning Post*, 31 July and 9 August 1798, and see Bass, p. 394.
2. *Letter/Natural Daughter*, p. 77.
3. *False Friend* II, p. 77, *Letter/Natural Daughter*, p. 41.
4. C. Kegan Paul, *William Godwin: His Friends and Contemporaries*, two vols, Henry S. King & Co., 1876, I, p. 154.
5. MR to William Godwin, 24 August 1800, Abinger Deposit Dep.b.215/2, Bodleian Library. Printed in full in *Selected Poems*, pp. 367–9.
6. Godwin's Journal, Vol. VII, Abinger Deposit, Dep.e.202, Bodleian Library, 9 February 1796.
7. *Ibid.*, 1 June 1796.
8. Published in *The Works of Mary Wollstonecraft*, edited by Janet Todd and Marilyn Butler, vol. 7, Pickering and Chatto, 1989, pp. 461–2.
9. Mary Wollstonecraft to MR, *The Collected Letters of Mary Wollstonecraft*, edited by Ralph M. Wardle, Ithaca & London, Cornell University Press, 1979, Letter 278 (undated), p. 370.
10. Mary Wollstonecraft to William Godwin, *ibid.*, Letter 268 (28 November 1796), p. 365.
11. *Ibid.*, Letter 272 (13 December 1796), p. 367.
12. *Works of Mary Wollstonecraft* 7, p. 523.

13. MR to William Godwin, 28 August 1800, Abinger Deposit Dep.b.215/2, Bodleian Library.
14. *Letter/Natural Daughter*, p. 65.
15. *Ibid.*, p. 81.
16. For a discussion of the literary aftermath of Wollstonecraft's work see Claire Tomalin, *The Life and Death of Mary Wollstonecraft*, revised edition, Penguin Books, 1992, pp. 297–314, though Tomalin does not include Robinson's *Letter*.
17. Bass, pp. 11–12 for the Tarleton family history.
18. *Morning Post*, 23 and 27 October 1799.
19. *Letter/Natural Daughter*, p. 191.
20. For interesting discussions, see Sharon Seltzer's introduction to *Letter/Natural Daughter*, pp. 26–32, and Eleanor Ty, *Empowering the Feminine*, Toronto, University of Toronto Press, 1998, pp. 74–9.
21. Quoted from the *Star* newspaper in Richard Holmes, *Coleridge: The Early Years*, Hodder & Stoughton, 1989, p. 106.
22. 'A New Song, To an Old Tune', *Morning Post*, 10 January 1798, signed T.B., short for Tabitha Bramble, one of Mary's pseudonyms.
23. *Morning Post*, 2 May and 6 July 1798.
24. 15, 18 January and 22 February 1800. Godwin's journal, Vol. IX, Abinger Deposit Dep. e 204, Bodleian Library.
25. S.T. Coleridge to Robert Southey, 25 January 1800, *Coleridge Letters*, I, p. 562.
26. *Memoirs*, pp. 138–9. *Selected Poems*, pp. 122–6.
27. *Selected Poems*, pp. 330–2, ll. 9–17.
28. For Coleridge's view of his poem see *Coleridge Letters* II, p. 904.
29. *Morning Post*, 5 and 8 March, 1800.
30. 'Theatricality in the Market-Place' in Judith Pascoe, *Romantic Theatricality: Gender, Poetry, and Spectatorship*, Ithaca and London, Cornell University Press, 1997, pp. 163–83, p. 172.
31. *Ibid.*
32. MR to Jane Porter, 27 August 1800, Misc. Ms. 2295, Carl H. Pforzheimer Collection of Shelley & His Circle, New York Public Library, Astor, Lenox and Tilden Foundations.
33. Quoted in *Selected Poems*, p. 54.
34. *Ibid.*, pp. 191–2, II. 49–56.
35. *Ibid.*, p. 56.
36. *Selected Poems*, pp. 340–2, ll. 1–10.
37. The illustrations can be seen in *Selected Poems*.
38. MR to Jane Porter, 11 September 1800, Misc. Ms. 2292, MR to Jane Porter, 27 August 1800, Misc. Ms. 2295, Carl H. Pforzheimer

Collection of Shelley & His Circle, New York Public Library, Astor, Lenox and Tilden Foundations.

39. Gerald Barnett, *Richard and Maria Cosway: A Biography*, Tiverton, West Country Books, 1995, p. 148.
40. *Memoirs*, p. 145.
41. *Morning Post*, 8 November 1799, 20 April 1800.
42. S.T. Coleridge to William Godwin, 21 May 1800, *Coleridge Letters* I, p. 589.
43. MR to William Godwin, 30 May 1800, Abinger Deposit Dep.c.810/2, Bodleian Library.
44. RA GEO/29858.
45. *Morning Post*, 3 July 1800.
46. *Ibid.*, 1 and 2 February 1798.
47. *Natural Daughter*, p. 222.
48. Letter of 23 April 1800, quoted in *Memoirs*, pp. 148–9.
49. MR to William Godwin, 24 August 1800, Abinger Deposit Dep.b.215/2, Bodleian Library. Printed in full in *Selected Poems*, pp. 367–9.
50. MR to William Godwin, 28 August 1800, Abinger Deposit, Dep.b.215/2, Bodleian Library.
51. Eliza Fenwick to Mary Hays, undated letter in A.F. Wedd (ed.), *The Fate of the Fenwicks: Letter to Mary Hays (1798–1828)* Methuen & Co. Ltd, 1927, pp. 10–11, p. 10.
52. There is still an Englefield Cottage on the A30 where Mary's cottage must have been, though it is a modern building.
53. MR to Elizabeth Gunning, 31 August 1800, Misc. Ms. 2291, MR to Jane Porter, 27 August 1800, Misc. Ms. 2295, Carl H. Pforzheimer Collection of Shelley & His Circle, New York Public Library, Astor, Lenox and Tilden Foundations.
54. MR to Jane Porter, 11 September 1800, Misc. Ms. 2292, *ibid.*
55. MR to Jane Porter, 27 August 1800, Misc. Ms. 2295, *ibid.*
56. *Morning Post*, 24 August 1800.
57. MR to James Marshall, 10 September 1800, Abinger Deposit, Dep.b.215/2, Bodleian Library.
58. MR to William Godwin, 10 October 1800, *ibid.*
59. MR to Jane Porter, 15 October 1800, Misc. Ms. 2293, MR to Jane Porter, 27 August 1800, Misc. Ms. 2295, Carl H. Pforzheimer Collection of Shelley & His Circle, New York Public Library, Astor, Lenox and Tilden Foundations.
60. *The Poetical Works of the Late Mrs Robinson*, Richard Phillips, 1806, III, p. 225.

61. *Memoirs*, p. 149.
62. See *Selected Poems*, pp. 182–288.
63. J. Wolcot to MR, 18 December 1800. Printed in the 1801 edition of the *Memoirs of the Late Mrs Robinson* 4, pp. 189–91.
64. *Memoirs*, p. 152.
65. Quoted in *George IV*, p. 785.

EPILOGUE

1. Godwin's Journal vol. X, 26 December 1800, Abinger Deposit, Dep.e.205, Bodleian Library.
2. Mary Robinson, *Poetical Works* 3, p. lvi.
3. S.T. Coleridge to Thomas Poole, 1 February 1801, *Coleridge Letters* II, p. 669.
4. *Morning Post*, 31 December 1800.
5. Jane Porter Ms Diary, 3 January 1801, M.b.15, Folger Shakespeare Library, Washington, D.C.
6. *Ibid.*, 4 January 1801.
7. Jane Porter, 'Character of the late Mrs Robinson', Misc. Ms 2296, The Carl H. Pforzheimer Collection of Shelley and His Circle, The New York Public Library, Astor, Lenox and Tilden Foundations.
8. Entries for 16 November, 24 December 1799, 2, 3 February, 2 April 1800. Godwin's Journal, Vol. IX, Abinger Deposit, Dep.e.204, Bodleian Library.
9. Jane Porter Ms Diary, 24 April 1801, Mb15, Folger Shakespeare Library, Washington, D.C.
10. Richard Polwhele, *The Unsex'd Females*, Cadell & Davies, 1798, p. 17. The couplet ran 'And ROBINSON to Gaul her Fancy gave,/And trac'd the picture of a Deist's grave', the reference being to Rousseau.
11. *Morning Post*, 21 May 1798.
12. *Oracle*, 22 September 1794.
13. Banastre Tarleton to John McMahon, 21 June 1801, RA GEO/29861.
14. *Ibid.*
15. MER to Robert Gray, 23 November 1801, RA GEO/29863.
16. Robert Gray to MER [draft], 24 November 1801, RA GEO/29865.
17. MER to Robert Gray, 26 November 1801, RA GEO/29866.
18. MER to Robert Gray, 3 February 1805, RA GEO/30287.
19. MER to Samuel Jackson Pratt, undated, Shelleyana 226, as note 7 above.
20. PROB 11/1096.
21. I am grateful to Rosemary Fisher of the Worcestershire Library & History Centre for this research.

22. *Monthly Review*, vol. 36, December 1801, pp. 344–50, p. 346.
23. S.T. Coleridge to MER, 27 December 1802, *Coleridge Letters* II, p. 904.
24. Pierce Egan, *The Mistress of Royalty; or, The Loves of Florizel and Perdita*, P. Egan, 1814, p. 143.
25. Eleanor Ty, *Empowering the Feminine: The Narratives of Mary Robinson, Jane West, and Amelia Opie 1796–1812*, Toronto, University of Toronto Press, 1998, p. 190, n. 4.
26. MER to Cadell & Davies, 13 August 1805, private collection, and MER to Messrs Longman *et al.*, 11 December 1809, Publishers Archives: *The House of Longman*, 1791–1914, Reel 1, British Library.
27. Both poems are printed in *Memoirs*, pp. 153–4.
28. Mr & Mrs S.C. Hall, *The Book of the Thames*, Charlotte James, 1859, p. 227.
29. MER to Robert Gray, 19 January 1805, RA GEO/30286.
30. Land tax listings, Buckinghamshire Record Office, Q/RPL/8/32–35.
31. MER to Robert Gray, 30 December 1814, RA GEO/30401.
32. Robinson could also theoretically have sued the Prince for 'crim. con.' (criminal conversation) and sought damages and a divorce.
33. MER to Robert Gray, 5 December 1815, RA GEO/30408.
34. *Ibid.*, and MER to Robert Gray, 1 January 1815, RA GEO/30402.
35. MER to Robert Gray, 18 April 1817, RA GEO/30412.
36. Elizabeth Weale to Robert Gray, 19 April 1818, RA GEO/30419.
37. T.E. Harwood, *Windsor Old and New*, The Ballantyne Press, 1929, p. 358.
38. PROB 11/1816.
39. William T. Whitley, *Thomas Gainsborough*, Smith, Elder & Co., 1915, p. 183.
40. Hibbert, p. 785.

Select Bibliography

The place of publication is London unless otherwise specified.

MARY ROBINSON'S WORKS

(SELECTED) ORIGINAL EDITIONS

Angelina; A novel, Hookham & Carpenter, 1796

Captivity, A Poem. And Celadon and Lydia, a Tale, T. Becket, 1777

The False Friend: A Domestic Story, T.N. Longman & O. Rees, 1799

Hubert de Sevrac, A Romance, of the Eighteenth Century, Hookham & Carpenter, 1796

Impartial Reflections on the Present Situation of the Queen of France by a Friend to Humanity, J. Bell, 1791

Letter to the Women of England on the Injustice of Mental Subordination with Anecdotes, by Anne Frances Randall, T.N. Longman and O. Rees, 1799

Memoirs of the Late Mrs Robinson, written by herself. With some posthumous pieces, ed. M.E. Robinson, R. Phillips, 1801

Modern Manners, a poem. In two cantos. By Horace Juvenal, James Evans *et al.*, 1793

Monody to the Memory of the Late Queen of France, T. Spilsbury & Son, 1793

The Natural Daughter. With Portraits of the Leadenhead Family. A Novel, T.N. Longman & O. Rees, 1799

Picture of Palermo, by Dr Joseph Hager (translation), R. Phillips, 1800

Poems, J. Bell, 1791

Poems II, Hookham & Carpenter, 1793

The Poetical Works of the late Mrs Mary Robinson including many Pieces never before published, 3 vols, R. Phillips, 1806

Sappho and Phaon, Hookham & Carpenter, 1796

Sight, The Cavern of Woe, and Solitude, T. Spilsbury & Son, 1793

Vancenza; or, The Dangers of Credulity, a Moral Tale, J. Bell, 1792

Walsingham; or, The Pupil of Nature. A Domestic Story, T. Longman, 1797

The Widow; or, A Picture of Modern Times, Hookham & Carpenter, 1794

SELECTED MODERN EDITIONS AND FACSIMILE REPRINTS

Letter to the Women of England and The Natural Daughter, ed. Sharon M. Setzer, Ontario, Broadview Press, 2003

Lyrical Tales, 1800, Oxford Woodstock Books, 1989

Perdita: The Memoirs of Mary Robinson, ed. M.J. Levy, Peter Owen, 1994

Poems, 1791, Oxford Woodstock Books, 1994

The Poetical Works, with a new Introduction by Caroline Franklin, 3 vols, Routledge/Thoemmes Press, 1996

Mary Robinson: Selected Poems, ed. Judith Pascoe, Ontario, Broadview Press, 2000

Walsingham, ed. Julie A. Shaffer, Ontario, Broadview Press, 2003

MODERN CRITICISM AND BIBLIOGRAPHICAL WORKS

Craciun, Adriana, *Fatal Women of Romanticism*, Cambridge, Cambridge University Press, 2003

The English Novel 1770–1829: A Bibliographical Survey of Prose Fiction Published in the British Isles, Volume I: 1770–1799, ed. Peter Garside, James Raven and Rainer Schöwerling, Oxford, Oxford University Press, 2000

Erdman, David V., 'Lost Poem Found: The co-operative pursuit & recapture of an escaped Coleridge "sonnet" of 72 lines', in *New York Library Bulletin* 65, 1961, pp. 249–68

Fergus, Jan, and Janice Farrar Thaddeus, 'Women, Publishers, and Money, 1790–1820' in *Studies in Eighteenth-Century Culture 17*, 1988, pp. 191–208

Griggs, Earl Leslie, 'Coleridge and Mrs Mary Robinson' in *Modern Language Notes 45*, 1930, pp. 90–5

Labbe, Jacqueline M. (ed.), *Women's Writing 9, No.1: Mary Robinson*, Triangle Journals, 2002

Levy, M.J., 'Coleridge, Mary Robinson and *Kubla Khan*' in *The Charles Lamb Bulletin, New Series 77*, 1992, pp. 156–66

McGann, Jerome, *The Poetics of Sensibility: A Revolution in Literary Style*, Oxford, The Clarendon Press, 1996

Pascoe, Judith, *Romantic Theatricality: Gender, Poetry, and Spectatorship*, Ithaca and London, Cornell University Press, 1997

Rivers, Isabel (ed.), *Books and their Readers in Eighteenth-Century England*, Leicester University Press, 1982

Setzer, Sharon M., 'Mary Robinson's Sylphid Self: The End of Feminine Self-Fashioning', in *Philological Quarterly 75*, 1996, pp. 501–20

——, 'The Dying Game: Crossdressing in Mary Robinson's *Walsingham*', in *Nineteenth-Century Contexts 22*, 2000, pp. 305–08

Stanton, Judith Phillips, 'Statistical Profile of Women Writing in English from 1660 to 1800', in *Eighteenth-Century Women and the Arts* (ed. Frederick M. Keener and Susan E. Lorsch), Westport, Connecticut, Greenwood, 1988, pp. 248–54

Ty, Eleanor, *Empowering the Feminine: The Narratives of Mary Robinson, Jane West, and Amelia Opie, 1796–1812*, Toronto, University of Toronto Press, 1998

BIOGRAPHY, MEMOIRS, LETTERS

Anon, *Public Characters of 1800–1801*, Richard Phillips, 1807

Anson, Elizabeth and Florence (eds), *Mary Hamilton afterwards Mrs John Dickenson at Court and at Home from Letters and Diaries 1756 to 1816*, John Murray, 1925

Archenholtz, J.W. von, *A Picture of England: containing a description of the Laws, Customs, and Manners of England*, 2 vols, Edward Jeffery, 1789

Aspinall, A. (ed.) *Mrs Jordan and her Family being the Unpublished Correspondence of Mrs Jordan and the Duke of Clarence, later William IV*, Arthur Barker, 1951

——, *The Correspondence of George, Prince of Wales 1770–1812*, 8 volumes, Cassell & Company, 1963

Ayling, Stanley, *George III*, Collins, 1972

——, *A Portrait of Sheridan*, Constable, 1985

Barnett, Gerald, *Richard and Maria Cosway: A Biography*, Tiverton, Devon, Westcountry Books, 1995

Bass, Robert D., *The Green Dragoon: The Lives of Banastre Tarleton and Mary Robinson*, Alvin Redman, 1957

Bingham, Madeleine, *Sheridan: the Track of a Comet*, George Allen & Unwin, 1972

Bleackley, Horace, *Ladies Fair and Frail: Sketches of the Demi-monde During the Eighteenth Century*, John Lane, The Bodley Head, 1929

Boaden, James, *The Life of Mrs Jordan*, 2 vols, Edward Ball, 1831

Brooke, John, *King George III*, Constable, 1972

Byrne, Paula, *Perdita: The Life of Mary Robinson*, HarperCollins, 2004

Cavendish, Georgiana, *Georgiana: Extracts from the Correspondence of Georgiana, Duchess of Devonshire*, ed. The Earl of Bessborough, John Murray, 1955

Coleridge, Samuel Taylor, *Collected Letters of Samuel Taylor Coleridge*, edited by Earl Stanley Gibbs, 2 vols, Oxford, The Clarendon Press, 1956

David, Saul, *Prince of Pleasure: The Prince of Wales and the Making of the Regency*, Little, Brown & Co. (UK), 1998

Davis, I.M., *The Harlot and the Statesman*, Bourne End, Buckinghamshire, The Kensal Press, 1986

Elliot, Grace Dalrymple, *Journal of My Life during the French Revolution*, The Rodale Press, undated
Fortescue, The Hon. John (ed.), *The Correspondence of King George III, 1760–1783*, Macmillan, 1928
Fothergill, Brian, *Mrs Jordan: Portrait of an Actress*, Faber & Faber, 1965
Fraser, Antonia, *Marie Antoinette*, Weidenfeld & Nicolson, 2001
Gontaut, Armand-Louis de, *Memoirs of the Duc de Lauzun*, trans. and ed. C.K. Scott Moncrieff, George Routledge & Sons, 1928
Gristwood, Sarah, *Perdita: Royal Mistress, Writer, Romantic*, Bantam, 2005
Hawkins, Laetitia-Matilda, *Anecdotes, Biographical Sketches and Memoirs*, F.C. and J. Rivington (eds), 2 vols, 1822
Hedley, Olwen, *Queen Charlotte*, John Murray, 1975
Hibbert, Christopher, *George IV*, Harmondsworth, Middlesex, Penguin, 1976
——, *George III: A Personal History*, Viking, 1998
Hickey, William, *Memoirs of William Hickey*, ed. Alfred Spencer, vols II & III, Hurst & Blackett, 1918
Hickman, Katie, *Courtesans*, HarperCollins, 2003
Holmes, Richard, *Coleridge: Early Visions*, Hodder & Stoughton, 1989
Huish, Robert, *Memoirs of George IV*, Thomas Kelly, 1831
Ingamells, John, *Mrs Robinson and her Portraits*, The Trustees of the Wallace Collection, 1978
Jones, M.G., *Hannah More*, Cambridge, Cambridge University Press, 1952
Kelly, Linda, *Richard Brinsley Sheridan: A Life*, Pimlico, 1997
McIntyre, Ian, *Garrick*, Harmondsworth, Penguin, 1999
Mayberry, Tom, *Coleridge & Wordsworth in the West Country*, Stroud, Sutton, 1992
Levy, M.J., *The Mistresses of King George IV*, Peter Owen, 1966
Lindsay, Philip, *The Loves of Florizel*, Hutchinson, 1951
——, *A Piece for Candlelight*, Hutchinson, 1953
Makower, Stanley V., *Perdita: A Romance in Biography*, Hutchinson, 1908
Manning, Jo, *My Lady Scandalous: The Amazing Life and Outrageous Times of Grace Dalrymple Elliot, Royal Courtesan*, New York, Simon & Schuster, 2005
Mitchell, L.G., *Charles James Fox*, Oxford, Oxford University Press, 1992
Norton, Rictor, *Mistress of Udolpho: The Life of Ann Radcliffe*, Leicester, Leicester University Press, 1999
Parissien, Steven, *George IV: The Grand Entertainment*, John Murray, 2001
Powell, David, *Charles James Fox: Man of the People*, Hutchinson, 1989
Price, Cecil (ed.), *The Letters of Richard Brinsley Sheridan*, Vol. I, Oxford, The Clarendon Press, 1966
Richardson, Joanna, *George IV: A Portrait*, Sidgwick & Jackson, 1966

Shelley, Frances Lady, *The Diary of Frances Lady Shelley 1787–1817*, ed. Richard Edgcumbe, John Murray, 1913

St Clair, William, *The Godwins and the Shelleys: The Biography of a Family*, Faber & Faber, 1989

Steele, Elizabeth, *The Memoirs of Mrs Sophia Baddeley*, 6 vols, Literary Press, 1787

Steen, Marguerite, *The Lost One: A Biography of Mary (Perdita) Robinson*, Methuen & Co., 1937

Stott, Anne, *Hannah More: The First Victorian*, Oxford, Oxford University Press, 2003

Taylor, John, *Records of my Life*, 2 vols, Edward Bull, 1832

Todd, Janet, *Mary Wollstonecraft: a Revolutionary Life*, Weidenfeld & Nicolson, 2000

Tomalin, Claire, *The Life and Death of Mary Wollstonecraft*, Weidenfeld & Nicolson, 1974

——, *Mrs Jordan's Profession: The Story of a Great Actress and a Future King*, Viking, 1994

Walpole, Horace, *The Yale Edition of Horace Walpole's Correspondence*, edited by W.S. Lewis *et al.*, Oxford and New Haven, Oxford University Press and Yale University Press, 1937–83.

Whitley, William T., *Thomas Gainsborough*, Smith, Elder & Co., 1915

——, *Artists and Their Friends in England 1700–1799*, 2 vols, Medici Society, 1928

Wollstonecraft, Mary, *The Works of Mary Wollstonecraft*, 7 vols, edited by Janet Todd and Marilyn Butler, Pickering & Chatto, 1989

THE THEATRE

Asleson, Robyn (ed.), *Notorious Muse: The Actress in British Art and Culture 1776–1812*, New Haven and London, Yale University Press, 2003

Benedetti, Jean, *David Garrick and the Birth of the Modern Theatre*, Methuen, 2001

Donkin, Ellen, *Getting into the Act: Women Playwrights in London 1776–1829*, Routledge, 1995

Highfill, Philip H., Kalmin A. Burnim, Edward A. Langhams, *A Biographical Dictionary of Actors, Actresses, Musicians, Dancers, Managers & Other Stage Personnel in London, 1660–1800*, 16 vols, Carbondale, Southern Illinois University Press, 1973–93

Hill, Aaron, *The Works of the Late Aaron Hill, Esq; in four Volumes . . . with an Essay on the Art of Acting* (Volume IV), 1754

Hogan, Charles Beecher, *The London Stage 1660–1800, Part V: 1776–1800*, Carbondale, Southern Illinois University Press, 1968

Pedicord, Harry William, and Bergmann, Frederick Louis *The Plays of David Garrick*, 5 vols, Carbondale, Southern Illinois University Press, 1981
Pedicord, Harry William, *'By Their Majesties' Command': The House of Hanover at the London Theatres, 1714–1800*, The Society for Theatre Research, 1991
Price, Cecil, *Theatre in the Age of Garrick*, Oxford, Basil Blackwell, 1973
Stone, George Winchester, *The London Stage 1660–1800, Part IV*, Carbondale, Southern Illinois University Press, 1968

GENERAL CULTURAL, HISTORICAL AND SOCIAL BACKGROUND

Anon, *Liverpool and Slavery: An Historical Account of the Liverpool-African Slave Trade by a genuine 'Dicky Sam'*, Liverpool, A. Bowker & Son, 1884
Ashton, John, *The Fleet, Its River, Prison, and Marriages*, T. Fisher Unwin, 1888
——, *The History of Gambling in England*, Duckworth & Co., 1898
——, *Florizel's Folly*, Chatto & Windus, 1899
Babits, Lawrence, *A Devil of a Whipping: The Battle of Cowpens*, Chapel Hill and London, The University of North Carolina Press, 1998
Barker, Hannah and Elaine Chalus (eds), *Gender in Eighteenth-Century England: Roles, Representations and Responsibilities*, Harlow, Addison Wesley Longman Limited, 1997
Barker-Benfield, G.J., *The Culture of Sensibility: Sex and Society in Eighteenth-Century Britain*, Chicago and London, University of Chicago Press, 1992
Barlow, Andrew, *The Prince and his Pleasures: Satirical Images of George IV and his Circle*, Brighton, Libraries and Museum, 1997
Black, Jeremy, *The English Press in the Eighteenth Century*, Beckenham, Kent, Croom Helm, 1987
Bonehill, John, 'Reynolds' *Portrait of Lieutenant-Colonel Banastre Tarleton* and the Fashion for War', in *British Journal for Eighteenth-Century Studies*, 24, 2001, pp. 123–44
Brewer, John, *The Pleasures of the Imagination: English Culture in the Eighteenth Century*, HarperCollins, 1997
de Castro, J. Paul, *The Gordon Riots*, Oxford, Oxford University Press, 1926
Campbell, Kimberley Chrisman, 'The Face of Fashion: Milliners in Eighteenth-Century Visual Culture', in *British Journal for Eighteenth-Century Studies 25*, 2002, pp. 157–72
Clayton, Timothy, *The English Print 1688–1802*, New Haven & London, Yale University Press, 1997
Donald, Diana, *Followers of Fashion: Graphic Satires from the Georgian Period*, Hayward Gallery Publishing, 2002
Flower, Raymond, *The Old Ship: A Prospect of Brighton*, Croom Helm, 1986

Ford, Boris (ed.), *18th Century Britain: The Cambridge Cultural History*, Cambridge, Cambridge University Press, 1992

George, Dorothy, *London Life in the XVIIIth Century*, Kegan, Paul, Trench, Trubner & Co., 1925

Harvey, A.D., *Sex in Georgian England: Attitudes and Prejudices from the 1720s to the 1820s*, Duckworth, 1994

Hayes, John, *Rowlandson: Watercolours and Drawings*, Phaidon, 1972

Hibbert, Christopher, *The French Revolution*, Allen Lane, 1980

——, *Redcoats and Rebels: The War for America 1770–1781* (reprinted from 1990), Harmondsworth, Middlesex, 2001

Jones, Donald, *Bristol Past*, Chichester, Phillimore, 2000

Jones, Vivien (ed.), *Women in the Eighteenth Century: Constructions of Femininity*, London and New York, Routledge, 1990

Keane, Angela, *Women Writers and the English Nation in the 1790s: Romantic Belongings*, Cambridge, Cambridge University Press, 2000

Levy, M.J., 'Gainsborough's *Mrs Robinson*: A portrait and its context', in *Apollo* 136, 1992, pp. 152–54

Mellor, Anne K., 'Making an Exhibition of Her Self: Mary "Perdita" Robinson and Ninteenth-Century Scripts of Female Sexuality' in *Nineteenth-Century Contexts 22*, 2000, pp. 271–304

Melville, Lewis, *Brighton, its Follies, and its Fashions*, Chapman & Hall, 1909

Musgrave, Clifford, *Life in Brighton: from the Earliest Times to the Present*, Faber & Faber, 1970

Murray, Venetia, *High Society: A Social History of the Regency Period, 1788–1830*, Harmondsworth, Penguin, 1998

O'Connell, Sheila, *The Popular Print in England 1550–1850*, The British Museum Press, 1999

——, *London 1753*, The British Museum Press, 2003

Perry, Gill, 'Women in disguise: likeness, the Grand Style and the conventions of feminine portraiture in the work of Sir Joshua Reynolds', in *Femininity and Masculinity in Eighteenth-century Art and Culture*, Gill Perry and Michael Rossington (eds), Manchester and New York, Manchester University Press, 1994

Picard, Liza, *Dr. Johnson's London: Life in London 1740–1770*, Weidenfeld & Nicolson, 2000

Pointon, Marcia, *Hanging the Head: Portraiture and Social Formation in Eighteenth-Century England*, New Haven and London, Yale University Press, 1993

——, '"Surrounded with Brilliants": Miniature Portraits in Eighteenth-Century England', in *The Art Bulletin*, March 2001, pp. 48–71

Porter, Roy, *English Society in the 18th Century*, revised edition, Harmondsworth, Penguin, 1991
——, *London: A Social History*, Hamish Hamilton, 1994
——, *Quacks: Fakers & Charlatans in English Medicine*, Stroud, Tempus, 2000
Ribeiro, A., *A Visual History of Costume: The Eighteenth Century*, B.T. Batsford, 1983
—— *The Dress Worn at Masquerades and its relation to Fancy Dress in Portraiture*, London and New York, Garland, 1984
——, *The Art of Dress: Fashion in England and France 1750–1820*, New Haven & London, Yale University Press, 1995
Russell, Gillian, '"Faro's Daughters": Female Gamesters, Politics, and the Discourse of Finance in 1790s Britain', in *Eighteenth Century Studies*, vol. 33, no. 4, Summer 2000, pp. 481–504
Waterhouse, Ellis, *Reynolds*, Phaidon, 1973
Wendorf, Richard, *Sir Joshua Reynolds: The Painter in Society*, National Portrait Gallery, 1996
Werkmeister, Lucyle, *The London Daily Press 1772–1792*, Lincoln, University of Nebraska Press, 1963
——, *A Newspaper History of England 1792–1793*, Lincoln, University of Nebraska Press, 1967
Wright, Esmond (ed.), *The Fire of Liberty*, The Folio Society, 1983
Wroth, Warwick, *The London Pleasure Gardens of the Eighteenth Century*, Macmillan & Co., 1896

Index

Index